Community and Political Thought Today

Edited by Peter Augustine Lawler
and
Dale McConkey

Westport, Connecticut
London

Library of Congress Cataloging-in-Publication Data

Community and political thought today / edited by Peter Augustine
　　Lawler and Dale McConkey.
　　　　p.　　cm.
　　Includes bibliographical references and index.
　　ISBN 0–275–96096–X (alk. paper)
　　1. Social ethics.　2. Communitarianism.　I. Lawler, Peter
Augustine.　II. McConkey, Dale D.
　　HM216.C6555　　1998
　　303.3'72—DC21　　　　98–14906

British Library Cataloguing in Publication Data is available.

Library of Congress Catalog Card Number: 98–14906
ISBN: 0–275–96096–X

First published in 1998

Praeger Publishers, 88 Post Road West, Westport, CT 06881
An imprint of Greenwood Publishing Group, Inc.

Printed in the United States of America

The paper used in this book complies with the
Permanent Paper Standard issued by the National
Information Standards Organization (Z39.48–1984).

10 9 8 7 6 5 4 3 2 1

Copyright Acknowledgments

The editors and publisher gratefully acknowledge permission for use of the following material:

Excerpts from Robert Bellah, Richard Madsen, William M. Sullivan, Ann Swidler, and Steven M. Tipton, *Habits of the Heart: Individualism and Commitment in American Life*, copyright © 1985, 1996 by the Regents of the University of California, are reprinted with permission of the University of California Press, Berkeley.

Excerpts from Richard Rorty, *Contingency, Irony, and Solidarity* (Cambridge: Cambridge University Press, 1989), are reprinted with permission of Cambridge University Press and Richard Rorty.

Excerpts from Leo Strauss, *Natural Right and History*, copyright © 1953, are reprinted with permission of the University of Chicago Press.

Part of Murray Jardine's chapter is based on the Introduction to his forthcoming book, *Speech and Political Practice*, and is used with permission of the State University of New York Press. All rights reserved.

Early and abbreviated versions of Bruce Frohnen's, Brad Lowell Stone's, Wilfred M. McClay's, and Peter Augustine Lawler's chapters appeared in the Spring 1997 *Intercollegiate Review* and are used with permission of the Intercollegiate Studies Institute, Wilmington, Delaware.

Some of Robb McDaniel's chapter is adapted from his "The Nature of Inequality: Uncovering the Modern in Leo Strauss's Idealist Ethics," forthcoming in *Political Theory*, and is used with permission of Sage Publications, Inc.

Contents

Acknowledgments

This book has its origins in a conference on communitarianism and civil society held in October 1996 at Berry College. Almost all of the contributors participated in that conference, and most of the book's chapters were presented in earlier forms there. The sponsors of the conference were Berry College's Departments of Political Science and Sociology, Oglethorpe University, the Berry College Student Government, and the Chautauqua Council, a Berry College student organization. We thank all of these fine organizations for their support. The sponsorship of the Intercollegiate Studies Institute deserves to be mentioned separately, in view of its generosity.

The conference was distinguished by large and varied student involvement. The Chautauqua Council handled expertly many of the conference's details, under the extraordinary guidance of David Lindrum. Jason Maxwell, Amber Still, Jocelyn Jones, and Lynsey Morris also made outstanding contributions, showing that maybe we at Berry College really do inculcate moral virtue. Oglethorpe's Brad Stone, a very unusual sociologist, also participated in the conference's planning. Donna Worsham, friend of the Berry freshmen, produced all the conference materials.

Lynsey Morris and Darrell Sutton did a great deal of careful proofreading. Kathy Gann whipped the manuscript into shape for publication with her routine excellence. Elizabeth Thompson prepared the Index.

Introduction

Human beings are mixtures of diverse qualities and possibilities. They are social and political beings, and a vital social and political order is at the foundation of all human flourishing. But they are also individuals, capable of distinguishing one's own good from the common good. They are to some extent alienated from society and political life, not to mention from the rest of nature or the cosmos, by their natures. A political order that does justice to the mixture that is human nature is some sort of mixed regime. That mixture, like human existence itself, is inherently rather unstable. It is always in need of thoughtful and practical attention.

Today, the particular concern of most political thinkers is the erosion of social and political life, the decline of community. Community is threatened by individuals who are excessively self-conscious, who relate to others too exclusively in terms of egoistic calculation. The source of that preoccupation with calculating selfishness is early liberal political thought. Liberal thinkers, such as Hobbes and Locke, wanted to free the individual from excessive absorption in patriarchal, theocratic, tyrannical community. Today's "communitarians," whatever their differences, are united by the perception that the liberation of personal selfishness has been too successful. People have become too concerned with rights, or their claims against others, and not concerned enough with their duties, or what is required of them as social and political beings.

The communitarian criticism of individualism begins with a moral revulsion against aggressive selfishness. But it continues with the observation that the liberated individual may be in constant pursuit of happiness but is too rarely actually happy. Alexis de Tocqueville, in *Democracy in America*, describes the relentlessly calculating American, for example, as pursuing enjoyment but never taking the time to actually enjoy. Enjoyment requires a suspension of calculation, or worried preoccupation with the future, and immersion in the present. But the aggressive individualist, most fundamentally, regards his environment as so hostile to his existence that he cannot afford to take time to enjoy.

The aggressive individualist believes that love or uncalculating connections with others is deluding and enslaving. Nobody can be trusted, and freedom is radically opposed to social dependence. So the social institutions that enlarge the human heart in the direction of love—the family, religion, local government, and so forth—atrophy under the influence of individualistic thought. But the human relationships formed by those institutions actually produce the experiences that most people, even today, say make life worthwhile. They are the genuine sources of human happiness. The history of American liberalism might be individuals becoming more wealthy, powerful, and free, but also more unhappy, lonely, and alienated. The communitarian movement, from one perspective, is a rebellion on behalf of love. Human love is usually expressed most intimately and satisfactorily in the family, then as religion or love of God, in personal friendships, and finally as the concern of one active citizen for another in political life. The social institutions that enlarge the heart are indispensable for satisfying ineradicable human needs, the needs the constantly calculating individual self-deceptively denies in his or her own case.

The history of American liberalism has also been in the direction of justice. Very few Americans or Westerners today deny that justice is somehow the recognition of the equal rights of all, and that rights are better understood and protected today than ever before. When we criticize the past, we do so on behalf of our theory and practice of justice. When we communitarians criticize the present, it is largely on behalf of love. This tension between the two undeniable human goods of love and justice in the modern world was first and best understood by Tocqueville.

Tocqueville says that modern democrats identify justice with equality. They are politically animated by love of equality and a corresponding hatred of privilege. It seems, at first, that they love justice, and love and justice are in harmony. But Tocqueville adds that this harmony, in truth, is only found in the case of God. He, able to love all human beings equally and intensely, does justice to each of them in his or her particularity. But the human power of knowing and loving is limited. So human love, unlike God's, is diluted when its scope expands. The fact is that our religion or our sense of justice may enjoin us to love all human beings equally, but we can do so only if we love each of them very weakly or abstractly. Love of equality, in many ways, undermines human love as it actually exists.

Love of one's own—family, friends, or country—leads one to favor one's own, and so to prefer their good to the egalitarian demands of justice. The very existence of the family works against egalitarian justice. Everyone knows, and studies show, that success in life is dependent more than anything else on the quality of one's parents. As long as the family exists, life-chances are arbitrarily unequal. The family, as Tocqueville explains, has depended in America on women not being sticklers for justice, preferring instead the good of those they love. Women's liberation, although surely just, has undeniably been at the expense of familial love. Today, both parents in the name of justice are encouraged to have economic and political lives and are warned not to be seduced into slighting their own self-fulfillment. So with every passing year they spend less time with their kids, and parents' love for their children is less of a barrier to divorce. The story of the struggle of the lonely single mom and the imperfectly suppressed and often destructive anger of the child of divorced parents no longer seems a social aberration. But we cannot ignore studies that show that marriage is especially good for the mental and physical health of men, and that when they choose divorce they often choose badly, against their long-term interest. We also still see women and even men sacrificing their just claims in order to spend their time socializing or civilizing their spouse and children.

The same sort of tension between love and justice can be found in political life. Tocqueville praises the strong participatory institutions of America's local government for their heart-enlarging effects. While a citizen may first get involved out of self-interest, what begins as calculation soon turns into affection. But local government has lost most of its power over the past several generations, and so citizen involvement has declined. There are many reasons for this development, but the most important has been the pursuit of justice. Local government did well in arousing the social passions of citizens, but it was also chauvinistic, meddlesome, inefficient, and racist. The national government is undeniably better at protecting rights, particularly the rights of minorities. American political life may be more just than ever before, but at the expense of civic spirit and affection. We actually seem to have a more just government because we have more apathetic citizens.

Our communitarian theorists criticize both aggressive individualism and personal and political passivity. The common explanation for their connection is that people have become so selfish that they have no time to be concerned with their social duties. But Tocqueville finds a deeper connection between selfish aggressiveness and apathy. The life devoted to the pursuit of self-interest and nothing more is too hard. There is no place for enjoyment or love. So individuals who attempt to live that life soon come to regard individuality as such as no good. They end up surrendering it, gratefully acknowledging their dependence on impersonal big government, public opinion determined by no one in particular, therapeutic expertise, and so forth. Marx was right, although not for the right reason, in anticipating that "bourgeois" individuality eventually becomes hateful.

Tocqueville named the doctrine that supports that surrender *individualism*, meaning an apathetic suppression of the social passions, pride, love, and hate, as more productive of human misery than anything else, as more trouble than they're worth. Apathetic individualism is a more perfect expression of self-reliance than aggressive individualism. The aggressive individual attempts to manipulate and control others to satisfy his or her bloated social desires. The apathetic individual is more self-reliant because he or she experiences no need for connection to others. Students of political philosophy can see that Tocqueville is accepting the Rousseauean correction to the incoherence of Lockean state of nature. Locke describes the natural human individual as asocial but in possession of social passions. But consistent asociality, Rousseau explains, would produce the apathy of contentment, an unconscious immersion in the goodness of the present.

So the deepest criticism of aggressive individualism is that it leads to the destruction of individuality or human liberty on behalf of what Tocqueville calls individualism. The concern of the authors in this book, in one way or another, is the perpetuation of the "moral ecology" on which human liberty depends to flourish. They know that the chief threat to liberty today is not smothering community but rootless apathy. Human liberty must be lovable, and so it must not be incompatible with human love.

The authors do not limit themselves to the concerns and thinkers of the "communitarian" movement. They mean to be relevant but not trendy, to think beyond current controversies to deeper issues. They include political scientists, political philosophers, historians, and sociologists. They are both conservative and liberal, as well as both supportive and critical of the new communitarian concern. They write from a variety of theoretical orientations. The dissident, Straussian, Voegelinian, Arendtian, Tocquevillian, traditionalist, Aronian-liberal, Aristotelian, Augustinian, Rieffian-antitherapeutic, and classical liberal perspectives are all represented. The authors also cover the range of contemporary political issues, including "moral ecology," federalism, postmodernism, therapeutic culture, justice, history, the liberal-communitarian debate, cultural literacy, the "great books," pragmatism, existentialism, philosophy and morality, citizenship, and globalism. One way to look at this book is as a comprehensive introduction to contemporary social and political thought.

1

The Concept of Moral Ecology

ALLEN D. HERTZKE AND CHRIS McRORIE

In Navajo legend Coyote, known as atse'hashkke or First Angry, symbolized the dark forces of chaos that might destroy a community dependent on harmony and peace for survival. As depicted by novelist Tony Hillerman, Coyote always waits for a chance to sow discord, selfishness, violence, and the breaking of rules and law.[1]

For years novelists, poets, and environmental thinkers have touted the Native American way of life as a model of how people can live in harmony with nature. Not as well appreciated is that a kind of moral ecology was interwoven with that reverence for nature. Living an ecological life meant not only living in harmony with nature but also with one another. Individual behavior deemed destructive to the community was thus checked by the kind of strong norms about right behavior that can operate in traditional societies—norms that were shattered when the indigenous population came into contact with advancing white civilization.

Today we see a flood of anguished commentary about the state of American culture—its violence, drugs, sexual promiscuity, anomie, family decline, and lagging achievement among the young. It seems that Coyote or, as orthodox Christians would suggest, Satan, has preyed on individual selfishness, lust, envy, and aggression to chip away at the fabric of community life. To many people, the moral environment today just seems coarser, cruder, more violent, and less healthy than in the past, especially for the young. Intriguingly, environmental analogies have begun to creep into this discourse on the culture. Consider the following examples. Conservative family advocate Gary Bauer referred to the "downstream effects" of pornography in analyzing its adverse influence on society.

Mona Charon depicted modern television as a "toxic waste dump" for its violence and unhealthy values, joining a host of media critics who now speak routinely of "cultural pollution" and the "trashing" of the airwaves. Columnist John Leo decried the "deregulation" of the moral environment he claims occurred in the 1960s. Movie critic Michael Medved went further by calling for a "cultural environmental movement" to check the adverse impact of the media on family and community life. Most vigorously, conservative propagandist Patrick Buchanan called upon his party to "Depollute and detoxify the culture so that Middle American can again drink freely from it and be nurtured and enriched, not nauseated and poisoned."[2]

The moral ecological understanding, however, is not restricted to conservative commentators and propagandists. Scholars Robert Bellah, Christopher Lasch, and Daniel Bell, among others, see cultural crisis resulting from an aggressive capitalist ethos seeping into communities and family life and degrading their sustaining norms.[3] A host of communitarian thinkers, such as Amatai Etzioni, Mary Ann Glendon, and Jean Bethke Elshtain, voice concern that a radical individualism threatens the ties of trust, civility, and cooperation that knit the human community.[4] This concern, moreover, is related to a growing scholarly conviction that the "social capital" so vital to well-functioning societies is mysteriously declining.[5] Other examples include those feminists who have made ecological linkages between an environment filled with pornography and the incidence of rape and sexual harassment,[6] and progressive clergy in black churches who share Jesse Jackson's view that the environment of the inner cities has deteriorated as people have abandoned the moral law in the Ten Commandments.[7]

Thus something more profound than the use of an occasional metaphor is occurring here. The critique of modern culture, as we will show, employs ecological language because its diagnosis of the problem mirrors that which emerged in the environmental movement. Both environmental analysts and cultural critics identify unrestrained individual freedom as a major source of disruption. Ironically, this diagnosis arises from within a rights-based liberal polity renowned for celebrating and protecting individual freedom. Yet this apparent paradox reveals an implicit Tocquevillian acknowledgment that within liberal societies the behavior of free persons can undermine the health of communities—whether biological or human. What links physical ecology and the moral realm, therefore, is an appreciation of interdependency that fosters a greater concern for the organic whole and a lesser stress on individual autonomy.

METHOD AND PURPOSE

Our prime purpose in this chapter is theory building; our procedure involves the first systematic formulation of empirical relationships inherent in the concept of moral ecology. We also offer initial corroboration of the theory as a means of illustrating the wide range of observable implications and testable hypotheses that are logically deduced from it. Finally, we offer some of the profound normative, policy, and philosophical implications of the empirical phenomena observed.

Our confidence in the potential explanatory power of the concept is fortified by the ways it conforms to standards of good theory as conceived by scientific theorists and epistemologists,[8] as well as the way it addresses deficiencies widely acknowledged in critical literature on the social sciences. For example, the concept of moral ecology responds to the complaint that in rejecting grand theories as non-falsifiable, social scientists have unwittingly succumbed to theoretical timidity.[9] Thus social science has a multitude of incredibly complex lower and middle level theories, but few successful attempts to weave them into broader explanatory frameworks. Moral ecology, on the other hand, appears to distill widely diverse relationships in an elegant and parsimonious theoretical formulation. As our discussion will illustrate, the concept of moral ecology synthesizes a vast empirical literature on media violence, family decline, and gambling, linking theories that encompass a wide array of observable phenomena. But in contrast to other grand theories, moral ecology suggests numerous testable (falsifiable) hypotheses. Thus it appears to offer incredible leverage, which is "explaining as much as possible with as little as possible."[10]

Ironically, the moral ecology also captures the complexity of social and political worlds that many linear or econometric models must reduce. It does so because it looks not to physics but to biology, which offers a more apt model for the social sciences because biologists do not purport to predict the direction of evolution given the complexity of variables and their interaction in the ecosystem.[11] Human responses to the moral environment (as to the physical ecosystem) have ethical weight and practical import because they determine the capacity for the system to sustain healthy life.[12] Finally, in a striking parallel to natural science, scholars operating with apparent independence have identified the phenomenon of moral ecology and identically named it.[13]

A final theoretical note: Even if moral ecology in some sense represents a distillation of ancient wisdom, its virtue lies in being more susceptible to empirical tests than, say, tenets of natural law or traditional religious morality. When moral ecologists speak of the "downstream effects" of pornography, when scientists speak of delicate biological communities, both partake of the insights from millennia of human experience and scientific exploration. What is being discovered, therefore, is a grand empirical framework that links diverse observable phenomena with profound normative and ethical implications. To see how this is occurring, let us explore more deeply the historical origins of the ecological insight.

INDIVIDUAL FREEDOM AND THE TRAGEDY OF THE COMMONS

In many respects the modern environmental movement contained a potentially radical analysis of the problems of liberal societies, an analysis that few appreciate even now. The first stirrings were felt around the turn of the century, when conservationists such as John Muir and Theodore Roosevelt fought to preserve the great natural wonders of North America for future generations to use and enjoy. With wise public stewardship of natural resources the aim, remedies included public ownership and management of national forests and parks. Meanwhile, in urban areas public health specialists called for government regulation to deal with untreated sewage, foul air, and unsafe drinking water. Both of these developments reflected a growing awareness of the problem of unrestricted individual freedom to plunder or pollute the natural world.

Later, a whole new branch of economics arose that reflected this understanding. Clean air and water, parks and wilderness reserves—these were "public goods" that an average person could not purchase in the marketplace; government had to provide them. Moreover, it became clear that the external costs of pollution—such as increased disease, lost livelihoods of fishermen, and the like— were not being borne by the polluter or the person who purchased manufactured products that created pollution. These external costs, resource economists suggested, must be internalized through government regulation, so that the purchaser of a consumer product would pay its true cost, including environmental cleanup. In this way, companies would have an economic incentive to do the right thing by the downstream community.

It is not hard to see how this understanding clashed with classical liberal notions of property rights. Within the Lockean tradition the idea that a landowner or business owner had the freedom to do what he wanted with his own property was next to sacred.

An even more far-reaching development, however, emerged in the new science of ecology that arose in the 1950s and 1960s. Developed by botanists and popularized by such figures as Aldo Leopold,[14] ecology was the science of describing the interaction of plants and animals within a specified physical setting. It was discovered that a symbiotic balance existed in ecosystems, in which the disruption to one member of the community could adversely affect all the others. Thus, indiscriminate use of pesticides would prove counterproductive because they could destroy birds and those insects that are natural predators of the insects one is trying to kill. A concern for habitats, spawning grounds, and migrating paths reflected this new science of ecosystems.

Critical to this new understanding was the notion of "threshold." An ecosystem, say a stream, has a certain carrying capacity for pollution; it can cleanse itself or dilute some toxins sufficiently to remain viable. But when pollutants reach a cumulative threshold beyond the carrying capacity of the ecosystem, serious long-term degradation occurs.

The ecological insight was both a tremendous scientific advance in our understanding of the natural world and a compelling rhetorical tool for the environmental movement. Environmentalists spoke of ecosystems as "delicate communities" that required unique understanding and care. If one happened to own land next to one of these ecosystems, then your use of that land ought to be constrained. Environmentalists, henceforth, would not just focus on large polluting companies, but also on smaller farmers, ranchers, loggers, miners, and other landowners, admonishing them that they did not have the right to destroy adjacent or downstream ecosystems by using their property in certain ways. When confronted with the predictable claim that a single landowner's impact was minimal, ecologists adduced the threshold effect—harm flowed from the cumulative interaction of many pollutants.

We can begin to see how environmental analogies might be picked up by critics of popular culture, concerned as they are that some individuals abuse their freedom to the detriment of family, community, and society. Implicit, though not always clearly articulated, is the deeper fear that we are approaching a dangerous threshold, in which moral contaminants push beyond the culture's carrying capacity to sustain healthy norms of behavior.

What then results, environmental thought tells us, is a "tragedy of the commons." As captured by ecologist Garret Hardin, the "tragedy of the commons"[15] explicitly posed the environmental problem as one of individual freedom. Imagine, Hardin suggested, a common grassland on which any farmer can graze his sheep. Now think of each individual's rational interest, which is to get as much benefit out of the grass as he can. What is rational for the individual, as Hardin showed, is potentially disastrous for the collective. Sheep are notorious for grazing down to the roots, so if they are allowed to overgraze an area it is literally destroyed. By acting rationally in their use of the commons, individuals tragically destroy it. Thus the problem was not just polluting technology or the lack of environmental legislation, but untrammeled individual freedom itself. Left to their own devices, people would abuse, pollute, or overpopulate the earth.

The Tragedy of the Commons became a powerful metaphor for the environmental problems of the modern era and a theoretical construct for empirical research. The commons could be our air and water, or it could be the delicate ecosystems that sustain life, such as the rain forest, or it could be spaceship earth itself. Hardin's metaphor has become a part of our language and thinking. And its central insight continues to haunt the liberal imagination: perhaps the practice of individual freedom, which all of us presumably desire, might, under certain circumstances, undermine the very basis of life itself, or certainly of the good life.

What we will show is that a kind of tragedy of the commons can operate in the moral realm as well, in the ecology of communities and families, in the delicate interdependent relationships of love, self-sacrifice, and civility that constitute a healthy society. Thus, some individuals and companies can be viewed as practicing their liberal freedom in ways that pollute this moral ecosystem, undermining its ability to sustain healthy lives. We are proposing that the moral ecology is a broadly applicable empirical theory, not solely a philosophical construct, that applies to a wide range of describable phenomena, middle level theories, and mounting empirical evidence. If so, then the insights of the environmental movement may be instructive as policy-makers and citizens strive to balance individual freedom with the broader health of society.

Now, a bit of fuzziness may surround the use of the term "moral ecology." Why not speak instead of "human ecology," "social ecology," or "community ecology"? Indeed, political theorists through the ages have pointed to the deleterious consequences of an atomized culture, in which people are cut off from the healthy structures of interdependency—family, neighborhood, church—that constitute a human or community ecology. Aristotle saw people bereft of social bonds as unable to achieve their proper telos; Tocqueville worried that a self-absorbed, atomized culture would sap civic life. Our response is that there is an obvious and intimate link between a healthy community or society and the moral ecology, one well documented in contemporary scholarship.[16]

An understanding of the phenomenon of moral ecology, however, nicely centers our theoretical framework on those aspects of individual behavior most commonly deemed the provenance of free moral choices—such as television and movie viewing, marital relations, sexuality, gambling habits, pornography, or use of intoxicants or hallucinogens. Moreover, it distinguishes the moral realm from particular institutions whose norms relate to more specific needs. The U.S. military, for example, exists as a culture of hierarchy and enforced group solidarity. Thus some advocates might speak of an "ecology" of military culture, in which the introduction of a counter-cultural force, say open gay lifestyles, threatens to disrupt the ecological balance. But however useful such norms as hierarchy and unit cohesion might be for military readiness, they do not necessarily represent a more general moral ecology. Thus by focusing on moral ecology we sharpen our theoretical focus on the general rather than the relativistic.

The key parallel between the current discourse on morality and the ecological movement concerns the collective and interactive impact of many polluters. Thus, the question of damage is not "Does this individual behavior cause harm?" but rather "How much does this behavior when multiplied cumulatively overwhelm the system?" This distinction, suggesting carrying capacity and threshold effects, is an integral part of understanding how thinking of morality in ecological terms entails a new understanding of morality as a national resource that is threatened or under-protected. Thus, while each of the three cases below provide solid empirical support for the moral ecology, it is in their cumulative interaction that the strongest case emerges.

MEDIA VIOLENCE

One of the clearest examples of an adverse ecological impact is the issue of media violence. Movies, television programs, even the nightly news contain graphic and often nihilistic depictions of violence that perpetuate models of aggressive behavior and acquiescence of violent resolution of conflict. Though some exposure to media violence may have limited effect, clear correlations have been found with greater exposure, especially among younger or more impressionable individuals, suggesting that there is a threshold level beyond which severe disruption to the moral ecology occurs.

Media violence is one of the most studied subjects in the social sciences, and the findings of this research are remarkably conclusive.[17] Indeed, the extant literature contains over 3000 separate publications reporting research on the impact of television violence,[18] including a number of congressional hearings and government reports.[19] The weight of evidence from these studies overwhelmingly supports a positive correlation between television viewing and real-world violence. Not only have these studies proven that television programming is dangerously violent,[20] but also that this violence affects behavior in viewers. The American Psychological Association report of 1992 is typical of findings, stating that "children and adults who watch a large number of aggressive programs also tend to hold attitudes and values that favor the use of aggression to resolve conflicts." Some studies focus on the short-term effects of viewing violent acts on television, which include physiological arousal, attitude changes, and activation of aggressive thoughts and emotions.[21] Longer term studies agree on certain dangerous correlations between heavy viewing and traits such as desensitization to violence, feelings of victimization, and more actual violence and crime.[22] There are even natural experiments, as when researchers tracked the behavior of children in a remote Canadian town that first got television in 1978. Using rigorous procedures and neighboring communities as control groups, researchers found a 160 percent increase in aggressive behavior by grade school children within two years of the introduction of television.[23]

Most studies on the effects on children of watching televised violence have documented what some researchers have dubbed "Mean World Syndrome"— the feeling that violence is more prevalent in the world than it is.[24] Viewers may become paranoid and feel like victims themselves, afraid to go out into the world. These feelings of victimization can have adverse effects on their daily interactions with other people and cause other moral ecological problems. Victims cannot develop the confidence needed to be successful in relationships and in dealing with conflicts. A general pessimistic feeling about the world also forestalls initiative for positive change. This pessimism affects other people and spreads, tainting the interpersonal relationships of an entire community.

Another related negative effect on viewers of media violence is that they can be desensitized to violence in general.[25] Violent acts are "no big deal." A desensitized individual feels less empathy for the victims of real-life violence and proves to be far less likely to intervene on the victim's behalf. While desensitization to violence does not necessarily mean that the viewer is more violent, it does make him more likely to accept violent acts done by others.

The most common detrimental effect found by independent research efforts is the teaching of aggressive modes of dealing with conflict, sometimes called Direct Effects.[26] This effect at its simplest level is a "copy-cat" phenomenon in which viewers mimic actions they see from television programs or the news.[27] Other, more subtle effects that children are particularly susceptible to are more widespread and more dangerous. The more common and troubling Direct Effect is that violence on television can send a message that aggressive behavior is an acceptable and normal reaction to problems. From a moral ecological perspective, this is especially true in households where the child does not receive alternate, positive scripts for behavior from parental role models. Abuse and violent conflict in the home reinforce negative scripts. Children cannot learn to deal with a problem calmly and peaceably if they have never seen a conflict resolved in that manner. A child who does have a loving home environment might see all of the violence that there is on television and still not internalize the negative scripts presented there because of the more powerful example of behavior presented at home. A child's moral ecological environment can remain unaffected by the pollutant of media violence unless it has already been weakened by a dysfunctional home environment.

The context of violence also has much to do with its effects on viewer behaviors. Children are more likely to emulate violent acts committed by the hero. A violent action that goes unpunished is more dangerous than one presented as a "bad" thing. The 1969 National Commission showed that effects of television violence could be checked if it was clear that the victim of the violence was suffering. These findings also raise questions about the effects of a new generation of ultra-violent, ultra-graphic video games in desensitization.

The issue of sexual violence has evoked enormous scholarship and commentary. The wider moral ecology of sexual norms and behavior deserves its own treatment (see the discussion on family decline in the next section), but what concerns us here is a special kind of media impact that scholars term the "eroticization of violence." The proliferation of graphic pornography has sparked scholarly attempts to assess its impact. Most revealing were studies by Edward Donnerstein, who found a dramatic desensitization among young men exposed to media depictions of violence and sexuality—rape, sexual torture, sadomasochistic rituals, and murder of women in erotic settings. Such men were notably insensitive to depictions of a rape trial, and they were much more likely than a control group to say they would commit rape if they could get away with it. Notably, Donnerstein found that some R-rated slasher films were more desensitizing than X-rated films that depicted no violence. Donnerstein summarized his findings in an ecological fashion: "The overall pattern of the data across the various laboratory and field experiments discussed in this chapter strongly supports the assertion that the mass media can contribute to a cultural climate that is more accepting of aggression against women."[28] Some criminal justice officials also see a direct link between pornographic culture and the incidence of rape.[29]

The ecological movement of the 1960s struggled with similar problems reconciling the freedoms of a rights-based society with the desire for a safe and flourishing community. Thus a media executive who exercises his right to produce violent programming is analogous to a large farmer using pesticide. Neither ruins the environment by himself, but both contribute to a larger problem of pollution that threatens the environment when it concentrates and mixes with other contaminants. A moral ecologist would argue that the media are damaging a fragile moral environment by constantly exposing audiences to behavior that it is destructive to emulate. Some scholars, indeed, have begun to characterize the problem of media violence as a public health issue that hits the most vulnerable members of society.[30] Particularly troubling, they find, is that inner city youth watch the most television and have the fewest resources to resist its often nihilistic messages. What is most striking, however, is that media violence is powerful enough to be empirically verified even before it is analyzed in terms of synergetic effects with other cultural depredations.

Given the huge weight of empirical scholarship, the anemic public response—ratings systems, occasional boycotts, periodic public shaming—is instructive. The power of the free market in the mass media has rolled on unimpeded in spite of four decades of congressional hearings, government reports, and massive scholarly studies strongly suggesting that graphic violence in the media has produced a more violent society and premature deaths. Moreover, that impact can be exacerbated by other ecological depredations, particularly the manifest erosion of family vitality that we catalogue below.

THE BREAKDOWN OF THE FAMILY

While a large consensus exists among scholars about media violence, less agreement is found on the contentious issue of "family decline." Nonetheless, a growing body of research and commentary suggests that disturbing trends are undercutting the viability of family as a source of moral norms, social stability, and economic advancement.

The potential adverse impact of weakened family structures on the moral environment is enormous, given the key role of the family in imparting to children the requisite habits, mores, confidence, and tools for success in school and beyond. Clearly specifying how and to what extent such depredation occurs, however, is a daunting task because of the inherent complexity of ecological relationships. This complexity is most manifest here because the family lies at the center of the moral ecological nexus, both shaping and being shaped. Or, to use a more scientific formulation, family decline is both an independent and a dependent variable, both a cause and an effect of moral ecological disruptions. For example, the extent to which children resist moral pollutants from the outside environment depends largely on how well their families have inoculated them. In turn, the ability of families to do so can be undermined by larger ecological forces. The interactions are dynamic and interactive—in a word, ecological.

This ecological complexity provides enough ambiguity for some to dispute the seriousness of changes affecting the American family in the last three decades or so.[31] But one thing is evident: the rapidity and scope of the change is without precedent. In an examination of five hundred years of the European experience regarding marriage, Arland Thornton concludes that an unprecedented and swift restructuring of the institution has taken place.[32] Thus even though particular family patterns change over time, mounting evidence suggests that rising illegitimacy rates, divorce, and eroding adult norms of sacrifice have fostered successive generations of fragile and vulnerable children (the suicide rate among teens, for example, has tripled since 1960).[33] From the perspective of children, therefore, family decline is real.

Within a generation the nation experienced a dramatic erosion in family structure. In 1960 nearly 81 percent of all children were living with both biological parents. By 1990 that figure was barely 58 percent, a result of the growing number of out-of-wedlock births and divorce.[34] Households headed by single mothers have tripled in that time, and more and more children are living today in step-families, whose effectiveness is mixed.[35]

One of the most striking indications of a change in the normative environment is the rise in illegitimacy. The rate of out-of-wedlock births for all Americans jumped from 5 percent to 32 percent between 1960 and 1995. Among the subset of African-Americans the number reached an astonishing 70 percent, while among whites the figure was 25 percent. These figures suggest a normative de-stigmatization of single parenthood, a change in the moral ecology with profound implications. How profound is indicated by the fact that three decades ago, when Daniel Patrick Moynihan issued his famous warning on the weakening of the "Negro family," the illegitimacy rate among blacks was almost precisely where it now is for whites.[36]

Another change is the rising divorce rate. Ever since the no-fault divorce laws of the 1970s there has been a sharp rise in the number of marriages ending in divorce.[37] For the first time ever, the number of families disrupted by divorce has exceeded those disrupted by a death as the rates for divorce have more than doubled in the last thirty years.[38] Divorce, like illegitimacy, has largely lost its earlier stigma. Increasing tolerance may be an inevitable part of the application of the American ideals of individualism and self-fulfillment to the contract of marriage.[39] And while debate rages on the impact of divorce, Barbara Defoe Whitehead's summary of the evidence suggests a profound and continuing disruption to children of divorce.[40]

Though the reasons for these changes are indeed complex, one of the most important has been the sexual revolution. Here, too, we see an ecological disruption of momentous consequence. A profound change occurred as individuals (rather suddenly) felt freed from long-standing taboos and moral norms regarding sexuality. In perhaps no other area of society has the idea of fixed moral laws been so quickly undermined. But now two decades of research and empirical evidence suggest that liberated individuals have indeed altered the moral ecology, with profound consequences for children. Thus while the sexual revolution may have been genuinely pleasurable for a number of adults, it has been disastrous for many children. Whitehead shows how the epidemic of out-of-wedlock births, divorce, and disease, along with their economic fallout, can be partially traced to the way this new practice of sexual freedom disturbed a delicate balance in the moral ecology.[41]

Another potential source of decaying family strength is the changing nature of the capitalist system. The emergence of a global economy has produced profound disruption in the web of social relationships in communities affected by plant closings or eroding jobs. The collapse of the "breadwinner" wage also means that most families depend on the income of both parents, taking time away from child-rearing and household tasks.[42] Government policy and business practices have arguably been slow to accommodate the needs of working parents for flex time or better group child care options.[43] At the same time, in an attempt to reduce costs, many companies are asking full-time employees to work more hours each week while the company employs more temporary and part-time labor without benefits. Less parental time with children, more young people subjected to adverse peer influences, and greater general stresses on families are adduced as consequences of this changing workplace. Though some scholars argue that harmful effects of these shifts have not been clearly shown,[44] a moral ecological understanding leads us to believe that these changes affect the family in ways that can only be fully appreciated when seen in light of other influences. In a deeper sense, the global triumph of capitalism poses potential disruption to cultural foundations that sustain the moral environment as hedonic marketplace values seep into heretofore non-market relationships.[45]

As we might expect, the decline of the family in turn threatens the moral environment because so many problems are linked to family success. Single-parent families generally do not have the economic resources of intact families and often live below the poverty line. As a whole, children who do not have the advantages of a two-parent family show lower educational achievement, more psychological and criminal problems, increased poverty, and a stronger tendency to repeat the patterns of illegitimacy and divorce.[46] The lack of a strong family unit means that the child has little support in combating the detrimental effects of other negative influences in the moral ecology.

Poverty is one of the most insidious problems attached to family breakdown. David Ellwood of Harvard University concludes in his book *Poor Support* that "the vast majority of children who spend time in a single-parent home will experience poverty," while the opposite is true of children raised entirely in two-parent homes.[47] William Galston claims in his report to President Clinton that "child poverty rates would be one-third lower if family structure had not changed so dramatically since 1960."[48] The optimistic view in the 1970s that a divorced mother could quickly become self-sufficient has proven to be a myth, with economic problems compounded by a lack of paternal support.[49] One of the lessons from the past three decades is that the most vulnerable members of society are most harmed by disruptions in the moral environment.

Poverty often leads to increased crime, but the erosion of family structure itself is an indicator of crime independent of poverty. In fact, studies show that criminal activity is linked more closely to the family environment than to poverty.[50] William Barr, a former U.S. Attorney General, joins mayors, police, and community leaders in asserting, "If you look at the one factor that most closely correlates with crime, it's not poverty, employment, education. It's the absence of a father in the family."[51]

Children from broken families also tend to have lower educational achievement, with length of time in a single-parent home intensifying the impact. Indeed, so strong is the relationship that lower-income children from intact families have been found to outscore children from high-income single-parent families.[52] These lower levels of education translate into lower occupational achievement, frustration, and poverty in a vicious cycle. The socializing mission of the schools is lost, compounding the loss of socialization in the family.

In sum, many of the traditional functions of families have been undermined,[53] as individual moral decisions, supported by laws and society, have initiated a disintegration of the family unit. The change in family structure is well documented, as is the corresponding decline in families' ability to successfully socialize and support the country's youth. Outside influences such as peers and the media now replace the family in teaching children about the world, and we have seen how these influences may already be polluted. To be sure, many children emerge from single-parent and blended families successful, happy, and well-adjusted, and it is obvious that not all two-parent families are good ones; but a growing body of research nevertheless indicates that the advantages of the traditional family are powerful and important in children's development, and thus to society's health.

THE STATE AS PUSHER: LOTTERIES AND GAMBLING

In 1964, New Hampshire began the first legal lottery of this century in an attempt to boost waning tax revenues. Since then, thirty-six other states have decided that the lottery is the least painful way of bringing in more money. Very few states have turned down a lottery referendum once it made it to the ballot, and the business is growing beyond lotteries to high-stakes gambling. Proponents of the lotteries tout it as an entertaining way to raise money for schools and internal improvements. Unfortunately, relatively little debate centers on the propriety of putting the state in the ambiguous position of encouraging gambling addiction.

In the cases of media violence and family decline, the state role, though limited by liberal norms, can ameliorate degradation through modest regulation of private activity, such as zoning, pornography, requiring program ratings, or restricting the ease of divorce when children are involved. In the area of state promotion of gambling, however, government activity is itself the culprit. Thus not only does the government fail to restrain the gambling vice but actively encourages it. While lotteries and casino gambling may provide state revenues and entertain some citizens, mounting evidence suggests profound deleterious effects on a populace tempted by the promise of a big strike. Thus the social and moral costs of state lotteries likely outweigh the revenue benefits.

Once again an environmental parallel emerges. One of the prime targets of environmentalists has been the government. Federal agencies, along with state and local governments, have engaged in rather massive projects—damming rivers, building highways, and constructing other public works. Out of concern for the harmful environmental impact of these projects, federal law now requires the filing of the famous, or infamous, Environmental Impact Statement, which can run to multiple volumes. This process, in turn, gives leverage to those who wish to delay, or block, state action. A clear parallel emerges in the growing number of public and private studies of the impact of state-sponsored and state-promoted gambling. Indeed, critics of the "state as pusher" of gambling have begun to call for a formal process, even a moral impact statement, before states proceed further in sponsoring lotteries or licensing casinos.

One problematic aspect of the state's legitimization of gambling is its effect on compulsive gamblers. Pathological gambling is "a chronic and progressive failure to resist impulses to gamble, and gambling behavior that compromises, and disrupts, or damages personal, family, or vocational pursuits."[54] This widely studied and very real disorder affects somewhere between two and ten percent of the population. Another ten to fifteen percent bet more than they can afford.[55] Problem gamblers progress into increasingly heavier wagers until they lose control of their gambling and it disrupts their lives. The *Washington Post*, for example, featured a profile of "Tom," who had played the lottery for two years before God began whispering in his head. Strangely, God's messages echoed many of the New York lottery's advertising slogans. Soon, lottery was a $300-a-day habit. Another woman entered counseling after losing her house to lottery debt.[56] Bankruptcy and divorce often follow compulsive gambling. Thus we see how the state actively encourages its citizens to pursue a vice with expensive social costs in lost worker productivity, disrupted families, and state spending on counseling and welfare.

Research confirms that state lotteries do promote behaviors that progress into the later stages of problem gambling.[57] Just as marijuana is often described as a "gateway drug" leading to heavier drugs and then serious addictions, lottery play might be described as "gateway gambling." Thus thirty-six states are in effect "pushers" of a potentially addictive product that for some provides a taste of more dangerous behaviors. Indeed, the growth of casino gambling has paralleled that of lotteries in America. Riverboat casinos, mountain resorts, and other gambling enclaves are springing up with less and less controversy every year. This phenomenon probably would not have occurred without the active involvement of state governments in the gambling business, redefining previous moral norms and allowing a more permissive view of gambling in general through lottery promotion.

The need to encourage gambling has placed the state in increasingly compromising positions. Faced each year with declining profit margins and inconsistent growth, states have employed Madison Avenue advertising campaigns to increase the purchases of current players and to attract new ones. One billboard in a Chicago ghetto reads: "This Could Be Your Ticket Out." Flashy commercials, billboards, and prime-time television shows such as California's "The Big Spin" send the message that gambling is fun and will let you escape from a world of troubles. The ads are ubiquitous, bombarding the non-player and the addict alike. Some states have even gone as far as to direct-mail free coupons for tickets in order to draw in more players. As Michael Sandel notes, this places the state in the position of aggressively promoting "a perverse civic education . . . a message at odds with the ethic of work, sacrifice and moral responsibility that sustains democratic life."[58]

That lotteries are a form of regressive tax is borne out by the advertising companies' own market research. This research leads them consciously to target low-income workers and problem gamblers with ad campaigns that appeal particularly to those who can least afford it. Known weaknesses in gambling addicts are carefully exploited by psychologist-advertisers who know that one symptom of addiction is a phobia about forgetting to place a bet on a lucky day. So we see the commercial where a man is not able to place his bet on the very day that his lucky numbers come up.

Studies by the *Journal of Business Ethics* have also found that most of the promotion for lotteries contains some aspect of misleading advertising.[59] Indeed, state lotteries are the only advertisers that are not governed by regulatory laws for truth-in-advertising. These laws require any sweepstakes to post odds of winning on every ad, but state lottery ads carefully omit their astronomical odds. Much of the advertising that states have commissioned would be classified as misleading or even false if challenged in a court of law. This advertising, moreover, represents an almost unprecedented competition between the state and private businesses over consumers' disposable income.

Debates over the merits of a lottery generally revolve around the financial expectations of this ambiguous money-distribution device, but there is also a subcurrent of debate that revolves around moral ecological concerns. Charles Clotfelter, a leading Duke University economist, finds one of the most distressing aspects of lottery advertising to be that government is squandering its already limited supply of moral capital by equating lottery purchases with a kind of civic virtue.[60] Exhortations to stay in school or immunize your children or say no to drugs carry less weight when the state is just as loudly telling you to buy more lottery tickets. Also, as the state promotes gambling, it alters the meaning of the American Dream. Instead of valuing hard work and education, people are told they should be trusting in fortune and get-rich-quick schemes. Corruption and crime are commonly associated with "harder" forms of gambling, and lotteries were originally outlawed in the early 1900s because of widespread lottery fraud.

Many lottery opponents, consequently, fear that the introduction of state lotteries will erode more general norms of public morality. Once again, the moral ecological insight shows why this fear is well grounded, especially in light of other diverse forces simultaneously chipping away at the moral fabric.

SCHOLARLY, PHILOSOPHICAL, AND POLICY IMPLICATIONS

As we have seen, the concept of moral ecology highlights the combined interactive effects of a wide array of normative depredations. Thus detrimental effects of media violence are amplified by the lack of parental involvement often characteristic of a broken home or a fatherless family. In turn, home life might be shattered by the disruption of a parent who becomes a compulsive gambler, or by an aggressive parent who learned violent scripts early in life. Linear cause-and-effect relationships thus will elude social scientists because effects have a web of causes. In the environmental metaphor, societal mores, families, churches, mediating institutions, businesses, and the state constitute the soil, air, water, flora, and fauna of the moral ecosystem. All interact and affect the other parts. In turn, a weakening in one part of the system will affect the capacity of the others to filter out moral pollutants. If moral depredations are allowed to accumulate, therefore, problems will become both hard to trace and difficult to address. In other words, as ecological damage erodes healthy norms, a dangerous threshold could be reached when the carrying capacity of the system is overwhelmed, causing the culture to spiral downward. Our inner cities provide a vivid glimpse of such a scenario.

For scholars the interactive and cumulative features of moral ecology, while daunting in their complexity, suggest a rich array of testable hypotheses and observable implications.[61] For example, we would expect to see the moral depredation greatest among the most vulnerable members of society, who lack resources to inoculate themselves against environmental influences. Corroboration for this hypothesis is found in the numerous studies and commissions on the status of America's children. What they suggest is that, in spite of enormous economic growth, America's children are, as a group, worse off than three decades ago. Most vulnerable to ecological disruptions, children today are far more susceptible to suicide and violence, early sexual activity, unhealthy habits, excess television viewing, substance abuse, declining educational performance, and obesity than in 1960. This dismal pattern led one commission to conclude that "America has orphaned" its young.[62]

Other hypotheses wait further exploration. For example, where we find resiliency against cultural pollution we would expect to find strong churches, neighborhoods, traditions, and mores that foster a healthy local ecological climate that shields people from wider influences. Another implication of the theory is that we would find some moral depredation throughout sectors of society, including among those at the high SES end, given how pervasive some forces are. Also, we expect to see greater moral depredation where state and local laws and norms are permissive, where multiple factors are at play, where the interactive effect would be strongest.

As a scholarly construct, therefore, the moral ecology is more concrete than culture, and more enduring than fleeting phenomena in the political realm.

Moreover, it responds to the lament about the inability of social science to explain transformations. Just as biologists do not predict the direction of evolution, but have explanations for why species will evolve, moral ecologists would not presume to predict precisely how complex interactions would ramify, only that they will. Thus, moral ecology represents both a timeless nomological insight and a more dynamic empirical construct than social and political theories that depend on a transient stability of the regime or a fragile epistemological framework.[63] Moral ecology, thus, appears to be a merging of natural law and empirical science.

The moral ecology also explains the disjointed nature of contemporary public discourse, as ecological arguments often clash with rights-based presuppositions. Liberal sex educators, for example, implicitly operate with individualistic assumptions, and thus they see a desperate need to teach about, and provide, contraception to stem unwanted pregnancies by already sexually active teens. Conservative critics, on the other hand, argue that technocratic approaches to sex education will disrupt the moral environment in which young people live and unintentionally increase sexual activity among those not emotionally ready for it, resulting in heartbreak, unwanted pregnancies, and abortion. On abortion, too, we see this disjointed discourse. Proponents of abortion rights see the issue through the liberal lens of the autonomous individual.[64] But one often hears in pro-life circles an ecological analysis similar to the one made by critics of sex education. Providing abortion on demand, they argue, has profoundly altered the moral environment by propelling the sexual revolution and undermining male responsibility. Where fear of pregnancy and the shotgun wedding restrained predatory male behavior, abortion now loosens the restraints on male irresponsibility.

Or take efforts to prevent the spread of AIDS. Some see the issue in technical terms as increasing condom use or clean needles. Others see such technical remedies as doomed to failure because they undermine moral restraints and monogamous relationships that offer the only sure solution. Thus moral ecologists are not surprised when the condom message fails to stem risky sexual behavior among some young gay men who, through a sense of youthful invulnerability or nihilistic fatalism, seem to resist the education efforts of their brethren.

Given the analysis so far, it is understandable that the concept of moral ecology is linked with conservatism, especially the cultural variety. But it would be a mistake to assume that moral ecology contains only conservative implications. Progressives, defenders of labor, even socialists could legitimately employ moral ecological insights in their critique of untrammeled capitalism. Indeed, in the global context one can make the case that corporations and their executives are increasingly unlikely to see themselves as tied to particular communities where enlightened self interest would foster concern with the wholesome development of society. The evidence, instead, suggests a largely amoral corporate environment, with its heavy focus on short-term profits, its lack of loyalty to workers, its unconcern about advertising messages (and their blatant appeals to the seven deadly sins), and its sponsorship of trash television and morally ugly music. In fact, the capitalist marketplace, as any parent instinctively knows, cannot constrain itself from exploiting children and teens for profit.

The moral ecology thus poses rich philosophical dilemmas. We have seen how both biological and moral ecologists share the perception that individual behavior, under certain circumstances, brings unintended harmful effects. Both confront the excesses of individual freedom in a liberal society. Classical liberal doctrine, we should remember, viewed individuals as autonomous rights-bearers floating in the state of nature, restricted in their freedom only when they bump into others. "It's my land and I will do as I please" is a phrase intimately linked in liberal thought to its cultural analogue, "It's my life and I will do as I please." An ecological understanding challenges this liberal notion with an understanding of interdependency and ecosystem health. Ironically, during the 1960s, when "individual liberation" was so celebrated (though more practiced by those who came after), environmental thinkers were cautioning about the potentially destructive consequences to the physical ecology of unrestrained individual freedom. As the cultural fallout of the 1960s continues into the 1990s, it is not surprising that environmental metaphors have entered the public lexicon. In response to the claim that cultural critics are attempting to "impose" their narrow sectarian morality, the moral ecological insight offers a better defense, perhaps, than previously inchoate invocations of "traditional values." Moreover, the growing empirical evidence briefly surveyed here lends powerful credence to the claim that the moral ecology is not a sectarian construct, but instead is a reasonably accurate depiction of real human dynamics. Since people are not only autonomous individuals, but social creatures as well, they are influenced by the moral environment around them; thus we understand the wisdespread angst about a coarsening of the culture that undermines civility, manners, even sportsmanship.

If the moral ecology exists, in other words, if individuals and business undertake behavior in their freedom that upsets the delicate balance of the normative environment, then a number of broad implications for policy follow. For example, a moral ecological understanding may contribute to the debate over the role of the courts in American life. Certainly our uniquely interventionist judiciary has altered the conditions of governance on issues ranging from vagrancy to pornography to family life, arguably weakening the capacity of local people to shape and protect their moral environment.

Defenders of the courts, of course, fear that the response to perceived moral depredations will be vigorously statist. That fear may be justified, given the history of the environmental movement. Garrett Hardin and other environmental thinkers, for example, saw no remedy to environmental disaster other than state regulation—"mutual coercion mutually agreed on."[65] Otherwise, the irresponsible would reap rewards at the expense of the responsible. Only coercive law could address the tragedy of the commons. This formulation, of course, underlies much of our environmental law today.

In the moral realm we have already seen tough criminal enforcement of drugs and mild government coercion in such areas as regulation of children's television, rating labels on music and movies, zoning of pornography, toughened child pornography laws, requiring a V-chip on television, and stiffening divorce laws.

Should the sense of cultural decay become more urgent, however, we could expect more harsh proposals, just as has occurred in the environmental arena. Indeed, some environmental radicals went pretty far: they advocated coercion against seemingly sacred liberal freedoms (especially procreation); they embraced triage and lifeboat ethics in development programs; and they accepted mass starvation as nature's solution to overpopulation. Indeed, elitists such as Hardin seemed to revel in shocking liberal sensibilities.[66] If there is an analogous vision among moral ecologists, it may be found among the radical Christian reconstructionists, who wish to replace the American constitutional order with a theocratic society.

Of course, just as many environmentalists rejected Hardin's draconian prescriptions, so most moral ecologists are not calling for Puritan penalties for adultery. Moreover, the lessons of the past decades of environmental politics teach us that draconian restrictions on freedom will be massively resisted. One alternative focus employs economics. Recall that one aim of environmental law is to internalize the costs of pollution that otherwise burden society. A cutting edge response to this concern has been to employ market mechanisms—to charge fees for pollution rights, thus either providing public treasuries with environmental cleanup money or encouraging companies to internalize those costs by adopting cleansing technology that avoids fees.

One can imagine how controversial such schemes might be if applied to the cultural and moral arena. But thinking about them is instructive. Magazine publishers, movie producers, television stations and the like would be asked to bear the cost of the moral pollution they promulgate. Violent programmers would be taxed the heaviest, given the mounting evidence of their deleterious impact on society. Violent, racist, misogynist lyrics similarly would be seen as costly to the culture they pollute, and cultural impact studies might be employed to determine the level of fees to be charged for their use. Divorce fees would similarly make sense, given the huge literature cataloging the adverse impact of family breakup on children. We can readily see how such would become a Puritan's dream or a liberal's nightmare.

But how far-fetched is such a scenario? We have already seen ideas floating around suggesting a financial reward to teenage girls if they remain un-pregnant till age 18. Or consider the implicit understanding of the moral ecology in so-called sin taxes, such as President Clinton's idea of having increased taxes on alcohol and tobacco to subsidize health care. A certain symmetry exists here because of the empirical connection between substance abuse and rising health care expenditures. Thus a new kind of economics could arise that would attempt to quantify the true cost of individual choices and internalize them. At minimum, one could imagine serious efforts to incorporate research on the adverse economic impact of compulsive gambling as a restraint on government promotion of the vice.

We are not proposing a rush to this scheme. As we are skeptical about the findings of economists when they quantify the value of a wilderness area or the cost of a dam, we would probably find the practical problems of such a scheme in the moral and cultural arenas insurmountable. Still, such a thought experiment reveals moral ecological insights. Just as clean air or pristine forests are public goods, something the average individual cannot purchase, a healthy moral climate can be similarly viewed as a precious public good, especially to parents—a public good that they cannot entirely create or purchase on their own. Should those who pollute such a public good not somehow pay the price?

Now, if draconian regulation is not desirable and the above economic measures impractical, where does that leave us? For many moral ecologists, particularly the neo-conservatives and communitarians, the answer lies in a revival of a robust civil society. Instead of governmental coercion, they look to those mediating institutions—churches, civic groups, youth groups, communities, neighborhoods, families, and local schools—that foster mores, teach moral codes, inoculate the young against cultural pollution, and embed individual behavior in a web of restraining relations. Not willing to abandon the classical liberal tenets of individual freedom and autonomy, they assert that governmental coercion or censorship may be less successful in shaping the culture than a recognition by the government of the value of mediating institutions. Government law and administration at all levels, they argue, should at minimum not undermine the vitality of mediating institutions and at best facilitate these agents of healthy socialization. Moreover, public agencies, notably public schools, can inculcate widely shared moral principals—such as honesty, integrity, courage of convictions, and kindness toward others. More broadly, scholarly analysis should focus on the way these mediating institutions are valuable public goods that deserve protection and nurture.

This more benign remedy, too, has its environmental analogy. Some public programs, such as soil conservation efforts, appear to work better when they rely less on regulation and more on education, landowner interest, peer pressure, and moral suasion. Critics of command approaches to the protection of endangered species also tout the successful record of voluntary environmentalism, as when Boy Scouts and 4-H members built millions of homes for the endangered wood ducks. Thus, the argument goes, merely strengthening voluntary associations and institutions will go a long way toward solving our moral ecological crisis. And one should not gainsay the influence of individual efforts, such as those of popular radio psychologist Dr. Laura Schlessinger, who dispenses moral advice to the confused or tempted. At the very least, all of us can ponder how we can become "better stewards" of the moral environment.

But there is a nagging sense that if the moral ecology is as real, vital, delicate, and interwoven as the concept suggests, remedies will not be so neat and painless.

A liberal society we are, but if we cannot handle degradation of the moral environment well within liberal norms, then more fundamental challenges may follow.

NOTES

1. Tony Hillerman, *Coyote Waits* (New York: Harper Paperbacks, 1990).

2. Bauer's statement is contained in an article entitled "The Moral Ecosystem," Focus on the Family Citizen newsletter (March 18, 1991); Charon's comes from a syndicated column, *Daily Oklahoman*, July 7, 1993. See Medved's *Hollywood Versus America* (New York: HarperCollins, 1992) on his diagnosis of video pollution; the specific quotation from Patrick Buchanan was cited in *Christian Science Monitor*, May 17, 1993, 3.

3. See Robert Bellah, Richard Madsen, William M. Sullivan, Ann Swidler, and Steven M. Tipton, *Habits of the Heart* (Revised edition. Berkeley: University of California Press, 1996); numerous works by Christopher Lasch, including: "Capitalism vs. Cultural Conservatism," *First Things* (April 1990), 15–23; *The True and Only Heaven: Progress and Its Critics* (New York: Norton, 1991); *Culture of Narcissism* (New York: Norton, 1991); *Haven in a Heartless World: The Family Besieged* (New York: Basic Books, 1979); and Daniel Bell, *The Cultural Contradictions of Capitalism* (New York: Basic Books, 1976).

4. See Amatai Etzioni, *The Spirit of Community* (New York: Crown, 1993); Mary Ann Glendon, *Rights Talk* (New York: Free Press, 1991), and Jean Bethke Elshtain, *Democracy on Trial* (New York: Basic Books, 1995).

5. See Robert Putnam, *Making Democracy Work* (Princeton, NJ: Princeton University Press, 1993); and "Bowling Alone: America's Declining Social Capital," *Journal of Democracy* 6 (January 1995): 65–78; "Tuning In, Tuning Out: The Strange Disappearance of Social Capital in America," *PS: Political Science & Politics* 38 (December 1995): 664–683.

6. See especially the works of Andrea Dworkin, *Pornography: Men Possessing Women* (New York: Plume, 1989); and Catharine MacKinnon, *Only Words* (Cambridge, MA: Harvard University Press, 1993).

7. See Allen D. Hertzke, *Echoes of Discontent* (Washington, DC: Congressional Quarterly Press, 1993), chapter 3.

8. On the epistemology of the scientific method we draw upon Karl R. Popper, *The Logic of Scientific Discovery* (New York: Basic Books, 1959), and *Objective Knowledge: An Evolutionary Approach* (Oxford: Clarendon Press, 1972). Popper stressed the importance of asserting falsifiable propositions or implications of a theory, the lack of which has doomed certain grand theories. In addition, he stressed that theories are better and deeper when they both encompass and surpass prior theories in relatively elegant and parsimonious fashion. The moral ecology appears to do just that, as it encompasses a number of theories from diverse fields that have attempted to explain the way media violence, gambling promotion, and normative change in the culture affect human responses.

9. David Easton, *The Political System: An Inquiry into the State of Political Science*, second edition (New York: Knopf, 1971). Easton's criticism of hyper-factualism has been addressed since his writing. But his implicit criticism of timid theorizing that never rises above the middle level remains prescient.

10. See Gary King, Robert Keohane, and Sidney Verba, *Designing Social Inquiry: Scientific Inference in Qualitative Research* (Princeton, NJ: Princeton University Press, 1994),

29. King et al. clarify that the quest for scientific inference involves "using the facts we know to learn about facts we do not know" (46). While this paper does not test hypotheses derived from the theory of moral ecology, our confidence in the richness of the theory is buoyed by the fact that so many diverse testable propositions can be readily derived from it.

11. Lawrence Dodd argues that biology is a better model for the social sciences because of the complexity of variables and the potential for change. See Lawrence Dodd, "Congress, The Presidency, and the American Experience: A Transformational Perspective," in James A. Thurber, ed., *Divided Democracy* (Washington, DC: Congressional Quarterly Press, 1991).

12. One scholar of science even suggests that the interdisciplinary study of ecology has direct ethical linkages to human behavior because the interdisciplinary study of ecology cannot bracket human influences. See Stephen Toulmin, *The Return to Cosmology: Postmodern Science and the Theology of Nature* (Berkeley: University of California Press, 1982), 228–229, 234, as cited in Bellah et al., *Habits of the Heart*, 284.

13. The term "moral ecology" has been used by several scholars, but heretofore without a systematic evaluation. As well as we can determine, Robert Bellah first used the term in *Habits of the Heart*, at various times interchangeably with the term "social ecology," to describe the "subtle ties that bind human beings to one another" (284). In turn, Michael Novak entitles a section of *The Catholic Ethic and the Spirit of Capitalism* (New York: Free Press, 1993), "Protecting the Moral Ecology." Novak explains Pope John Paul II's warning to American Catholics (that the U.S. media may be undercutting the moral virtues necessary for democracy and capitalism to work) to mean that the media represent "a form of pollution in the moral order even more destructive than the pollution of the physical environment." "There is," he says, "an ecology in morals as well as in the biosphere." Novak also ends a 1997 essay on cultural crisis with a call to recognize the moral ecology, but without specifying what that might mean. See Michael Novak, "Truth and Liberty: The Present Crisis in Our Culture," *Review of Politics* 59 (Winter 1997): 5–23. Allen Hertzke used the term in *Echoes of Discontent* prior to having read specific passages of Bellah and Novak, and it is possible that Bellah and Novak latched onto the formulation independently of one another. The fact that several scholars coined the same theoretical construct, apparently independently of one another, provides one kind of corroboration that a genuine empirical phenomenon has been identified.

14. See especially Aldo Leopold, *The Sand Country Almanac* (New York: Oxford University Press, 1987), originally published in 1949.

15. Garrett Hardin, "The Tragedy of the Commons," *Science* 162 (13 December 1968), 1243–1248.

16. There is a growing literature in public health on indicators of healthy communities and how they appear to influence individual healthy behaviors.

17. Confidence in the ability of the social sciences to discover truths about human behavior has been severely tested by often ambiguous or contested findings. Sociologists, psychologists, political scientists, and the like rarely agree on theories of human behavior. Moreover, studies full of qualifications to maintain academic integrity frustrate policymakers who search in vain for hard data on which to base decisions. Nonetheless, the academic community has produced an uncharacteristically strong consensus about the impact of media violence and behavior. See especially Leonard Berkowitz, *Aggression: Its Causes, Consequences, and Control* (St. Louis: McGraw-Hill, 1993); A. C. Huston, E.

Donnerstein, H. Fairchild, N. D. Feshback, P. A. Katz, J. P. Murray, E. A. Rubenstein, B. Wilcox, and D. Zukerman, *Big World, Small Screen: The Role of Television in American Society* (Lincoln: University of Nebraska Press, 1992); National Institute of Mental Health, *Television and Behavior: Ten Years of Scientific Progress and Implications for the 80s,* vol. 1 (Washington, DC: U.S. Government Printing Office, 1982); John P. Murray, "Children and Television Violence," *Kansas Journal of Law and Public Policy* 4 (1995), 7–14; Brandon S. Centerwall, "Television Violence: The Scale of the Problem and Where to Go From Here," *Journal of the American Medical Association* 267 (10 June 1992): 3059–3063; Deborah Prothrow-Stith, *Deadly Consequences* (New York: Harper Perennial, 1991); and most recently, National Television Violence Study Council, National Television Violence Study, Summary of Findings and Recommendations, Mediascope, http://www.mediascope.org/mediascope/ntvs.html.

18. Carl Cannon, "Media Violence Increases Violence in Society," in Leone Bruno, ed., *Violence in the Media* (San Diego: Greenhaven Press, 1995).

19. Since 1952 numerous congressional hearings have explored the problem of media violence. The Surgeon General issued reports in 1972 and 1979 that firmly established the correlations mentioned in this paper. In 1969, the National Commission on the Causes and Prevention of Violence reported to President Lyndon Johnson that television was violent and that violence was adversely affecting viewers, a finding echoed by the Attorney General's 1984 Task Force on Family Violence. Dozens of government agency reports reinforce the research of other major organizations. See *Progress Report of the National Commission on the Causes and Prevention of Violence to President Lyndon B. Johnson* (Washington, DC: U.S. Government Printing Office, 1969), Publication No. 0–331–948.

20. Determining the level of violence in television programming is often seen as a necessary first step in evaluating effects. Huston et al., in *Big World, Small Screen,* calculated that the average child sees approximately 12,000 violent acts a year. Levels have risen over the last two decades, as noted by B. Hattemer, "Violence in the Media Causes Youth Violence," in *Violence: Opposing Viewpoints,* edited by S. Barber and K. L. Swisher (San Diego, CA: Greenhaven Press, 1996).

21. Expanding on the more primitive theories of "modeling," scholars note that the translation of violence on television to violence in real behavior is more complex than simple learning, but that the acquisition of aggressive "scripts" is an important part of the process. See Berkowitz, *Aggression;* R. P. Abelson, "Script Processing in Attitude Formation and Decision-Making," in *Cognition and Social Behavior,* edited by J. S. Carroll and J. W. Payne (Hillsdale, NJ: Lawrence Erlbaum, 1976); and Hattemer, "Violence in the Media."

22. Studies around the world, from Canada to South Africa, show correlations between television violence and real-world effects. See George Gerbner, "Violence and Terror in the Mass Media," UNESCO Report No. 102, Paris, 1988. This report summarizes findings from many countries. Others with similar findings include: L. Bogart, "Violence in the Mass Media," *Television Quarterly* 8 (1969): 36–47; Centerwall, "Television and Violence"; National Institute of Mental Health, *Television and Behavior,* Huston et al., *Big World, Small Screen;* V. Viemero, "Violence Viewing and Adolescent Aggression: A Longitudinal Study," paper presented at the International Television Studies Conference, London, April 10–12, 1986, ED 294555; C. Kruttschnitt, L. Heath, and D. A. Ward, "Family Violence, Television Viewing Habits, and Other Adolescent Experiences Related to Violent Criminal Behavior," *Criminology* 24 (1986): 235–267; and L. R. Huesmann

and L. D. Eron, eds., *Television and the Aggressive Child: A Cross-National Comparison* (Hillsdale, NJ: Lawrence Erlbaum, 1986).

23. L. A. Joy, M. M. Kimball, and M. L. Zabreck, "Television and Children's Aggressive Behavior," in *The Impact of Television: A Natural Experiment in Three Communities*, edited by T. M. Williams (Orlando, FL: Academic Press, 1986).

24. George Gerbner may have been the first to use the term, but others have found the Mean World Syndrome a useful model, including Murray, "Children and Television Violence," and the large research team for Mediascope, which described it as "increased feelings of victimization."

25. Berkowitz, *Aggression*.

26. Like Mean World Syndrome, researchers disagree about the terminology, though their conclusions remain strikingly similar. Murray refers to Direct Effects as the complex modeling and script building that TV violence activates. The violence on TV justifies and teaches aggressive behavior that may be mimicked or incorporated into the viewer's value system in some other way.

27. The National Commission in 1969 concluded that national violence rates rise predictably after a violent newscast or program, but that such violence is generally confined to individuals who were already disturbed. Nonetheless, one could argue that a more wholesome moral ecology might prevent some individuals from crossing the line.

28. Edward Donnerstein, "Pornography: Its Effect on Violence Against Women," in *Pornography and Sexual Aggression*, edited by Neil Malamuth and Edward Donnerstein (Orlando, FL: Academic Press, 1984). After the experiment the young men were resensitized. The quote is from page 40.

29. The District Attorney of Oklahoma County, Bob Macy, cited a dramatic reduction of reported rapes when the city cracked down—through a combination of legal sanctions and zoning—on the previously thriving sex industry, which included numerous porn shops and video stores, nude dancing lounges, and open prostitution rings. From a 1996 interview with the authors.

30. Deborah Prothrow-Smith sees media violence as one of several factors—but a tangible one—that cause destructive behavior and thus should be viewed as a public health problem. Prothrow-Smith even mentions that the effects of TV violence are magnified when poor children have few other safe recreational activities and often lack a real-life male role model. Deborah Prothrow-Smith, *Deadly Consequences* (New York: Harper-Collins, 1991).

31. Critics of the traditional two-parent family consider current trends evolution rather than disintegration and question what interest there can be in preserving this outdated institution, if it can even be preserved. See Judith Stacey, "Good Riddance to 'The Family': A Response to David Popenoe," *Journal of Marriage and the Family* 55 (August 1993): 545–548; and Edward Kain, *The Myth of Family Decline: Understanding Families in a World of Rapid Social Change* (Lexington, MA: Lexington Books, 1990). These voices, we conclude, remain unpersuasive in light of the growing body of evidence that family decline is real and problematic. The best summary of that evidence is in *Promises to Keep*, edited by David Popenoe, Jean Bethke Elshtain, and David Blankenhorn (Lanham, MD: Rowman and Littlefield, 1996).

32. Arland Thornton, "Comparative and Historical Perspectives on Marriage, Divorce, and Family Life," in Popenoe, *Promises to Keep*.

33. William Bennett, *Index of Leading Cultural Indicators* (Washington, DC: Heritage Foundation, 1993).

34. David Blankenhorn, *Fatherless America* (New York: Basic Books, 1993), 18–19.

35. Barbara Defoe Whitehead cites a wide variety of Social Science research, including the National Commission on Children, and the National Survey on Children, in summarizing the problems with stepfamilies as replacements for the original family of two biological parents. These include lack of as strong a commitment to stepchildren, feelings of isolation from the new stepfamily, increased risk of abuse, and anxiety and uncertainty resulting from both the original change into the stepfamily and possible future family breakups since stepfamilies are far more likely to break up than are other families. See Barbara Defoe Whitehead, "Dan Quayle Was Right," *Atlantic Monthly* 271 (April 1993): 47–84.

36. The National Center for Health Statistics of the U.S. Department of Health and Human Services released figures on birth rates for 1995 on October 4, 1996. Of all births, 32 percent were out of wedlock, with the racial breakdown revealing illegitimacy rates of over 25 percent for whites, 41 percent for Hispanics, and 69.5 percent for blacks.

37. Moira Eastman concludes from her studies that divorce is associated—for adults as well as children—with "increased rates of poverty, mental illness, suicide, physical illness, mortality, depression, drug abuse, cigarette smoking, homelessness, juvenile crime, and school failure." Moira Eastman, "Myths of Marriage and Family," in Popenoe, *Promises to Keep*.

38. David Popenoe, "American Family in Decline, 1960–1990: A Review and Appraisal," *Journal of Marriage and the Family* 55 (August 1993): 527–545.

39. Michigan is leading several states in rethinking its no-fault divorce laws in an implicit understanding of the moral ecology. Michigan State Representative Dalman is quoted in *The New York Times* as saying that people "must begin to see the connection between divorce and other problems," such as poverty and juvenile delinquency. Dirk Johnson, "No-Fault Divorce Is Under Attack," *The New York Times*, February 8, 1996, A8.

40. Barbara Defoe Whitehead, "Dan Quayle Was Right," and "The Decline of Marriage as the Social Basis of Childbearing," in Popenoe, *Promises to Keep*, 3–14.

41. Whitehead, "Dan Quayle Was Right."

42. Indeed, 1980 saw the first time that more married women were employed than not. Jane Riblett Wilkie, "Marriage, Family, and Women's Employment," in *Marriage and Family in Transition*, edited by John N. Edwards and David H. Demo (Boston: Allyn and Bacon, 1991).

43. Ibid., 143.

44. Ibid., 155.

45. One hypothesis is that the potential disruptive effects of these capitalist values will vary from cultural context to context. Thus, while Daniel Bell in *The Cultural Contradictions of Capitalism* may have been prescient in identifying hedonic tendencies in modern capitalism that can disrupt the moral ecology, some cultures and even nations may be better equipped to minimize such effects while others will find themselves extremely vulnerable.

46. Regarding psychological problems, Deborah Dawson found that children were twice as likely to need professional psychological help and generally scored more poorly on a number of wellness indicators when they did not live with both biological parents. Nicholas Zill et al. independently reached the same conclusions in his work with children whose parents divorced. Deborah Dawson, "Family Structure and Children's Health and Well-being: Data from the National Health Interview Survey on Child Health," *Journal*

of Marriage and the Family 53 (1991): 573–84. Nicholas Zill, Donna Morrison, and Mary Jo Cairo, "Long-term Effects of Parental Divorce on Parent-child Relationships, Adjustment, and Achievement in Young Adulthood," *Journal of Family Psychology* 7 (1993): 91–103.

47. David Ellwood, *Poor Support* (New York: Basic Books, 1988), 46.

48. William Galston and Elaine Kamarck, "A Progressive Family Policy for the 1990s," in *Mandate for Change* (Berkeley, CA: Berkeley Books, 1993). This book was prepared by the Progressive Policy Institute.

49. Whitehead, quoting McLanahan, in "Dan Quayle Was Right."

50. Edward L. Wells and Joseph H. Rankin, "Families and Delinquency: A Meta-analysis of the Impact of Broken Homes," *Social Problems* 38 (February 1991): 71–89.

51. Wade Horn, *Father Facts* (Lancaster, PA: The National Fatherhood Initiative, 1995), 23. The issue of fatherless families is given full length treatment by David Blankenhorn, *Fatherless America: Confronting Our Most Urgent Social Problem* (New York: Basic Books, 1995).

52. University of Illinois researchers go as far as to conclude that generally "the longer the time spent in a single-parent family, the greater the reduction in educational achievement. Their numbers transcend the problems of poverty associated with single-parent (and therefore usually single-income) families." See Sheila Krein and Andrea Beller, "Educational Attainment of Children from Single Parent Families: Differences by Exposure, Gender, and Race," *Demography* 25 (1988): 221–233. Astone and McLanahan found lower-income children with "intact" families outscored children from high-income, single-parent families. See Nan Marie Astone and Sarah S. McLanahan, "Family Structure, Parental Practices, and High School Completion," *American Sociological Review* 56 (1991): 309–320.

53. Popenoe, in "American Family in Decline," notes how families in the past provided apprenticeship in a trade, religious socialization, education, and some security for the aged. Now, however, he sees only childbearing or emotional support, and not always that.

54. American Psychological Association, *Diagnostic and Statistical Manual of Mental Disorders* (Washington, DC: APA, 1980), 291.

55. Joseph Hraba, Waiman Mok, and David Huff, "Tonight's Numbers Are . . . Lottery Play and Problem Gambling," *Journal of Gambling Studies* 7 (1991): 178.

56. Wolfe Shenk, "Everyone's A Loser," *Washington Monthly* (July/August 1995).

57. Hraba et al., "Tonight's Numbers Are . . . ," 192.

58. Michael J. Sandel, "Bad Bet," *New Republic* (March 10, 1997), 27.

59. James M. Stearns and Shaheen Borna, "The Ethics of Lottery Advertising: Issues and Evidence," *Journal of Business Ethics* 14 (January 1995): 50.

60. Charles Clotfelter, *Selling Hope: State Lotteries in America* (Cambridge, MA: Harvard University Press, 1989).

61. King et al., in *Designing Social Inquiry*, suggest that social science research should seek to derive as many observable implications of a theory as possible. And even though the inherent complexity of interactions inhibits the kind of predictions found in physics, nonetheless, numerous observations derived from the theory can be made. A useful emendation of King's formulation, we think, is Lawrence Dodd's suggestion that biology is a better model for the social sciences because it does not purport to predict how the ecological interactions will evolve, only that they do evolve in ways we can observe. See Dodd, "A Transformational Perspective."

62. On children see Richard Louv, *Childhood's Future* (Boston: Houghton Mifflin,

1990); David Blankenhorn et al., *Rebuilding the Nest* (Milwaukee: Family Service America, 1990); Victor R. Fuchs and Diane M. Reklis, "America's Children: Economic Perspectives and Policy Options," *Science* (January 1992): 41–46; Carnegie Commission Report, *Ready to Learn: A Mandate for the Nation* (Princeton: Princeton University Press, 1992); and National Commission on Children, Senator Jay Rockefeller, Chair, *Beyond Rhetoric: A New American Agenda for Children and Families* (Washington, DC: Government Printing Office, 1991). The quote is from Ernest Boyer, commenting on the findings of the Carnegie report. See Ernest Boyer, "America Has Orphaned Its Young," *Los Angeles Times* (8 December 1991), M5. These studies do not dismiss the importance of economic forces, but they do stress the pivotal nature of the family, community, and moral environment in which children live.

63. Dodd, "A Transformational Perspective."

64. Of course, a broader analysis supporting abortion rights underlies the rights-based rhetoric. Feminist analysis suggests that without abortion rights guaranteeing reproductive control for women, they will not be able to fully participate in all spheres of society; the glass ceiling will remain. This broader analysis, however, appears less ecological and more liberal in its aims and understanding.

65. This was how Hardin phrased the remedy in his essay "Tragedy of the Commons."

66. "The freedom to breed," he said in one of his memorable phrases (ibid.), "is intolerable." To Hardin, therefore, China's brutal population control effort is a positive model.

2

Are Communitarians "Premodern" or "Postmodern"? The Place of Communitarian Thought in Contemporary Political Theory

MURRAY JARDINE

Communitarian political theory and policy analysis have gained increased prominence in American academic and public debate over the past decade. The term "communitarian" itself, however, still seems to be only vaguely defined. To some, the term implies a backward-looking nostalgia for an idealized communal past that would restore old social hierarchies and limit individual freedom; to others, it sounds suspiciously like a kind of closet socialism that would replace the market economy with centralized regulation in the name of community. The theoretical basis of communitarianism is hardly less confusing: communitarians cite with approval an incongruous collection of theorists that includes Aristotle, G. W. F. Hegel, sometimes Jean-Jacques Rousseau, and occasionally even John Dewey. Is there a unifying theoretical perspective to communitarian thought other than a vague dissatisfaction with modern individualism? Does communitarianism look mainly to the past or mainly to the future? I will argue that a coherent theoretical basis for communitarianism can be developed, but that much current communitarian thought seems incoherent because it appears to draw upon two incompatible theoretical models. I will do this by placing the concerns of communitarian thinking in the broader context of late twentieth-century political theory. Examining the major issues in contemporary political philosophy should, I think, illuminate the central thrust of communitarianism.

The essential concern of present-day political theory could hardly be more fundamental: it amounts to nothing less than finding a new basis for political order. To state the situation most briefly (and drastically), there is widespread agreement among contemporary philosophers, theologians, and political theorists that we are, at the end of the twentieth century, also at the end of an era. On this view, modern Western bourgeois culture, which had its beginnings with the Protestant Reformation in the sixteenth century, developed more completely during the Enlightenment of the seventeenth and eighteenth centuries, and reached the peak of its coherence in the nineteenth century, has in the twentieth century become increasingly incoherent and self-destructive. Specifically, by the late twentieth century, the central idea spawned by the Enlightenment, the idea of progress, has become increasingly implausible. That is to say, the very foundation upon which modern bourgeois civilization is constructed has crumbled. Hence the sense of an ending—a sense which, far from being confined to a few academics, pervades popular culture as well, in forms ranging from the meaninglessness articulated by alternative rock to the millennarian expectations of fundamentalist groups.

To explain more fully, the modern conception of progress assumes that human beings can, both individually and collectively, control their own fate more or less independently of God or nature; more specifically, most versions of the idea of progress state that humans can, through science and technology, understand and control their environment to the point where they can progress toward and possibly achieve a realm of freedom where individuals are not subject to hierarchical command, and can choose and pursue their own personal goals to the extent that they do not impinge on other individuals' freedom to do the same. The doctrine of progress has taken relatively moderate and cautious forms (as in Anglo-American liberalism) as well as much more radical versions (such as revolutionary Marxism); in any case, central to all notions of progress is the idea that humans can make the world demonstrably better, and that betterment means individual freedom in some sense. It has been frequently argued by twentieth-century political theorists that the modern idea of progress is derived from, or rather is a this-worldly perversion of, Christian eschatology, which promises the freedom of God's Kingdom, but this interpretation is not universally accepted.[1]

In any event, the idea of progress, which in the nineteenth century triumphed over older, more pessimistic conceptions of the human condition, was mortally wounded by the cataclysms of the first half of the twentieth century. The unprecedented slaughter of World War I, the total economic collapse of the Great Depression, and the limitless human degradation of World War II have made the idea of human progress toward cosmopolitan freedom seem naive at best, and, to the extent that these disasters were caused by fanatical attempts to bring about progress, positively sinister at worst. To be sure, the half-century since the end of World War II has been one of relative peace and unprecedented prosperity, but it has also been characterized by a profound sense of cultural exhaustion; it seems that the failure of this era's material affluence to bring any real sense of human happiness has completed the destruction of the progressive ideal begun by the catastrophes of the previous half-century. Perhaps the best indicator of this pervasive mood within Western societies has been the reaction to the collapse of communism in eastern Europe. What should have been, from the standpoint of moderate progressivism, the most significant event of the century—

the more-or-less worldwide acceptance of the liberal democratic formula for freedom—has been greeted with, on the whole, utter indifference.[2]

Somewhat more concretely, many specific reasons can be (and have been) given for the theoretical incoherence and practical demise of the progressive dream. I will not digress into a full discussion of these issues but will simply give a few examples.

First, it has become clear in the twentieth century that although technology can often solve existing problems, pathologies, or other sources of human dissatisfaction, it invariably creates new problems when it does so. To take perhaps the most obvious example, the poverty and epidemic disease that were the curse of humanity in pre-industrial societies have been substantially (although not entirely) conquered by economic development, but in their wake have arisen complicated and potentially even more threatening problems of environmental pollution and depletion of natural resources. Similarly, the modern rights and liberties that have freed individuals from the (frequently harsh) hierarchical authority of the past seem to have resulted in profound feelings of insecurity and alienation—so much so that in the twentieth-century whole nations have voluntarily—indeed, enthusiastically—submitted to tyrannical control as a way of escaping such disorientation.

Another familiar example of the contradictions at the core of the progressive ideal is the profoundly disappointing twentieth-century discovery that technology can control and destroy as readily as it can free and build. The philosophers of the eighteenth century who proclaimed the doctrine of progress did not anticipate the machine gun, much less the atomic bomb. A more subtle manifestation of this paradox is that although modernity has made individuals formally free and equal from a legal and political standpoint, modern technology has vastly increased the potential for detailed control of individuals in their work environments and even as consumers. Modern individuals are subjected to systems of technical examination and psychological manipulation unimaginable in premodern societies.

These issues are perhaps best illustrated by public reactions to the revolution just beginning in computers and related fields such as biotechnology. Although the third industrial revolution, as it has been called, has generated some utopian expectations, it has also caused considerable apprehension about the dislocative effects of the new technologies as well as their vast potential for misuse. The initial experiments in cloning, in particular, have been greeted mainly with a collective shudder at the possibility of horrors exceeding even those of the Holocaust.

The most important reason, however, for the demise of the idea of progress would have to be its own self-destructive internal moral logic. If the idea of individual freedom—that each individual should be free to choose and pursue his or her own goals—is taken with full seriousness, it ultimately becomes impossible to determine any common standards for, or limits upon, human actions. The modern liberal limitation that individuals should be free to pursue their own goals as long as they respect the equal freedom of others to do the same is really of no help, since two individuals may, precisely because of their freedom from authority, have radically different understandings of what this actually means. The conception of autonomous individual agency contained in the idea of progress leads logically to a situation where individuals can have utterly different, incompatible perceptions of reality and therefore of what constitutes an acceptable limitation of human freedom.

Friedrich Nietzsche, writing slightly more than one hundred years ago, was the first to recognize this situation, which he called the "advent of nihilism." Nihilism, according to Nietzsche, was the end result of the Enlightenment, with its dream of progress toward human autonomy through scientific rationality. By attempting to turn themselves into gods, controlling their own destiny, humans would instead turn themselves into beasts, or rather something worse than beasts, with unlimited power to control and to destroy but with no moral constraints on the use of that power. What seemed a century ago to be the raving of a madman has now become, as we said earlier, the most conventional of academic and even popular wisdom; the term "postmodern," referring vaguely to the collapse of the modern moral order, has become a commonplace. To understand more clearly what communitarian thinking is about, then, it will be helpful to consider in slightly more detail the modern Enlightenment understanding of political order, as well as the major alternatives that have emerged following its demise.

Any vision of political order inevitably embodies certain assumptions about the structure of reality and how human beings attain knowledge of that reality; indeed, because they shape the vocabulary of social practice, these assumptions largely determine the possibilities inherent in a human society. The breakdown of a political community is really the collapse of a cosmology. Hence any attempt to understand a political order must examine the epistemological and ontological assumptions underlying that order.

Modern political theory and practice are inextricably tied to the Enlightenment conception of acceptable knowledge. For modernity, valid knowledge must take the form of exact, exhaustively specifiable, impersonal "facts." Such "objective" knowledge can be obtained only if the knowing subject—the human being who ascertains facts—ruthlessly eliminates all unexamined assumptions and prejudices from the mind and proceeds by well-defined logical procedures to derive truth, that is, facts, from an unbiased examination of the relevant experiential evidence. Ontologically, reality is structured in such a way that it can be exhaustively described by such facts, and experiences that purport to describe dimensions of reality which cannot be so treated are regarded as derivative or even unreal. Progress results from the accumulation of proven, factual knowledge and its application to concrete human problems.

As has been extensively documented in the twentieth century, the Enlightenment project of obtaining exact, impersonal, objective knowledge has failed, mainly because it is impossible for the subject to obtain the independence from context required by this epistemological model. Human beings inescapably approach any cognitive task from within the confines of a "paradigm," or particular set of presuppositions, and cannot subject their assumptions or methodology to full critical assessment. The application of the Enlightenment model of acceptable knowledge has thus had the effect of actually shrinking the domain of intelligible human experience. In the seventeenth and eighteenth centuries, what is now called "religious belief" conflicted with the model of exact, impersonal knowledge and was relegated to the realm of mere opinion; by the late nineteenth century, morality, which the Enlightenment philosophers had thought could be placed on a firm, secular footing by skeptical rationalism, was in serious danger of becoming a matter of subjective value; and by the mid-twentieth century it had become an open question whether even the hardest sciences could meaningfully be described as objective. This potential disintegration of even scientific knowledge into a thoroughgoing subjectivism is, at one level, what has caused the breakdown of any limits to human action in late modernity, as it has become difficult, if not impossible, to determine the relative validity of competing truth claims and thus rule out any belief system and its practical implications as unacceptable.

Politically, the Enlightenment's normative model has conceived of human societies as collections of autonomous individuals pursuing their own personal goals subject only to a neutral framework of laws that prevents these individuals from interfering with each other's actions. The task of political theory in this model is to maximize individual freedom by articulating a set of neutral, impersonal rules that does not favor any individual or group of individuals, or any particular way of life, over others. This is the basic project of modern liberalism, although liberals notoriously disagree over precisely what institutionally embodied set of rules—whether the free market of nineteenth-century liberalism or the activist state favored by twentieth-century liberals—actually maximizes individual autonomy. Marxism differs from liberalism only in that it assumes that destroying the oppressive and discriminatory institutions of capitalism will eventually eliminate the need for any rules and thus for the state that enforces them, replacing regulation with voluntary cooperation. Political progress for both liberalism and Marxism consists in applying scientific knowledge to develop the material resources and institutional framework necessary to allow full individual autonomy. In either case, the essential political ideal—the society of independent individuals pursuing their goals without subordination to hierarchical command—corresponds to the modern conception of acceptable knowledge in several ways.

The autonomous individual pursuing his (or more recently, her) own independently chosen goals corresponds to the autonomous subject achieving neutral, unbiased knowledge, as does the liberal political theorist, establishing universal, neutral rules to order the society of autonomous individuals, or the critical Marxist, using a scientific understanding of the historical process to unmask ideological delusions embedded in the liberal's supposedly neutral rules. Additionally, the idea that individuals should be autonomous to pursue their own goals is itself partly a result of the relegation of questions about ultimate human ends to the realm of the subjective; since such questions lie outside the public sphere of objectively ascertainable facts, their resolution must be left up to the private judgment of each individual person. The collapse of the idea of neutral, purely objective knowledge has meant the collapse of the modern liberal political project as well, as it brings about the recognition that any set of rules inevitably privileges certain individuals, groups, or ways of life, which in turn has led to the despairing conclusion that since reality is ultimately only a chaos of subjective interpretations, no true knowledge is possible and human societies are finally ordered only by sheer power.

Practically, as we have already briefly mentioned, although modernity at its best has achieved some impressive successes in limiting arbitrary personal power and improving the material conditions of life, the modern attempt to create a society of autonomous individuals has ultimately had the paradoxical result of vastly increasing the potential for tyranny. Even at the earliest stages of the Enlightenment, Thomas Hobbes had observed that the logical outcome of conceiving society as a collection of purely isolated individuals was perpetual conflict, or a "war of all against all," which would require an authoritarian government to maintain order. A more subtle analysis was made by Alexis de Tocqueville in the nineteenth century when he suggested that the attempt to replace older ascriptive hierarchies with neutral, impersonal rules would eventually have the effect of subjecting every conceivable detail of everyday life to bureaucratic regulation—a system of "administrative despotism" rather than violent authoritarianism. In the twentieth century, various social commentators, most notably Max Weber and more recently Michel Foucault, have refined Hobbes's analysis even further by cataloging the ways in which the attempt to liberate the individual from premodern hierarchies and social roles through enlightened education has actually turned each individual into an object of administration by an army of experts. Finally, as numerous sociological studies have demonstrated, the conditions of isolation and anomie produced by modern individualism are indeed fertile ground for demagoguery and ideological fanaticism. The combination of these practical results of the goal of individual autonomy and the breakdown of any ethical or even epistemological limits has turned this century into an orgy of destruction, both in the worldwide ideological wars of the first half of the century and more recently in the wanton waste of the consumer economy as it attempts to anesthetize the malaise experienced throughout contemporary Western societies.[3]

In terms of a theoretical response to the situation of late modernity, it seems to me that it is possible to discern the emergence of at least three different approaches to reconstructing political order.

As we have seen, Nietzsche was the first fully to comprehend the disintegration of modernity into nihilism. He did not view this situation with despair but rather saw it as an epochal opportunity. Accepting that reality is indeed nothing more than a chaos of interpretations, and that all political order is a form of domination, Nietzsche saw that power rests with the strongest, which for him meant the most persuasive—those who could create the most aesthetically appealing interpretation of the human condition. The collapse of modern scientific rationalism and its illusion of utilitarian truth would allow the recreation of an aristocratic order based on the persuasive capacities of an artistic elite.

In the twentieth century, there have been two major appropriations of Nietzsche's philosophy. One has been the vulgarization found in the Nazi and fascist pseudo-aristocracies. The other, originating with Martin Heidegger's response to Nietzsche, associated with such theorists as Foucault and Jacques Derrida and sometimes referred to as "postmodernism," has, contrary to both Nietzsche and Heidegger, an egalitarian political vision. For these thinkers, the recognition that reality is a chaos of interpretations implies that one who wants to live most fully should be open to "otherness"—that is, to other interpretations of the world and their practical manifestations which bourgeois rationalism has suppressed and silenced. Additionally, the postmodernists see Nietzsche's insight into the inevitability of power and domination as a tool with which any hierarchy can be discredited. Political orders such as modern technocracies, which legitimate themselves through supposedly objective truth-claims, can be shown to be nothing more than interpretations of the world that benefit those in power. Hence egalitarian freedom would be found not in the easily-corrupted utopias of Marxism and anarchism, but rather would take the form of a continual effort to deconstruct the disciplinary matrix of any social system that might develop; liberation comes not from tearing down the existing society and replacing it with a new one but from creating tolerance and autonomy by constantly discrediting would-be structures of domination. The postmodernists see the Nietzschean insight as liberating, but in a different way than Nietzsche did. If attempts to construct neutral systems of rules based on supposedly objective truth have paradoxically intensified the potential for domination, perhaps recognizing the relativity of truth and thus the inevitably of domination may actually permit its amelioration through an aesthetic appreciation of the other.[4]

The postmodernist project is open to at least four crucial objections. First, and most fundamentally, it could be argued that postmodernism is not really *postmodern* at all but rather only a kind of disappointed modernism, since, like Nietzsche, it does not really question the Enlightenment conception of valid knowledge but simply draws the conclusion that since no knowledge claims can meet the modern standard of objective truth, there is ultimately no truth. Second, from a practical standpoint, it is not clear why recognizing reality as a chaos of competing interpretations implies openness and tolerance. This was not Nietzsche's conclusion. If domination is inevitable, why attempt to limit it? Why not simply engage in ruthless domination? The assumption that we would want to avoid or limit domination seems to be a product of the Western humanist tradition, with its idea of a rationally structured reality, which the postmodernists claim to repudiate. Third, to the extent that contemporary Western, and espe-

cially American, societies already have developed a substantially aesthetic orientation, as manifested in the consumer capitalist economy, a postmodernist
politics may simply be co-opted by the forces it proposes to critique. What could
be more postmodern than MTV? Finally, and more ominously, a postmodernist
politics, by attempting to discredit existing structures of domination, could destroy political orders, such as liberal capitalism, where domination is at least
somewhat restrained, and allow them to be replaced with overtly tyrannical political movements, whether of the left or of the right, whose leaders have simply
answered the second question raised above with an unbridled assertion of the
will to power. This is to say that postmodernism does not really seem to have
resolved the issue of limitations on human action that is the fundamental issue
of late modernity. Or, to paraphrase Allan Bloom, those who have given Nietzsche a tolerant, egalitarian interpretation do not seem to realize that they may
be playing with fire.[5]

A different response to the breakdown of the Enlightenment project has been
to revive the classical conception of political order as articulated paradigmatically
by Aristotle. This "neoclassicist" approach is most closely associated with political theorists such as Leo Strauss and his followers. In the classical cosmology,
reality is a fixed, hierarchical natural order where every being has a place and a
function. Human knowledge comes from practice, from participating in the natural order by fulfilling the purpose appropriate to one's place. The political community is concerned not with achieving maximal autonomy for individuals but
rather with teaching individuals the virtues appropriate to their places in the
society and thus in the cosmos. Individuals achieve happiness not by pursuing
self-chosen goals but by virtuously fulfilling their naturally ordained role.[6]

The classical model of political order is compelling in many ways, but from
the standpoint of late modernity it has at least two fatal flaws. First, however
much we may have become disillusioned with the modern goal of individual
autonomy, the hierarchical social organization implied in premodern political
theory is not palatable to us because we fear its potential for arbitrary personal
power. Indeed, this is so partly because of the breakdown of the modern idea of
neutral knowledge: we suspect hierarchies precisely because of the capacity for
domination inherent in claims to epistemological privilege. Any postmodern
political order, it seems, must be democratic in some sense, although perhaps not
in the manner envisaged by liberalism and socialism.

Second, and even more importantly, the unchanging natural order that is the
fundamental assumption of classical political theory has been one of the prime
casualties of modern science. This is true in two senses—first in that we now
know that we can indeed control and change nature through science, and more
fundamentally in that we now realize that "nature" is not something that exists
independently of us, but rather is (at least partly) our own interpretive construct.[7]
Indeed, this is where lies one of the crucial contradictions in the Enlightenment
paradigm. Early modernity assumed a fixed natural order (albeit one that was

mechanistic rather than functional), but it also assumed that humans could understand this order well enough to control it—without realizing that such control would itself imply a changeable nature. It is precisely the late modern recognition of the extent of human agency, wrought partly by the development of science, that has made establishing moral and epistemological limits such a difficult task. If the Enlightenment ideal of progress represents a denial of human finitude, it nevertheless must be admitted that the premodern anthropology underestimates human capacities. We cannot reestablish moral limits on human action by crawling back into the cosmic womb.

A corollary to this second objection is that the classical cosmology is problematic because it may well be the precursor of the Enlightenment model of acceptable knowledge. The classical conception of an unchanging natural order, independent of human agency and with a definitive, context-neutral meaning for each component of that order, is very similar to the modern notion of an impersonal, acontextual fact. In both cases knowledge which does not transcend human interpretation to reach the level of pure, detached theory is regarded as mere opinion. The modern rejection of the transcendent as undemonstrable may not be so much a rebellion against Plato as his logical successor.[8]

The third discernible response to the breakdown of the modern project is represented by recent developments in the philosophies of language and science, both of which have been heavily influenced by the later work of Ludwig Wittgenstein, by political theorists such as Eric Voegelin and Hannah Arendt, whose work in certain ways parallels and even anticipates these developments, and by more recent political theorists such as Jürgen Habermas, Charles Taylor, and Alasdair MacIntyre, who have explicitly or implicitly built on Wittgensteinian foundations. Recent philosophy of language and of science have recognized that adequate descriptions of these phenomena will not be found through reconstructions of them in terms of strictly specifiable logical relations, but rather in explications of the overall context of these activities, including the structures of the communities that sustain them. Obtaining reliable knowledge is not a matter of somehow abstracting oneself from any context to achieve objectivity, but of learning the communal practices appropriate within various contexts. Or, to put it in Habermas's terminology, the model of human rationality that is emerging from these endeavors is communicative rather than subject-centered.[9]

Richard Bernstein has argued that these developments can be described as an attempt to go "beyond objectivism and relativism." By objectivism, Bernstein means the Enlightenment conception of acceptable knowledge already described, that is, that which takes the form of exactly specified, impersonal facts. As we have seen, relativism is simply the flip side, or logical outcome, of objectivism, since once we have taken the objectivist model of acceptable knowledge as our standard, the discovery that no knowledge claims can meet this standard forces us to conclude that there can be no valid knowledge. Recent philosophy of science and of language, however, have shown that we can have reliable knowledge that does not conform to the objectivist Enlightenment model, and that regarding the world as a chaos of interpretations is not the only alternative to objectivism.[10]

Politically, the theorists whom I have grouped together differ significantly, but it can be said that the emerging model of rationality just described implies that human existence should be understood in the context of a community, rather than in terms of isolated individuals, and that political communities can order themselves not through neutral ahistorical rules, or through a natural hierarchy, but through communicative activities, or in other words, through speech. For Habermas, this means paradigmatically debate about the common good, and much of his theoretical attention has been directed at an explication of how to structure such debate. Others, most notably MacIntyre and theologian Stanley Hauerwas, have been concerned with reviving virtue as a central ethical category, and have argued that the stories that make up a community's history can provide the examples of virtuous action that can guide the individual members of the community.[11] This model of political order is similar to Aristotle's, except that the historical narratives of a community take the place of his functional natural order. In this understanding, political order is not something given in the eternal structure of the cosmos, but rather something humans speak into existence, just as human activities generally are not governed by any natural telos, but instead are structured by communicative contexts.

We might say that if this approach is epistemologically "beyond objectivism and relativism," then from a moral standpoint it attempts to go beyond the dichotomy represented by neoclassicists and postmodernists, that is, that either there is an unchanging, natural moral order independent of human agency or else all human conceptions of morality are arbitrary conventions. That is, from this standpoint, any community's moral understandings are to some extent conventions, but these conventions are by no means arbitrary; the human capacity to create a world through speech does imply that there are ways to make moral judgments with a reasonable degree of confidence. Or, we might say that this position is *truly* postmodern in that it articulates a way of thinking that attempts to go beyond the standard modern dualisms, unlike postmodernism, which seems to be really only a type of disappointed modernism.

This rough threefold classification should make it more clear why communitarian thinking frequently seems rather poorly defined. It will almost certainly have occurred to the reader that communitarians and their ideas appear, at least, to draw on both the second, neoclassicist model, and the third model which attempts to go "beyond nature and convention." Or rather, to state it more clearly, communitarians in general seem to have a political vision—a democratic community based on narrative traditions and committed to debate about the common good—congruent with many aspects of the third model, but frequently employ rhetoric that suggests they are reasoning from something like the second model.

An excellent example of this occurs in Robert Bellah's book *Habits of the Heart*, one of the definitive statements of the communitarian outlook. Bellah argues that American culture exhibits four basic elements or traditions—the older biblical and civic republican understandings of human social existence, which were oriented toward the maintenance of local communities, and the more recent, purely modern utilitarian and expressive individualist models of society, committed to maximizing individual freedom, understood in, respectively, economic or aesthetic terms. Bellah argues that American society needs to recover the older communal traditions to stem the tide of social disintegration evident in the late twentieth century. In this sense he sounds like a neoclassicist. Certainly his conception of education, for example, seems very close to the neoclassicist model:

The American college through much of the nineteenth century was organized on the assumption that "higher learning constituted a single unified culture." The purpose of college education was to produce a "man of learning" who would have "an uplifting and unifying influence on society." Literature, the arts, and science were regarded as branches of a single culture of learning. It was the task of moral philosophy, a required course in the senior year, usually taught by the college president, not only to integrate the various fields of learning, including science and religion, but even more importantly to draw the implications for the living of a good life individually and socially.[12]

This understanding of learning seems to assume something like the classical cosmos where every being and every type of knowledge has a place, and it wants to produce something very much like the classical ideal of the well-rounded, public-spirited gentleman. In fact, Bellah explicitly contrasts this model with the specialized professionalism of the twentieth century and the impoverished public life that results from it. Elsewhere, however, Bellah clearly wants to disengage himself from the hierarchical implications of the classical model:

There are both ideological and sociological reasons for the growing strength of modern individualism at the expense of the civic and biblical traditions. Modern individualism . . . has come into confrontation with those aspects of biblical and republican thought that accepted, even enshrined, unequal rights and obligations—between husbands and wives, masters and servants, leaders and followers, rich and poor. As the absolute commitment to individual dignity has condemned those inequalities, it has also seemed to invalidate the biblical and republican traditions. . . . We thus face a profound impasse. Modern individualism seems to be producing a way of life that is neither individually nor socially viable, yet a return to traditional forms would be to return to intolerable discrimination and oppression. The question, then, is whether the older civic and biblical traditions have the capacity to reformulate themselves [in a more egalitarian way] while simultaneously remaining faithful to their own deepest insights.[13]

Here Bellah clearly sounds more like our third position "beyond nature and convention." He wants to restore community and public life, but in a democratic manner that recognizes the equality and dignity of every person. What emerges from this analysis appears to be a situation where Bellah and other communitarians, as we have said, have in mind something like the third position but (as Bellah himself implies) frequently lack the conceptual vocabulary to express this and end up falling back on formulations borrowed from the neoclassicist school of thought, which, with its model of community (albeit an organic, hierarchical one), bears a superficial resemblance to the ideas of MacIntyre, Hauerwas, and others.

How then can communitarians make their positions and reasoning more clear, both to themselves and to others? I believe there are at least two ways they can do so. The first would be to employ something like the classificatory model I have presented here: instead of speaking in a reactive manner about the destruction of traditional communities by modern individualism, it would be more helpful to talk about a modern individualist culture that has some impressive accomplishments but which has exhausted its constructive possibilities, and the need for a new ("postindividualist," perhaps) culture that can retain the constructive achievements of modernity while reconstructing new egalitarian forms of community. By doing this, communitarians could clearly distinguish themselves from the neoclassical school and could respond effectively to criticisms that they are wallowing in hopeless nostalgia.

Second, communitarian thinking could be made more coherent if it addressed more explicitly the epistemological dimension we have discussed. Communitarians need to make it more clear that their goal of democratic community represents an epistemological alternative to the objectivism of modernity as well as to the proto-objectivism of the neoclassicists or the relativism of the postmodernists. This could allow them to articulate more clearly and explicitly a vocabulary appropriate to and formative of the structure and functioning of new democratic communities which would escape the moral dualism of nature and convention.

Let me explain more clearly what I mean by briefly examining one possible approach to this task. In my discussion of the movement beyond objectivism and relativism, I mentioned that theorists such as MacIntyre and Hauerwas have argued that communal narratives can, in a sense, take the place of Aristotle's finite cosmos by providing individuals with a sense of place in a community but at the same time allow the construction of more flexible, democratic communities than classical political theory seems to allow. There is in fact a body of literature that gives an indication of why this might be so. Anthropologists, psychologists, and others have studied the differences between premodern oral cultures, which have little or no writing, and modern literate cultures, where, thanks to the printing press, all or most of the population has at least basic reading ability. Although there are of course many benefits to literacy, there is also strong evidence that the heavily visual orientation produced by literacy (as well as more recent visual means of communication such as television and computers) can contribute significantly to an objectivist conception of knowledge. With literacy, one tends to take the relative stasis and impersonality of the written word, as opposed to the dynamic and personal spoken word, as an epistemological paradigm, so that one conceives of valid knowledge as that which somehow exists independently of any human interpretation (as a written or printed word on a page appears to do) and dismisses knowledge dependent on interpretation as mere subjective "opinion." It is hardly accidental that the initial sharp distinction between true, objective knowledge and mere opinion was first made by the highly literate classes of ancient Greece and that the even more extreme dichotomy between facts and values became the prevalent mindset during a period of universal literacy and heavy reliance on visual means of communication. The discovery that all knowledge is formed by interpretation has, as we have already discussed, resulted in the relativism of late modernity. If we want to escape the objectivist/relativist dichotomy, and the nature/convention dualism that derives from it, this analysis implies, certainly not a return to a nonliterate state, which would be absurd, but rather an attempt to redress somewhat the imbalance between vision and hearing in our everyday experiential orientation. A greater reliance on sound, and specifically human speech, could decrease our tendency to understand knowledge, including moral knowledge, in the rigidly dualistic manner characteristic of modern visual culture.[14]

If this is the case, and a reorientation toward sound might help us escape the dualisms of modernity, then the narrative-based communities discussed by MacIntyre and Hauerwas, which would entail greater use of oral communication, could be one way to achieve such a reorientation. At the same time, such communities could avoid the hierarchies of the past by recognizing the capacity of every person to formulate narratives that can contribute to debate about the common good. Such a conception could preserve and even enhance the modern commitment to equality while abandoning modernity's narrow and ultimately destructive conception of acceptable knowledge as well as the utopianism that the modern notion of individual autonomy generates. Stated another way, it could recapture the more flexible, practice-oriented model of moral reasoning and education employed by premodernity without reviving the rigid hierarchies of the past. Communitarians could present themselves, not as nostalgically yearning for a vaguely-defined communal solidarity destroyed by modern individualism, but as working toward a new kind of democratic community, based on a new model of knowledge, in turn derived from a different sensory orientation, to replace the exhausted visually-based objectivist (now relativist) individualism of modernity. Such an approach would clearly establish communitarianism as looking toward the postmodern future—without, however, the illusions of modern progressivism.

NOTES

1. See, for example, Eric Voegelin, *The New Science of Politics: An Introduction* (Chicago: University of Chicago Press, 1952) and Karl Löwith, *Meaning in History* (Chicago: University of Chicago Press, 1949). For an alternative interpretation, see Leo Strauss, *Natural Right and History* (Chicago: University of Chicago Press, 1953).

2. See Francis Fukuyama's strangely prophetic "The End of History?" *The National*

Interest (Summer 1989): 3–35. Fukuyama argues that the end of communism signals the essential worldwide triumph of liberal democracy but that the new world order of individual freedom will be, frankly, a meaningless bore.

3. Broad overviews of the development and later demise of modern liberal rationalism can be found in Thomas A. Spragens, Jr., *The Irony of Liberal Reason* (Chicago: University of Chicago Press, 1981); Roberto Mangabeira Unger, *Knowledge and Politics* (New York: Free Press, 1975); William M. Sullivan, *Reconstructing Public Philosophy* (Berkeley: University of California Press, 1986); and John H. Hallowell, *The Decline of Liberalism as an Ideology* (Berkeley: University of California Press, 1943). For more general discussions of the breakdown of modern scientific rationalism, see Richard Bernstein, *Beyond Objectivism and Relativism: Science, Hermeneutics and Practice* (Philadelphia: University of Pennsylvania Press, 1988) and Alfred North Whitehead, *Science and the Modern World* (New York: Macmillan, 1925). In addition to the classic discussions of Tocqueville and Weber, influential sociological studies of modern individualism include Robert Nisbet, *The Quest for Community: A Study in the Ethics of Order and Freedom* (Oxford: Oxford University Press, 1953); David Riesman, *The Lonely Crowd: A Study of the Changing American Character* (New Haven, CT: Yale University Press, 1961); Richard Sennett, *The Fall of Public Man: On the Social Psychology of Capitalism* (New York: Random House, 1974); Christopher Lasch, *The Culture of Narcissism: American Life in an Age of Diminishing Expectations* (New York: W. W. Norton, 1978); and Robert Bellah et al., *Habits of the Heart: Individualism and Commitment in American Life* (Revised edition. Berkeley: University of California Press, 1996).

4. Early statements of postmodern themes can be found in Martin Heidegger, *Nietzsche*, vol. 4: *Nihilism*, trans. Frank A. Capuzzi, ed. David Farrell Krell (San Francisco: Harper and Row, 1982) and especially in Martin Heidegger, "The Question Concerning Technology," in *Basic Writings*, ed. David Farrell Krell (New York: Harper & Row, 1977), 283–318. Definitive works by Jacques Derrida include *Speech and Phenomena: And Other Essays On Husserl's Theory of Signs*, trans. David B. Allison (Evanston, IL: Northwestern University Press, 1973) and *Of Grammatology*, trans. Gayatri Chakravorty Spivak (Baltimore: Johns Hopkins University Press, 1976). Michel Foucault's position is most fully developed in *Discipline and Punish: The Birth of the Prison*, trans. Allan Sheridan (New York: Vintage Books, 1979); *The History of Sexuality*, vol. I: *An Introduction*, trans. Robert Hurley (New York: Random House, 1979); and *Power/Knowledge*, ed. Colin Gordon (New York: Pantheon Books, 1980). See also Jean-Francois Lyotard, *The Postmodern Condition: A Report on Knowledge*, trans. Geoff Bennington and Brian Massumi (Minneapolis: University of Minnesota Press, 1984).

5. See Allan Bloom, *The Closing of the American Mind* (New York: Simon and Schuster, 1987), 154.

6. See for example, Strauss, *Natural Right and History*.

7. Leo Strauss argues that the fundamental question for political theory is whether nature is functional or mechanistic (see *Natural Right and History*, 7–8), but this misses the point. The real question is whether it is meaningful to talk about a "nature" independent of human agency in the first place.

8. A more detailed discussion can be found in Jürgen Habermas, *Knowledge and Human Interests*, trans. Jeremy J. Shapiro (Boston: Beacon Press, 1971), 301–317.

9. See Voegelin, *The New Science of Politics*; Hannah Arendt, *The Human Condition* (Chicago: University of Chicago Press, 1958); Habermas, *Knowledge and Human Interests* and *Theory and Practice*, trans. John Viertel (Boston: Beacon Press, 1973); Alasdair

MacIntyre, *After Virtue: A Study in Moral Theory*, 2d ed. (Notre Dame, IN: University of Notre Dame Press, 1984); and Charles Taylor, *Sources of the Self: The Making of the Modern Identity* (Cambridge, MA: Harvard University Press, 1989).

10. See Bernstein, *Beyond Objectivism and Relativism*.

11. See MacIntyre, *After Virtue* and Stanley Hauerwas, *A Community of Character: Toward a Constructive Christian Social Ethic* (Notre Dame, IN: University of Notre Dame Press, 1981) and *The Peaceable Kingdom: A Primer in Christian Ethics* (Notre Dame, IN: University of Notre Dame Press, 1983).

12. Bellah et al., *Habits of the Heart*, 298–299.

13. Ibid., 143–144.

14. The discussion here is quite simplified. For a more detailed treatment, see Walter J. Ong, S. J., *Orality and Literacy: The Technologizing of the World* (London: Methuen, 1982), *The Presence of the Word: Some Prolegomena for Cultural and Religious History* (New Haven, CT: Yale University Press, 1967); Eric A. Havelock, *Preface to Plato* (Cambridge, MA: The Belknap Press of Harvard University Press, 1963); as well as my "Sight, Sound, and Epistemology: The Experiential Sources of Ethical Concepts," *Journal of the American Academy of Religion* (Spring 1996): 1–25, and *Speech and Political Practice: Recovering the Place of Human Responsibility* (Albany, NY: SUNY Press, 1998).

3

How Much of Communitarianism Is Left (and Right)?

MARC STIER

Communitarianism is a doctrine that seems, at first glance, to cut across the usual categories with which we apportion the political spectrum. Both leftists and rightists are concerned about the excessive individualism of contemporary life. They are apprehensive about the decline of civic knowledge and participation. They are uneasy about the imbalance between what we demand from and what we are willing to give to public life. While they wish to protect our liberties, they have misgivings about the consequences of freedom for the ties that bind us to each other. They would like to see a greater emphasis on virtues rather than rights. And they worry that an excess of individualism threatens the very rights that makes individualism possible.

Trouble begins, however, when communitarians begin to offer specific proposals to enhance civic virtue and communal life. At this point, communitarians often find themselves in the cross-fire that results from two divisions between the left and the right today. First, while some leftists and some rightists are comfortable talking about civic virtue, they often have rather different virtues in mind. Second, leftists and rightists drawn to communitarian ways of thought differ on how economic policies and institutions ought to be reformed so as to strengthen civic virtues and communities in America. These conflicts are so serious that anyone who wants to make a case for communitarianism that has broad appeal would do well to avoid them. That is precisely what so many communitarians do. The difficulty, however, is that, given the seriousness of these conflicts, communitarians will not get anywhere unless they address them.

This chapter is written, in the first place, for those who find the communitarian critique of liberalism plausible, but who wonder how communitarians should act in the political world as it exists today. I will present an overview of the kinds of changes in our institutions, practices, and policies that communitarians should pursue. And I will ask where communitarians should stand with regard to the conventional divisions between left and right found today in our polity. I put forward the following proposals in a very tentative manner and with full recognition that many communitarians would disagree with part or all of what I say. Indeed, my own thoughts are still unsettled on many of these issues, especially since they involve a wide range of complex problems about which no one can be expert. But, to stimulate thought and reflection, I will try to make the case for a particular strategy for communitarians as directly and forcefully as I can, leaving aside many of my own doubts and questions.

One final prefatory note: Given the aims of this chapter, I will not rehearse the communitarian analysis of the problems of the contemporary liberal democracies. That is not to say that I find the most common communitarian views unproblematic—I do not. But I shall suppose enough agreement about essential ideas among those of us who from time to time call ourselves communitarians— or who are, at least, unembarrassed by being called communitarians—that it is profitable to raise the question of what concrete goals communitarians should pursue today. In the first part of the chapter I will say a few words about the two divisions between left and right in contemporary American politics. Then, in later parts, I will make some suggestions about where communitarians should stand with regard to these conflicts.

POLITICAL CONFLICT IN CONTEMPORARY AMERICA

Augustinians, Aristotelians, and Liberationists

The virtues are all the rage these days. They have made the cover of a news magazine. And they have made William Bennett rich. Bill Clinton and Bob Dole both called for their renewal. But they did not necessarily agree in their definition of the virtues or perhaps even in the list of virtues to which they would subscribe. There are also people who are deeply suspicious of the revival of talk about the virtues. We can best understand the contemporary dispute over morality and the virtues as one between an Augustinian view on the right, a counter-Augustinian liberationist view on the left, and an Aristotelian view in the center. Central to this conflict is a profound disagreement about human nature.

This is not the place for a full account of these three views. At the risk of caricature, let me provide a rough sketch of the contestants. The religious right's immense frustration with the direction of contemporary America implicitly rests on their Augustinian view of the double nature of human beings.[1] Augustinians hold that the appetitive part of our soul is the product of mere nature, that is, our bodies. It consists of extremely powerful, and never entirely satisfied, bodily desires that are one, but not the only, source of our urge for domination over the world around us and, especially, over other human beings. Our first nature underlies a second that is the product of the socialization and acculturation of the higher, rational part of our soul. In any decent polity, the desires of our first nature will, in fundamental ways, be in conflict with those of our second nature. Indeed, Augustine takes this conflict to be both the result, and an indication, of original sin. That our bodies are in conflict with our souls also means that conflict between human beings is endemic. Civic peace is hard to maintain precisely because it is difficult to keep the lustful and tyrannical desires of the body firmly in their place.

For Augustinians, government is essentially the imposition of authority. And that is true whether we are talking about governing ourselves or governing others. The tyranny of our desires can only be controlled by a stronger, and opposed, tyranny. The soul rules over the body essentially by repressing our unruly desires. This effort involves, in part, the elevation of our bodily desires, for example, by allowing sexual fulfillment within the confines of marriage. However, marriage constrains even as it provides an outlet for our bodily desires. Even if we have been properly brought up, it is always difficult to accept these constraints. To be trained to repress ourselves is to come to exercise authority over our desires. At the same time, it is to accept the authority of our parents, our community, the state, the church, and, ultimately, God, over ourselves. To accept authority, then, is to become the agent of authority in the struggle with our lower desires for control over our lives.

When Augustinians look at contemporary America, they tremble. They fear that liberal regimes have given up all efforts to encourage us to accept and become the agent of the proper authorities. And they worry that those in authority are unlikely to be the kinds of people who have mastered their own lower ends.[2] The consequences of ever more free speech, ever more shameless advertising, legal abortion, and the breakdown of taboos against infidelity, divorce, and homosexuality encourage everyone to identify with their first, rather than their second nature. The result of this liberation from traditional authority is, for Augustinians, readily apparent. People are ever more inclined to serve their own ends at the cost of neglecting their responsibilities to others. The result is the many social pathologies to which communitarians frequently point.

So, when Augustinians call for the revival of community, they would like to see the traditional virtues and authorities reestablished. To attain that aim, they are willing to place limits on freedoms that many of us think liberal governments are obliged to protect and extend.

This Augustinian view of community is opposed by two other tendencies of thought. The first is the counter-Augustinianism of those I call liberationists. Their ideas are most directly influenced by romantic, Nietzschean, or Freudian thought. But liberationists are, in a way, descendants of Augustinianism as well. Liberationists accept the dual view of human nature while reversing the Augustinian valuation of the two parts of the human soul. Augustinians call for repression, liberationists for the emancipation of our lower ends. Augustinians call for reestablishing traditional authority, liberationists for overthrowing it. Though this is not the place to make the case, I would agree with the Augustinians that liberationist thought is partly responsible for the ills that afflict our political community. But this should not lead us to conclude that communitarians must be Augustinians, for there is another tendency of thought opposed to liberationism, one that I will call Aristotelian.

The Aristotelian tradition differs from the Augustinian in two important ways. First, while they acknowledge that human beings can suffer from a tension between our lower and higher ends, Aristotelians do not think that this conflict is a product of some implacable bodily desires. For, on the Aristotelian conception, all of our desires, including our natural bodily desires, are subject to the shaping force of culture. This is true for two reasons. Aristotelians hold that reason and/or language is so central to human beings that even our most basic bodily wants must be articulated in rational or linguistic terms before we can act on them.[3] This metaphysical claim is supplemented by a psychological claim. Rather than being asocial or tyrannical in our first nature, as Augustinians typically assume, Aristotelians believe that men and women naturally seek to be a part of their polity and society. Given this view of human nature, according to Aristotle, it is conceivable that a man might have the virtue of *sophrosune* (often translated temperance) as opposed to being merely *enkrates* (continent). The latter exercises self-control but suffers from his efforts. The former, on the other hand, acts on the proper desires without pain or strain. This, Augustinians claim, is impossible for sinful man, without the grace of God.

A second important difference between Augustinians and Aristotelians is that the latter do not seek to restore the deference to authority characteristic of traditional communities. Aristotelians hold that, under the conditions of modern life, commitment to the common good requires active participation in community affairs, not just the passive acceptance of traditional authorities. Life under liberal regimes demands autonomy and self-determination. If that demand cannot be met through communal activity, it will be met solely through individual activity, of a kind that will sometimes undermine community life. Moreover, only active participation in political and social life gives people the experience, knowledge, and trust in each other that can sustain communal life under the ever-changing circumstances of modernity. Aristotelians are not opponents of authority. Liberationists threaten communitarian aims precisely because no form of communal life is possible without authority. But Aristotelians call for authoritative decisions to be made in a democratic and participatory manner.

Perhaps it would help make my characterization of these three political and moral views clear if I briefly give an example of how they lead to concrete political conclusions. Take, for example, the issue of homosexual marriage. Augustinians are, of course, resolutely opposed. While liberationists are likely to support the idea, they do not do so with any great enthusiasm. Indeed, many liberationists are dubious about the commitments and restraints entailed in any marriage, gay or straight. Aristotelians, however, are likely to insist that the intense and committed relationship of marriage is central to the good life of most men and women today, gay or straight.

Augustinians and Aristotelians are not different in all respects. Both reject liberationist views. And both uphold many of the same virtues and a commitment to the common good. That is one reason for thinking that Augustinians and Aristotelians might be able to put aside their differences and agree on some communitarian proposals. As we shall see, however, they would first have to recognize just how much they have in common.

Liberal Egalitarians and Libertarians

Consider now a second division between leftists and rightists concerning government control over economic life. Here two ideological tendencies, which I will call liberal egalitarianism and libertarianism, define most contemporary political debate. Liberal egalitarians believe that men and women have a moral claim either to a job that pays an appropriate wage or, if they are not able to work, to a decent minimum income. Thus they support the redistribution of income by means of a minimum wage, social welfare benefits, publicly provided jobs, and the organization of labor unions. Liberal egalitarians also believe that both the common good and distributive justice are served when the state provides important goods and services and regulates market relationships. So they favor governments that invest in education and infrastructure, create parks and control pollution, protect the health and safety of consumers and workers, and take other similar actions.

To one degree or another, libertarians reject all of these aims. They argue that both distributive justice and economic growth are served when governments refrain from interfering with the workings of the market. They hold that business enterprises can more efficiently provide most of the goods and services we get from government, not only because government monopolies tend to be wasteful but also because high taxation distorts economic incentives and reduces economic growth.

COMMUNITARIANISM AND CONTEMPORARY POLITICAL CONFLICT

With this sketch of ideological debate in contemporary America before us, we can now turn to the question of to what extent the concerns of communitarianism are congruent with any of these ideological positions. I will start with the human good and the virtues and then turn to political economy.

The Human Good and the Virtues

It will come as no surprise that I find the Aristotelian view of human nature and the good community more plausible than either the Augustinian or libertarian views. Though the Augustinian (and counter-Augustinian) view is deeply embedded in our culture, empirical support for it is not all that strong.[4] Yet I believe that communitarians must welcome any and all efforts to restore the balance between responsibilities and rights. This means that Aristotelian communitarians should be supportive of the efforts of Augustinians to pursue their own vision of a good community—and vice versa. How can we all be supportive of those visions of political and social life we call into question or reject? We can accomplish this by welcoming a genuine pluralism, one that is open to a wide variety of local attempts to create a more communitarian form of life.

Communitarians must allow local communities—both local governments and the various intermediate associations and organizations, including business enterprises—the greatest leeway to adopt institutions, practices, and policies that reflect a partisan, and even religiously inspired, vision of the virtues and the good community. Whether we are Augustinians or Aristotelians, we must allow local communities to teach doctrines we disagree with; to encourage or restrict certain action in ways we find questionable; and even to adopt institutions and practices we think harmful. We must also insist that no local political community infringe upon the rights of those who disagree with the majority view. However, we will not have strong local communities if we do not allow them to reflect the aims of their members. Thus we must make sure that we do not expand rights so far as to overly limit what local communities can do.

Communitarians must also be willing to see public funds used for an immense variety of purposes. I shall argue that intermediate associations must receive substantial support from the state. This means, however, that state aid will be provided to intermediate associations that pursue ends rejected by many, and perhaps a majority of, citizens. Moreover, some of this aid will have to go, directly or indirectly, to the religious associations that have such central importance in our civil society. This, too, will raise the hackles of many. But a communitarian civil society will have to be tolerant of the various kinds of communities citizens try to create.

Many questions can be raised about my proposal. Are we to have a great deal of state and local variation in laws governing abortion or pornography and obscenity? And what about institutions and practices that draw distinctions between the sexes? I cannot answer these or other similar questions here. I think that the dividing line in principle is fairly clear. Communities have the right to pursue their own vision of the common good by teaching and education, by encouragement and condemnation, by setting limits on what people do in the common spaces, and by using their own funds to support one rather than another set of activities. However, they do not have the right to prevent individuals from pursuing their own vision of the good in private. Nor can they discriminate against people for irrelevant reasons.

There will, I know, be many objections to granting local communities, and especially governmental organizations, the right (and the funds) to pursue policies and activities that embody a particular vision of the common good and the virtues, especially where that vision is based in religious teachings. But, if we are serious about reviving communal life, we have to accept that some governments and intermediate associations will pursue ideals of community we find mistaken, disagreeable or wrong. When we take part in disputes in our communities, we should be prepared to fight for our views. But, if we take communitarianism seriously, then for three reasons, we must be willing to accede to judgments different from our own.

First, if we really do believe that the future of liberal democracy in the United States depends on restoring a greater commitment to the common good, we must be prepared to allow local communities to define and pursue their own conception of the common good. For reasons I will discuss in more detail in a moment, social solidarity and a commitment to the common good of the kind necessary to inculcate the civic virtues is possible only when the members of a community share a particular conception of the good. In a political community as multifarious as our own, some people are bound to be disappointed with the direction of their local community. However, while a local majority should act with tact and consideration, making allowances for different views, they should not forbear taking the actions necessary to the pursuit of the common good as they see it.

Second, the various issues between Augustinians and Aristotelians are still open. I have my own views on these matters. But I cannot say, though, that I find the alternatives to my own views unreasonable. The difference between Augustinians and Aristotelians rests on important questions about the nature of human beings and about what will result from different forms of political and social life. We cannot confidently address these issues unless we can examine the consequences of variation in political and social life. So some pluralism in the kinds of communities formed in states and localities will, in the phrase of Brandeis, be a laboratory in which we can test the claims of Aristotelians, Augustinians, and Liberationists.

Third, if communitarianism is to have any impact on this country, it is important that we temper the struggles between Augustinians and Aristotelians, struggles that divert us from the much more important task of rejecting liberationist views. This conflict has already done a great deal of damage. And both sides are guilty. Augustinians, by and large, do not take Aristotelian views of a good polity and society seriously. They are always quick to lump us with the liberationists. For example, anyone who has read Andrew Sullivan's *Virtually Normal* should be able to see that the case for homosexual marriage rests on a rejection of the liberationist understanding of human nature.[5] Yet Augustinians take the marriage of gays and lesbians to be as threatening to the ideal of heterosexual marriage as the bathhouses.[6] Similarly, Augustinians fail to see that one can legitimately support abortion as a right while, at the same time, agreeing that abortion is not the virtuous choice in many circumstances. Aristotelians, for their part, often can see no difference between the public condemnation of pornography or the labeling of raunchy CDs, on the one hand, and the censorship of speech, on the other. We Aristotelians should support an expansive notion of civil liberty and reject policies we find silly or pernicious, without calling our opponents fascists. Moreover, we should give up our reliance on the courts and engage our opponents in the struggle of everyday legislative politics. For the

Augustinians are right at least in this: On issue after issue liberationists, often with the tacit support of Aristotelians, have been hiding behind the Constitution, unwilling to make their case to the people. And they have been hypocritical in doing this. When the Augustinians want to label obscene albums or to insist that the NEA not fund offensive works of art, liberationists, along with some Aristotelians, scream "censorship" and call for government neutrality about the good. But they forget about government neutrality when it comes to labeling cigarettes and food or requiring motorcyclists to wear helmets.

Political Economy

It is possible to finesse the disputes between Aristotelians and Augustinians by making room for a wide range of different conceptions of the human good and the virtues. But politico-economic issues are not so easy to finesse. Here, I think, communitarians must support institutions and policies that will, ultimately, radically change our political economy. And in doing so, communitarians will have to break with many of the most cherished ideas of the two dominant tendencies of thought on these issues.

That the basic principles of libertarianism have nothing to offer communitarians should be obvious. But to say that they should reject libertarianism is not to say that they should embrace liberal egalitarianism. Perhaps the best way to see why communitarians should have qualms about liberal egalitarianism is to consider a third, communitarian, view of the proper role of government in the economy. The conception I put forward here owes a great deal to two traditions of thought. The first tradition is especially prominent among theorists influenced by Catholic political and social thought and, in particular, by the doctrine of subsidiarity.[7] It focuses on the importance of mediating—or, as I prefer to call them, intermediate—associations in attaining a good and just form of political and social life. The second tradition that contributes to the political economy I will defend can be called, for lack of a better term, social democracy. While those who call themselves social democrats (or democratic socialists or market socialists) have supported some liberal egalitarian ideas, they have also criticized this doctrine along lines that parallel those found in Catholic political and social thought.[8] Taken together, these two lines of thought lead to harsh criticisms of many of the social welfare, public goods, and regulatory programs favored by liberal egalitarians. A communitarian political economy would hold that these institutions, practices, and policies undermine civic virtue and solidarity.

First, liberal egalitarianism undermines the sense of *responsibility* that characterizes citizens with civic virtue. It turns active citizens into passive consumers, who demand much from government but are unwilling to do their share in providing for the common good or for the well-being of their friends and neighbors or, in some cases, for themselves. Second, liberal egalitarianism undermines the *accountability* of government by vesting power in large bureaucracies that are not only unresponsive to the citizenry but whose successes and failures are hard for citizens to recognize. Third, by insisting on *uniformity* in public policy, these bureaucracies ensure that government-provided goods and services do not meet the particular needs of different localities or citizens. Fourth, liberal egalitarianism limits public *participation* in government, undermining the prime source by which citizens come to understand their own political and social life. Fifth and last, because of these and other failures, liberal egalitarian institutions, practices and polices undermine public *support* for the ends they mean to serve.

I cannot explore each of these problems in any depth here. However, if we are to understand these difficulties and what might ameliorate them, we must consider at least a few details of the communitarian case against liberal egalitarianism. The critique of liberal egalitarian welfare and social welfare policies is the most developed part of communitarianism. It holds that large bureaucratic social welfare programs undermine the responsibility of both the recipients of government aid and of the citizenry at large. Indeed, these two effects are intertwined. Both arise because social welfare programs undercut the efforts of the intermediate associations that were once charged with the care of those who could not care for themselves. Unlike government bureaucracies, intermediate associations can ensure that the truly needy are aided in the proper way—with jobs or goods or money or medical treatment or counseling or other kinds of support—while resisting the demands of those who are unwilling to do what they can for themselves. They can assist people who need help, without undermining their initiative and self-respect. Moreover, these intermediate associations draw upon the participation of the better-off members of a local community, educating them about the situation of the worse-off. For this reason—and because they are careful not to waste money—social welfare programs run by intermediate associations help to generate the broad public support they need to survive and flourish.

The communitarian critique of the social welfare state can be extended to the liberal egalitarian approach to providing public goods.[9] Communitarians claim that large government bureaucracies have a distressing tendency to escape from public accountability and to insist on an undesirable uniformity of the goods they provide. Liberal egalitarians well know that government bureaucracies often come to serve their own interests, or those of special interest groups. So liberal egalitarians say we must try harder. We must add more inspectors and watchdogs, place limits on the revolving door between government service and business enterprises, and limit campaign contributions. These, however, are rarely more than temporary palliatives. And some of these reforms add to the inefficiency of public enterprises.

The real problem is that while government bureaucracies are very good at some things—such as distributing money to individuals and other government agencies—they are very bad at other things—such as providing specialized goods and services. It is often difficult to determine whether a bureaucratic agency is doing a good job of providing such goods and services. Those who have the responsibility to oversee such agencies—high government officials, the press, and the citizenry—do not have the time or the incentives to carry out this task on a regular basis.

One way to make the oversight of government agencies easier is to insist that government agencies follow uniform procedures and provide uniform goods and services. Uniformity is sometimes desirable. We expect the IRS to treat us all uniformly. In other cases, the uniformity of government-provided goods and services can be very frustrating, especially when people are divided about what public or individual goods and services they desire. Consider, for example, the public schools. In a country as divided as our own about what moral education means, there is no hope that any program of real substance can be adopted. Much the same is true with regard to academic programs. Parents who seek a demanding and challenging education for their children are bound to be disappointed. Many Americans are reluctant to see elementary or high school children work very hard and thus pressure elementary and high school teachers to make their courses less demanding. But, at the same time, parents insist that their children must learn what they need to know to function as citizens and workers.

In the first case, where different groups of parents want different things from the schools, there is no way in which public schools, as presently designed, can satisfy everyone—except by doing as little as possible. In the second case, where the very same parents make contradictory demands on the schools, schools should respond by making parents recognize their inconsistency; but they find it easier to evade accountability by creating a pretense of teaching and learning. And that explains why most Americans are happy with the schools their children attend at the same time that, by most measures, the quality of education in America is pitiful.

A final problem with large public bureaucracies is that support for the provision of common goods is undermined because most citizens are unaware of just how much they receive from the government. Students at public universities at which I have taught have no conception of just how much of their education is subsidized by taxpayers. They typically think that they or their parents are paying for 90 percent of the costs when, in fact, they are paying for no more than 10 percent. This disjunction between what people think they receive and what they do receive from government goes far to explain why Americans think *both* that they should receive more from government *and* that they pay too much in taxes.

There is no way to overcome the disabilities that results from the dominance of large bureaucratic agencies. So communitarians should call for radically decentralizing the provision of public goods and services. One way to do this is by devolving power and funds to lower levels of government and to nongovernmental agencies and associations. Devolving power to lower levels of government in large cities means creating neighborhood councils that have control over a range of important government goods and services.[10] Another way to decentralize government enterprises is to privatize government in conjunction with the creation of a voucher system to help individuals pay for important public goods and services. Decentralization has been offered as a remedy for the provision of such things as public parks, police services, and education. And privatization has been held up as a possible solution for other services such as sanitation, or, in conjunction with vouchers, education and health care. Decentralizing and privatizing the provision of public goods and services are not cure-alls. But they are plausible means of reversing the problems created by large, bureaucratic government programs.

Since privatization is likely to be more controversial among communitarians, let me briefly discuss the consequences of a voucher system for the public schools. A case can be made that the public good would be better served by allowing people with broadly different conceptions of the good of education to pursue their own aims, provided that we also ensure that they can come to see the consequences of their choices. Uniformity would be a thing of the past, as a variety of schools provide different kinds of moral and academic education, suited to the aims and goals of different parents and students. Of course, governments would have to insist that all students are taught basic skills, and more importantly, our civic ideals. But a testing scheme could certainly be devised to ensure that this is accomplished.[11] Done properly, these minimal expectations would not prevent the development of a wide range of experimental and alternative schools. Some of these schools might well remain mediocre. But alternatives would be available, and their consequences more open to view. Parents will have a better idea of what particular schools aim to achieve and how they plan to meet these aims. Thus parents will have to, and be more able to, accept responsibility for their children's education. At the same time, principals and teachers will be more accountable for the kinds of education they provide.

Schools that are focused on a particular vision of education—and that are smaller than many public schools today—will also encourage a much greater level of parent involvement and participation.[12] Liberal egalitarians often doubt that this will occur, for they think that when markets allow people to exit from institutions they dislike, their incentive to voice their complaints by means of democratic participation is diminished.[13] But participation is encouraged when people believe that taking part can make a difference. This is much more likely to be the case when schools are small, and the aims of the parents and students who attend them are congruent. Under these conditions, parents can have a greater impact when acting by themselves. And, they will have an easier time finding other, like-minded, parents with whom to work in both contributing to and changing the schools their children attend. In addition, market forces will encourage principals and teachers not only to meet the demands of parents but also to draw them into the schools.

A final good consequence of a voucher system is that parents would, for the first time, truly recognize just how expensive public education is and how much they receive from government. This might strengthen support for education spending. Some well-off parents would probably supplement public funds in order to send their children to schools that cost more than the voucher. But given the "savage inequalities" that characterize public schools today, the inequality in the resources used for the education of each student would probably be much less under a voucher system.[14] Indeed, since there are diminishing returns to money spent on education, a high universal voucher would greatly reduce such inequality. And a universal program of vouchers, like other universal programs such as social security, would generate a powerful demand for higher levels of education spending on the part of all parents, rich and poor. Supplemental scholarships for the poor could further reduce inequality.

It may seem that, in calling for decentralization and privatization, the communitarian political economy I have been defending makes common cause with libertarianism. But while communitarians question the means liberal egalitarians adopt, they by and large accept their ends. Moreover, a program of decentralization and privatization would still require a substantial central government. While communitarians admire local government, intermediate associations, and voluntary organizations, they must recognize that a high level of public funding will be needed to make these alternatives work. Public funding is necessary to overcome four problems that afflict the provision of any common goods.

The first difficulty is the free rider problem. Even virtuous citizens will balk at contributing to those organizations and associations that provide common goods when they believe that many, if not most, of their fellow citizens are not doing their share. Second, because of the competition for economic investment, state and local governments find it difficult to raise taxes to support the provision of common goods either directly or by aiding intermediate associations. They thus need financial support from the federal government. Third, members of historically oppressed classes, ethnic groups, and races are relatively lacking in resources. The intermediate associations that work on their behalf—and on behalf of equality for women—have proportionately fewer resources. There is thus good reason for government to support the associations—such as historically black colleges— that aim to overcome these disparities. Fourth and finally, inner city governments are very much disadvantaged by their inability to tax the suburbanites whose economic success would be inconceivable apart from the goods and services provided by city governments, and apart from the large population of unskilled workers who live in these cities. In an ideal world, boundaries between cities and suburbs would be broken down at the same time that a great deal of political authority is decentralized. But we will probably have to make do with mechanisms for the redistribution of funds from suburbs to urban areas.

Communitarianism, then, should favor central government support for a variety of intermediate associations and organizations, including local government. This support might be provided in many ways. Special purpose or block grants are the common alternatives. Another possibility, however, is for government to offer substantial, refundable tax credits, perhaps with matching grants, for individual contributions to intermediate associations that can plausibly claim to serve the common good or distributive justice.[15] This would diminish the hold of central government on intermediate associations and allow for indirect government support for a variety of good works. This program might also encourage citizen involvement in intermediate associations.

Communitarians should also support government aid to individuals. They must recognize that without substantial government funding, the distribution of goods like education and health care would be terribly unjust. And there are good communitarian reasons to reduce the huge inequalities in income that flow from unfettered market relationships. Gross disparities in income cut the poor off from participation in the mainstream of community life. And they create pockets of wealth filled with people who have no grasp of how the other 95 percent lives. Communitarians then, should support redistributive policies such as income supplements for low-paid workers and publicly supported jobs. The latter might best be provided by intermediate associations and organizations that use federal funds to hire hard-to-place workers. While communitarians would like these associations to provide various forms of help to those who are sick and disabled or who are too young or too old to join the workforce, it is likely that a central government would also have to provide them with a minimum income.

The communitarian political economy I have sketched would require important changes in our institutions, practices, and policies. But we have not yet come to the most dramatic reforms communitarians should endorse. Communitarians must insist that we recognize that business enterprises are political entities that should be evaluated by moral as well as economic criteria. Business enterprises have a tremendous effect on the common lives of those who work within them and on the communities in which they are located. Thus business enterprises should be considered political entities. And, for four reasons, they must be governed by people committed not just to profit but to serving the ends of the workers of the corporation and the broader community as well.

First, insofar as communitarians are concerned with reducing the extreme and growing inequality of income found in the contemporary liberal democracies, they should worry about the disparities in the economic rewards received by those at the top and bottom of corporate hierarchies, disparities that serve no useful economic purpose.[16] New forms of corporate governance are necessary to correct this problem.

Second, communitarians must be concerned with the consequences of business enterprises devastating communities by moving in search of cheap labor. If those who govern our business enterprises took a larger view of their task, the profit motive would be moderated by other aims, without burdensome or inefficient regulation.

Third, communitarians have vigorously criticized the way in which contemporary economic life has undermined the family.[17] Careerism on the part of both men and women and an unwillingness to make sacrifices in their standard of living has led to a dramatic decline in parental interaction with and supervision of children.[18] Day care has replaced the intense parent-infant bond. Television has become the universal baby sitter. The consequences of these trends are likely to be unpleasant both for individuals and for the community as a whole. However, cheerleading for family values will not reverse these trends. As currently governed, corporate America is extremely resistant to the changes that would help restore the balance between work and family. Part-time work is still very difficult to come by for professional and managerial men and women. And the costs of working part time—in terms not just of income and benefits but, more importantly, of career prospects—are far greater than a family-friendly political community should allow.[19]

Fourth, and most importantly, work is one of the most important forces shaping our lives and character. If we seek human beings who are committed to the common good, we must create forms of political and social life in which men and women can take part in collective efforts to secure a common good. We simply cannot expect men and women to exhibit the civic virtues if much of their lives takes place in circumstances that are antithetical to the inculcation of such virtue. That, however, is an accurate description of life in most business enterprises today.

There are, roughly speaking, two ways in which the governance of business enterprises could be changed so as to recognize their political and moral character. Since they reflect the two different views of human nature and virtue we considered above, we might as well call them the Aristotelian and Augustinian approaches.

Aristotelians call for the democratization and decentralization of work. They argue that work is the arena in which men and women have the most direct and constant experience of politics in Aristotle's sense: ruling and being ruled in turn. Most of us, however, are ruled a great deal more than we rule. Oligarchy at work keeps people from the experience of making difficult judgments about the common good and justice. But it is precisely in deliberations of this sort that civic virtue is learned, developed, and exercised. We cannot expect men and women who work in an oligarchy eight hours a day to develop the knowledge, skills, and self-assurance necessary to take part in democratic self-government during the other eight hours they are awake. Nor can we expect them to develop the generosity of spirit and commitment to the common good that characterizes those with civic virtue.

Those who adopt an Augustinian view of human nature will argue for a more hierarchical and paternalistic view of the way in which business enterprises should be governed. The aim of Augustinian institutions and practices would be to encourage all who work in a business enterprise to accept certain goals and a particular ethos, as well as the authority of the elite that guides the corporation in living up to these ideals. Such a business enterprise might not be democratically structured. But the governance of that enterprise will be based upon consent, not contract. Consent will often take the form of deference on the part of low- and mid-level workers to the upper-level elite that make the fundamental decisions about corporate policy. However, this deference will be conditional upon the paternalistic concern of the elite for the well-being of all of those who work in the corporation. Business enterprises that seek to motivate men and women by means of inculcating respect for certain core values can do so without the pettifogging regulation or narrow market incentives typically found in American corporations. Such an enterprise will thus be open to the ideas and innovations of its workers. That means that many decisions about how to attain the agreed goals of a business enterprise will be made in a more or less decentralized and consultative, if not democratic, fashion.

Whether an Aristotelian or Augustinian approach to creating communitarian business enterprises is to be preferred is an open question. Each might be appropriate in different circumstances. My sketch of the Augustinian approach is, of course, modeled on Japanese management techniques, in which hierarchy and strong corporate cultures are combined with decentralization and broad consultation. Whether such a form of business enterprise can be adopted in our circumstances depends on why it has been successful in Japan. Some authorities point to the distinctive features of Japanese capitalism, in particular, the interlocking ownership of corporations and the dominance of investment banks over the stock market as a source of capital. These arrangements are said to make some space for the civic virtue of Japanese managers and workers by reducing their need to create short-term profits. Other analysts hold that the relatively closed and homogeneous character of Japan has allowed for the preservation and adaptation of what we in the West tend to think of as a premodern ethos.

On any account, it is hard to see how the Japanese form of corporate governance can be adopted in the United States without a great deal of modification. It would not be impossible to change the institutional framework within which our business enterprises operate. But it is not likely that the Augustinian pattern of paternalism and deference can be instituted here, given our individualist culture and our history of intensely conflictual labor-management relationships. Thus I tend to think that our business enterprises can be transformed into real communities only if we adopt the Aristotelian strategy. I could be wrong about this, and I would welcome attempts to create Augustinian forms of business enterprise in America. Assuming I am right, however, we communitarians should support the radical measures of devolving power within business enterprises and giving workers a greater say in the decisions that shape their work process and workplace.

How we should decentralize and democratize business enterprises is open to debate. In response to changes in technology and consumer demand, corporations are already decentralizing. They are turning more authority over to their various divisions, creating internal capital markets, and spinning parts of themselves off entirely. This costs many people jobs. However, over time, decentralization might bring not only economic benefits but also allow for greater democratization.

There are many paths to democratization in the corporation. We might strengthen labor unions or move directly to instituting democratic procedures at work. If we choose the latter route, we can start at the bottom, with the work process, and move up. Or we can start at the top and move down. Or we could

adopt both approaches. In any case, democratic decision making can be implemented in a variety of ways. All of the questions that come to the fore when we
discuss the proper form of democratic government will arise along with a movement for greater worker's control. Debates will take place about direct and representative democracy, about geographic versus functional representation, about
how much independent authority should be granted to managers, and about
whether some form of checks and balances is necessary in corporate government.
Decisions about these matters will reflect the circumstances of different business
enterprises and the workers within them, and the importance they give to the
variety of desires that men and women can seek to satisfy in work. And they will
also be guided by the policies of central governments, which must be concerned
with protecting the rights of property owners and securing sufficient levels of
investment. I do not mean to endorse any particular answers to these questions
here. Nor do I think that we should rapidly move to transform our political
economy. There are many steps between the weak labor unions we have today
and a full-fledged system of workers' control. Thus there is room for experiment
and a gradual transition to a new kind of political economy. It is not clear where
we should end up on this continuum, and it is doubtful that all large business
enterprises should end up at the same place. But we do know a good deal about
how the experience of work under oligarchy impoverishes our individual and
common lives today. And there have been enough positive results from experiments with various forms of workers' control to take these ideas seriously and
begin to implement them in a more sustained way.[20]

For some communitarians, this brief for workers' control of corporations will
seem to come, as it were, out of left field. But there is a close fit between the
broader communitarian perspective I have presented here and the creation of
business enterprises that are explicitly political and moral in nature. Communitarians aim to invigorate intermediate associations and to place many important political and moral tasks in their hands. We can best do this, however, if
we can rely on those functional associations, such as business enterprises and
churches, that have a reason for being other than to take on these responsibilities.
For it is precisely such functional organizations that have the money, the large
and continuing membership, and the organizational structure to take on added
tasks. Or they can use their own resources to support and subsidize other intermediate associations. Business enterprises already play this role. Health care and
a great deal of training in the United States is provided by corporations. And,
business enterprises once played an important role in providing housing and
supporting community life. Given the resources available to corporations and
how central work is to most of us, it makes eminent sense for these tasks to be
taken on by corporations.

The goal of decentralizing and democratizing business enterprises has ties to
another aspect of communitarianism, its critique of bureaucracy. This critique
can, and should, be directed against bureaucracy in the private as well as the
public sphere. Nothing in America resembles the lumbering, sclerotic Soviet

economy as much as IBM's hapless attempts to adjust to the world of personal computers. Markets and democratic procedures, the two means by which the power of large, unresponsive bureaucracies can be reduced, should be brought to bear not just on the liberal egalitarian state but on the large bureaucratic corporation as well.

The politico-economic agenda I have proposed for communitarianism is, in some ways, radical in nature. Communitarianism does not and should not challenge the fundamental institutions and practices that define liberalism. It should recognize the values of basic human rights, constitutional government, civil liberties, the separation of powers and checks and balances, and a market economy. But communitarianism should call into question many of the ideals of contemporary leftists and rightists and the institutions and practices they have created. And it should suggest new and even radical alternatives. The problems communitarians seek to address will not be solved just by reinvigorating bowling leagues or reviving Memorial Day parades.

COMMUNITARIANISM, PLURALISM, AND MULTICULTURALISM

Some communitarians will, I think, be dissatisfied with my emphasis on local pluralism in the last part of this chapter. For many communitarians suggest that we have too much pluralism already. They worry about the disintegration of the political and social life in the nation as a whole. When they look at our politics today, they focus on the baneful effects of what has become known as multiculturalism.

The Threat of Multiculturalism

A multicultural politics is one in which human beings are divided into identity groups that define themselves in a special way. Those within the group are said to have a shared identity that is exclusive in two respects. First, each group claims to have a privileged understanding of all matters concerning itself, one that cannot be questioned by those outside the group. This claim has startling ramifications, for identity groups also claim that their view of everything else in the world is shaped by their own identity or perspective. Taken seriously, this claim leads to the conclusion that there is no possibility of rational debate, or even serious communication, between the members of different identity groups.

Extreme formulations of multiculturalism make a second claim of exclusivity. While they insist on the distinctiveness of different identity groups, they deny the possibility of legitimate differences among the individuals within each group. Three terrible outcomes result from this second kind of exclusivity. First, identity politics quickly degenerates into dogmatism. Politics within the group focuses on charges of apostasy and heresy. Second, identity politics leads to fragmentation as we divide ourselves into ever finer group identities. That, however, is a recipe for political impotence and frustration, since democratic politics is the art of combination, of compromise, and of coalition building. When the group in question is already an oppressed minority, there is a third troubling outcome: The tyranny of identity groups can limit the opportunities for individuals to gain the experience and knowledge necessary to make it in the wider political community.

I can well understand why someone who is worried about multiculturalism would find many of the claims of this paper problematic. For will not many of the diverse, strong, local communities I call for understand themselves in one or both of these exclusive ways? If, for example, we adopt a voucher program for schools, won't many of these schools teach or preach a form of identity politics? Will we all be better off if most Americans go to schools run by the most extreme supporters of Afrocentrism or Christian fundamentalism? How will such schools teach students to live, work, and politic with those who have different ideas and ways of life? And how will they prepare students to enter the mainstream of political and social life—assuming it continues to exist? These are real concerns. Let me respond first by saying something more about why the aims of communitarians require us to make room for a diversity of views of the common good and the virtues. Then I will try to show why the communitarianism I defend is unlikely to lead to the extreme multiculturalism we are right to worry about.

Exclusivity, Solidarity and Moral Education

One of the most unsatisfactory features of much communitarian political thought is that it fails to specify the exact location at which we are to hope for or try to create a more communal form of political and social life. Too often, communitarians assume that what we should aim at is a greater sense of solidarity everywhere, from the neighborhood to the country as a whole, or even beyond. And they expect that communities at each level will encompass and meld together the incredible diversity of people in the United States today.

The vision has its appeal. But it flies in the face of everything we know about what real, solidaristic communities look like. One of the oldest lessons of political theory is that the most intensely solidaristic communities are also the most exclusive. Commitment to the common good is only possible when people hold some ends in common and look at things more or less in the same way. Moreover, civic virtue is impossible without mutual knowledge and trust. And this cannot be created when men and women have widely divergent ends. Indeed, we cannot even formulate an account of the virtues specific enough to serve as a basis for socialization apart from a concrete vision of a political community with common ends.

So if we want to encourage civic virtue, a commitment to the pursuit of common goods and to those with whom we pursue these goods, we must take part in, and raise our children in, communities that are constituted by a particular vision of the good. Moreover, there is reason to think that this kind of community is necessary even if our only aim is to encourage people to live within the minimal moral constraints of liberal democracy. Liberal critics of communitarianism often ask why liberal morality is not sufficient. They ask why we cannot just raise our children to respect the rights of others. The difficulty with this standard, however, is that, when taken by itself, it is so thin as to be inadequate to the process of socialization.

Liberalism supposes that human beings can be motivated, and thus should be taught, to obey liberal moral principles for their own sake. I do think that we can act on the basis of moral principles for their own sake. However, because the morality of liberalism is so thin, it does not define a satisfactory way of life. To be able to respect others and themselves, children need to be taught to meet a thicker standard, one that is intrinsically tied to a particular way of life. A child will lack self-esteem if she has no sense of what is important in life and, thus, what kind of life she should lead. A child will be detached from others if she does not take part in communal activities in which everyone must live up to some ideal way of acting. A child will not have the kind of self-control necessary to a moral life if he is never asked to do more than respect the rights of others. And a child will feel entitled to more than he deserves, if his desires are always satisfied but nothing is asked of him.

Even if they are taught to respect the rights of others, adults who have been brought up in this way are not likely to do so all the time. Because they lack self-esteem, they will be determined to gain recognition from others, perhaps by seeking, in any way possible, those instrumental goods—money, prestige, and power—that are the only widely regarded measure of our worth. Because they cannot control themselves, they will fail to live up to their own expectations or those of others. They will respond to the ensuing frustrations in explosive ways. Because they are entitled, they will frequently see themselves as being treated unfairly. Because they are detached from others, their own good will be divorced from the good of others. Thus, adults who have been raised outside of the setting of a real community are likely to find that respecting the rights of others will be a barrier to satisfying their own desires. Those who think they can get away with it will be tempted to violate these rights in pursuit of money, status, and power.

So the minimal moral standards of liberalism do not, by themselves, support the kind of socialization that produces adults likely to meet those standards. But even if people raised in this way remain, at first, committed to the moral standards of liberalism, a life regulated by the morality of liberalism and nothing else would still work to undermine that commitment. There is much nastiness and evil that we can do to others in pursuit of our own interests without violating anyone's rights. Decencies will no longer be common if we are reduced to liberal morality alone. Such a world will be hostile and unpleasant for most people. They will eventually wonder why they should respect the rights of people who treat them badly. Soon enough, first a few, and then even more, people will begin to cut corners. We cannot count on people not to lie, cheat, or steal to get ahead when they expect little in the way of support and much in the way of rabid competition from their fellow human beings.

If this understanding of what makes for a moral community is correct, then the only way to meet the problems that motivate communitarian thought is to ensure that a significant part of our lives is spent with others who have similar aims and purposes. And that is why, in a pluralistic community like our own, communitarians must encourage a diversity of strong local communities with their own view of the common good and the virtues. That means we will have to take the risk that some of these local communities will have the exclusivist form welcomed by multiculturalists and feared by true democrats. But, there are good reasons to think that most of us will not look for or find ourselves in exclusivist communities. Nor will we adopt the multiculturalist ideology. For strong communities can also be what I will call partial and contested communities.

Partial and Contested Communities

Even if we try to create many close-knit local communities, that does not mean we will live our whole lives in enclaves of like-minded people. For in the pluralist world of liberal democracy, there are all kinds of overlapping communities. Among others, there are communities based in a certain territory, a workplace, a profession, a racial, ethnic, or national group, a sexual identity, a mutual concern, a recreational interest, or an ideological affinity.[21] Some of these communities involve face-to-face interaction, while others are largely virtual in nature. Moreover, almost all of us are members of more than one such community. These local communities are, by and large, made up of people who share certain ends and a point of view. They are exclusive, but only within a certain sphere of life. They are strong but partial communities. They do require their members to be committed to certain broadly defined ends. But these ends do not, by themselves, define each individual member of the community. Most of the members of each such local community are members of others as well.

Communitarians have expressed concern about the existence of overlapping communities to which we commit only a part of ourselves. These partial communities seem to some communitarians to be a pale reflection of the intense and thus exclusive communities of civic republican lore. And, make no mistake, they are very different from the Spartan model. But if we value freedom and democracy we should reject the civic republican model and not hanker after Sparta. The two kinds of exclusivity I criticized when discussing contemporary identity politics is exactly what characterizes Sparta and all the other golden ages for which civic republicans pine. On the other hand, the aims of communitarians can be attained within partial communities. For they can be places in which the civic virtues are taught. And this is true even for partial communities which seem far from the civic republican ideal. The virtues can surely be taught in religious, ethnic, and ideological communities. But they can also be taught in professional associations and even in recreational communities. There is a hacker's ethic and a skier's ethic. And, in each, one can find particular understanding of most of the traditional virtues.

Many strong local communities will be not only partial but contested. The members of a local community will, of necessity, be committed to certain ends. But there can also be important divisions about how this end is to be understood or interpreted and how it is to be realized or made concrete. Indeed, much of the vitality of a particular community, whether full or partial, will be found in the internal debates and struggles that characterize it. A vital community will come together when challenged by outsiders. But it will also be open to discussions about how best to meet that and other challenges. Computer people are, by and large, united against the threats of government censorship of the Internet. But there are disagreements about how to meet that threat (as well as the usual ideological differences, such as those between Macintosh and PC users).

The baneful effects of multiculturalist exclusivity will also be moderated if our strong communities are democratic in nature. For exclusivist ideas are most often the product of free-floating (or academic) ideologues who are not closely tied to any real community. Strong democratic communities will produce leaders who truly reflect the aims and aspirations of their members. These aspirations will not generally lead people to embrace either form of exclusivity.

Given the pluralism of American political and social life, and the continuing importance of overlapping and partial local communities, there is little reason to worry about the, admittedly scary, ideas of extreme multiculturalists. Consider, for example, what would be the likely result of the widespread adoption of a voucher system for the support of independent schools. Many such schools would be based upon religious and ethnic identity. There will be Jewish and Catholic schools, as well as schools supported by both mainstream and fundamentalist Protestants. There will be Afrocentric schools and schools that aim to serve the members of other ethnic groups. But not all of the students and teachers will be drawn from a particular identity group. And even those who are will differ in many ways, and especially in the extent of their commitment to an exclusivist view of that group. There will also be many other kinds of schools. There will traditional and progressive schools. There will be science and math academies and schools devoted to the humanities or performing arts or athletics. Some schools will have a strong component of public service. Others may stress personal development and reflection. These schools will all draw on a population that is, in many ways, diverse. We can also expect that, most of all, there will be neighborhood schools that serve a local population. Indeed, most of the more specialized schools will be diverse precisely because they also function as neighborhood schools for a residential community.

There is no need to worry that too many schools will be exclusivist in orientation. For one thing, we should not assume that students who are taught to follow a particular moral or religious view of the good will become closed-minded bigots. Most people with strong religious and moral views reject the exclusivist view of reasoning. They confidently believe that they can defend their own views against all comers. Moreover, people with strong moral and religious commitments are often committed to questioning their own views. It is precisely because

they take morality and religion seriously that they are drawn to explore alternatives to their own ideas, if only to better understand what they have been
taught. After ten years of teaching in the South, I have come to recognize that
among the students most open to the political philosophers I teach are those
brought up with a strong religious faith. They are closer to the spirit of true
inquiry than the amiable and aimless students who, in their willingness to let
everyone go his own way, never take seriously any alternatives to their own views.

Another reason not to worry is that the extreme forms of identity politics are
unlikely to influence many parents. Identity politics is easy for academics who
can win fame and fortune by making outlandish claims. It is a great deal harder
for parents concerned about the academic, moral, and civic education of their
children. Such parents will recognize that their children will have to get on with
people very different from themselves. And they will act accordingly. No doubt
a few parents will, for a time, come under the sway of one or another silly ideological or pedagogical notion. But that happens already. And, today, parents
sometimes have a hard time freeing their children from the influence of teachers
with those ideas.[22]

It is possible that even though most schools will remain pluralistic in many
respects, there will be some tendency toward more uniformity, if not exclusivity,
in some schools. This cuts against the old idea that the public school provides
the training ground for pluralist democracy. There is something to this idea. If
politics is to go well, people must be able not just to tolerate but to listen to
other points of view and to recognize the legitimacy of the claims made by groups
other than their own. If the central problem of American life today truly were
the inability of the members of different groups to understand and work with
one another, I might have second thoughts about the kind of education program
I have endorsed. But our situation is far different from that found earlier in this
century. We do not have to worry about how to create citizens out of children
who have been raised in a diverse set of strong communities with distinctive and
powerful cultural commitments of their own. Rather, our difficulty is to overcome
the apathy, withdrawal, and cynicism that too frequently characterize the culture
of our country as a whole.

Nor should we worry if committed and engaged students do not interact with
every type and kind of person in their schoolyard. For, if we have strong local
communities, the diversity of America will be very hard to miss. We will find it
one place or another—if not in our own schools then in interscholastic events;
if not on our local street then downtown or at the mall; if not in the books we
find at home, that at the library, the movie theater, or on television. And young
people who are encouraged to think beyond themselves and look to the common
good will find the diversity of America in its most important place, in the political
life of towns and cities that encompass more than one strong community and in
their participation in state and federal politics as well.

Federal and State Politics Under Communitarianism

What, on the pluralistic communitarian view I am presenting, will political and social life be in the country as a whole? The hope of some communitarians to give people a strong sense of solidarity with our country as a whole is forlorn. Indeed, the stronger local communities become, the less important a broader identity is likely to be. Communitarians, then, should follow the path of Horace Kallen, who rejected the demands of assimilationists that immigrants give up their distinctive identities.[23] America is now a nation of nations, of sects, of associations, of groups, and of interests. It will be even more so if, by adopting communitarian institutions, practices, and policies, we encourage people to identify with their strong local communities.

But will there then be nothing it means to be an American? Americans will still share political and moral ideals that remain distinctive in giving us our broader identity, even if we also recommend their universal adoption. And there will be certain partial communities that will have large numbers of members. Many of us will follow the national pastime[24] or talk about the latest movie or television show or about what we heard on the nightly news. There will be no one partial community to which one must belong in order to be a part of the American nation. But there will be an overlapping series of communities to which many Americans will belong. Most of these large communities will play a rather small and less intense part in our lives. Our attention to them will be sporadic. We will only pay close attention when, say, the home team is on a winning streak or the playoffs have begun. But they will help cement our identification with our city and country as a whole.

One of these broad communities is focused on the politics of the federal government. What will it be like, when the communitarian utopia is attained? In some respects it will not be much different from what it is today. That is to say, it won't be utopian at all. Federal politics will continue to have extremely important consequences for all of us. But given our individual ends—and, one hopes, our commitments to strong local communities—most of us will ignore much that goes on in the federal government. The various communities and associations to which we belong will pay attention to federal politics. Thus, to the extent that we are members of local communities that are democratically governed, we will be drawn from a concern with our own community to federal politics. This has important consequences, to which we will return. But we can probably expect that most of us, most of the time, will be more concerned with the decisions made in our local community than with the decisions made by Congress.

Federal politics will, undoubtedly, remain conflict-ridden as different interests and the proponents of various ideologies struggle with one another. Communitarianism will not eliminate such struggles. Indeed, it may make them worse when the engaged—or enraged—citizens of strong local communities turn their attention to the federal government. These citizens will bring with them their passion for the common good as well as their belief that they know where the common good lies. That passion and belief are likely to be intense, precisely because it will be shared by the other members of a strong local community. And, because these communities are already organized locally, and because many of them will already have representatives in their state capitol or Washington as well, it will be much easier for people to overcome the difficulties of initiating collective action.

So how will we deal with these conflicts? In large part, by the same means we employ today. Most Americans will remain committed to the practices that constrain our political conflicts: to the rule of law, to civil liberty and tolerance, and to the procedures of government found in the Constitution. This respect for the formalities of our politics will continue to be coupled with a fundamental moderation in ideology. Political leaders, and many of their followers, will continue to recognize the need to compromise in order to form the coalitions that make for effectiveness in what will remain a pluralist form of politics. Communitarianism will not fundamentally change these features of our politics. We can hope, however, that the moral education provided in strong communities will strengthen our commitment to them. That could dramatically improve the quality of our political and social life, if only by reducing the crime rate, in and out of politics. And we can also hope that respect for our central government will increase once the liberal egalitarian state is reduced in stature and people come to welcome federal subsidies for their own local communities.

Many communitarians have higher expectations. They hope to elevate our politics as a whole. It is possible that civic virtue will, to some extent, carry over from local communities. People might come to state and federal politics and ask what they can do for their country. And they might be more willing to trust the members of other communities. This could make it easier to secure those common goods that can only be attained if all give a little. A commitment to the common good and trust in others might be the consequence of the broader knowledge of, and experience in, political life gained by members of participatory local communities. This civic virtue would also be enhanced if decentralization and privatization enable people to recognize just what they get from government. It might also come about because of the enhanced sense of security people have in strong communities, for the members of such communities would not be facing a large powerful state on their own. Instead, they would be associated with a local community that they could expect to protect their interests. At the same time the decentralization of political power would to some extent diminish the reliance of the members of these communities on the federal government. That could reduce political conflict and also make interest groups more willing to sacrifice their own good for the good of all. With a more virtuous, knowledgeable, trusting, and secure citizenry, we might even find that the slogans and proposals of candidates would not be quite as oversimplified and free with the truth as they are today.

I share the hopes of communitarians who look to civic virtue and a sense of solidarity to improve our politics. And I think that, for the reasons I have presented, these hopes could be met. But I have also suggested some reasons to worry that the conflicts between strong communities might be more passionate. Knowledgeable and committed citizens are more likely to discuss and debate political issues. But they are also more likely to demonstrate and protest. Indeed, as Michael Walzer has pointed out, their riots are likely to be more organized and focused.[25] So strong political communities might make people less willing to trust or compromise with others. I expect that the factors that would lead away from this possibility are stronger than the ones that lead to it. But we cannot be entirely sure. And, indeed, the strength of these factors might change over time. So it seems to me that we should move toward a more communitarian regime with both eyes open. We should not over-hype what we expect from communitarianism, particularly in state and federal politics. And we should beware of the dangers. If a more communitarian political community created strong local communities throughout the land, we could be confident that human life would be more fulfilling and the basic institutions of liberal democracy would be more secure. Any improvement in politics at the federal and state level beyond this is gravy.

CONCLUSION

When I began this chapter, I was not yet sure whether I should or could call myself a communitarian. I was uncertain about what a communitarian believes and supports. And I did not know how communitarianism could play a positive role in reviving our political and social life. As I went along, however, I became more and more comfortable saying "we" when I talked about what communitarians should think or do. Of course, this is in large part because, in this chapter, I get to say what communitarians should think and do. And, anyway, writing a chapter that suggests a positive path to follow is always a dangerous thing. One's own ideas for political and social transformation can create a peculiar kind of auto-intoxication, especially when they contain a hint of optimism. That is, I suppose, why academics—who are supposed to be self-critical above all else—prefer to be restrained and pessimistic, dour, and, these days on the left, sour as well.

The main point of this chapter is that there may well be a reasonable set of ideas about restoring virtue and community to our politics, ideas that would help us avoid the name calling and sterility of so much contemporary political debate. I do not know whether most of those who call themselves communitarians would agree with the proposals I have made here. But communitarianism sounds like a good name for these ideas. It is a banner under which many of us might just be willing to, if not march, then walk, more or less together.

NOTES

I could not have written this chapter without the help, advice, and love of Diane B. Gottlieb and Katja Gottlieb-Stier. I am indebted to the work of Michael Walzer, Jean Elshtain, and Charles Taylor for the fundamental perspective on political and social life that guided me in writing this chapter, as well as for more than a few of my specific arguments. See, among their many other works: Michael Walzer, *What It Means to Be an American* (New York: Marcel Publishers, 1992); Jean Bethke Elshtain, *Democracy on Trial* (New York: Basic Books, 1995); and Charles Taylor, "The Politics of Recognition" in his *Philosophical Arguments* (Cambridge, MA: Harvard University Press, 1995). Walzer, Elshtain, and Taylor should not, however, be held responsible for what I have done with what I learned from them.

1. I can give no more than a potted account of this argument here. I call this view Augustinian because it is Augustine who is in large part responsible for making it so central to our civilization. Some would argue that we should call this view Platonic. In my view, however, a careful reading of *The Republic* and *Symposium* would lead us to reject this conclusion.

2. This concern partly explains the peculiar fascination that people have with the sex lives of our politicians.

3. I can do no more than gesture to this argument here.

4. In addition, I stand with most Jews in rejecting the notion of original sin.

5. Andrew Sullivan, *Virtually Normal* (New York: Vintage, 1996).

6. In my view, neither homosexual marriage nor the bathhouses are a threat to the *practice* of heterosexual marriage. But the conception of the place of sexuality in human life implicit in the practices found at the bathhouses is such a threat. Note, however, that the identical conception is implicit in the practices found at the heterosexual equivalents of the bathhouses, not to mention at many fraternity houses.

7. See Richard John Neuhaus, *The Naked Public Square: Religion and Democracy in America* (Grand Rapids, MI: W. B. Eerdmans, 1984); Michael Novak, *The Catholic Ethic and the Spirit of Capitalism* (New York: Free Press, 1993); and *The Spirit of Democratic Capitalism* (New York: Simon and Schuster, 1982).

8. Long ago Michael Walzer presented a social democratic argument for the "hollowing out" of the welfare state and its replacement by local, participatory, and often voluntary organizations. See his "Dissatisfaction in the Welfare State" in his *Radical Principles* (New York: Basic Books, 1980).

9. It can be extended further to the regulatory activities of the state. I can't discuss this here, however.

10. In most cases, it is probably important for these neighborhood councils to have a broad rather than a narrow mandate. That is, they should play a role in many policy areas, such as governing local public schools, police protection, sanitation, planning, and so forth. The difficulty of political bodies with narrow mandates is that they are often neglected by many citizens who are not particularly concerned with one area of public policy. This leads to neighborhood councils being dominated by one faction in a community with a very particular interest. This is a reason for the ineffectiveness of community control of the elementary schools in New York City.

11. Since the aim would be to test schools, not students, a series of intensive tests could be given to randomly selected students or all of the students at certain grade levels rather

than to an entire student body. Thus there would be no reason for these tests to consist solely of multiple choice questions.

12. As we shall see in the next section, this communitarian argument about political economy links up with a powerful argument for pluralism, that is, for allowing different local communities to pursue their particular vision of the human good and the virtues.

13. This analysis and the terms "exit" and "voice" are drawn from Albert Hirschman, *Exit, Voice and Loyalty* (Cambridge, MA: Harvard University Press, 1970). Many parents who are disadvantaged will, no doubt, find it difficult to guide the education of their children. But intermediate associations such as churches might take it upon themselves to investigate the alternatives and make recommendations to parents. Moreover, market forces can (and typically do) work well when only a small minority of people are willing and able to make informed choices about what goods to consume. Their actions are signals to others.

14. Jonathan Kozol, *Savage Inequalities* (New York: Crown, 1991). At this point liberal egalitarians often say that, rather than a voucher system, we need a political movement to equalize school spending. Given how invisible state and local budgetary decisions are to most people, and how politically connected upper income households are, there is simply no prospect of such a movement arising or being successful in most states and cities anytime soon.

15. A proposal along these lines was made in Samuel Bowles and Herbert Gintis, "From the I.R.S. to the P.T.A." *The New York Times* (April 19, 1995), A23.

16. A good discussion of this issue can be found in Robert H. Frank and Philip J. Cook, *The Winner-Take-All Society* (New York: Free Press, 1995).

17. Amatai Etzioni has a particularly good discussion of this in *The Spirit of Community* (New York: Simon and Schuster, 1993), chapter 2.

18. Ibid., 62–67.

19. An excellent analysis of these problems can be found in Juliet B. Schor, *The Overworked American* (New York: Basic Books, 1991).

20. There are some theoretical reasons to accept, and some empirical evidence to support, the notion that socially controlled enterprises are more productive than either privately or publicly owned enterprises. Among many works which discuss this question see Paul Blumenberg, *Industrial Democracy: The Sociology of Participation* (New York: Schocken, 1973); Jaroslav Vanek, *The Participatory Economy* (Ithaca, NY: Cornell University Press, 1971), chapters 3, 4, and 8, and *General Theory of Labor-Managed Market Economies* (Ithaca, NY: Cornell University Press, 1970); John F. Witte, *Democracy, Authority and Alienation in Work* (Chicago: University of Chicago Press, 1980); and Christopher Eaton Gunn, *Worker's Self-Management in the United States* (Ithaca, NY: Cornell University Press, 1984), 103, 106.

21. The importance of recreational communities should not be overlooked. They play an important role in the lives of many people. I once made this point to Michael Walzer about downhill skiing. He asked whether there were any magazines devoted to skiing. My response was that there were two such journals, which differed, of course, in their ideological persuasion.

22. There will, no doubt, also continue to be some exclusivist schools that prepare students to live in an exclusivist local community, such as Amish and Hassidic Jewish schools. As they have done in the past, debates will continue about the extent to which these schools should prepare their students for a life outside these communities. But these exclusivist communities are never likely to attract more than a few. And, unless we are

prepared to sacrifice the freedom of people to live very differently from the majority, we cannot stand in the way of parents creating schools that reflect their distinctive traditions.

23. Horace Kallen, *Culture and American Democracy* (New York: Arno Press, 1970 [1924]).

24. It is basketball, isn't it?

25. Michael Walzer, "Civility and Civic Virtue," in his *Radical Principles* (New York: Basic Books, 1980), 89.

4

Does Robert Bellah Care About History?

BRUCE FROHNEN

It may seem odd, perhaps even unfair, to ask whether a sociologist like Robert Bellah "cares" about history. In one sense he obviously must. The institutions and practices that are his objects of study are shaped by historical events and circumstances. In another way the sociologist clearly does not care about history. A sociologist is not, after all, a historian, interested in recapturing as fully as possible the truth about past events for its own sake.

But particularly in *Habits of the Heart* Bellah repeatedly resorts to the authority of one historical figure—the French statesman and philosopher Alexis de Tocqueville—in setting forth his arguments concerning America's cultural ills. More important, he describes American character through analysis of what he claims are the historically rooted traditions of individualism and republicanism. Finally, Bellah points to "communities of memory"—that is, groups bound together by a shared sense of their history—as the proper cure for the ills afflicting our society.

It is fair, then, to ask whether Bellah presents credible accounts of Tocqueville's thought, American traditions of thought and action, and the grounding of communities of memory. If, as I will argue here, he does not, this raises further, more interesting questions: Is Bellah merely attempting to mislead us for his own political purposes? Or does Bellah truly believe that historical truth and historical practice do not matter? And if, as I will argue is the case, he believes the latter, to what end does he make historical references and analyses in his work?

I will begin by arguing that Bellah uses references and terms from Tocqueville for distinctly un-Tocquevillian ends, and that he knows that he is being untrue to Tocqueville's vision. Next I will argue that Bellah, far from caring about the traditions set in motion by the "biblical/republican" tradition, sees it merely as a discontinuous "voice" that can guide us, ideologically, to actions he finds politically more palatable than current individualistic practices. I then will argue that Bellah's communities of memory actually rest on political argument and patriotic myths not grounded in true historical experience. Further, his recent overt use of economic class analysis demonstrates hostility toward tradition as an arbiter of proper social constructs.

For Bellah, history is the source of useful models and myths to be used to encourage the people to proper, civic minded action. Truth, in this view, is beside the point. Indeed, the historical record is Bellah's enemy. In his own view America's inherited institutions, beliefs, and practices are by and large hostile toward his vision of the good life. As an intellectual, Bellah believes his task is to replace this record with stories that will convince Americans to abandon individualism and its capitalist bases in favor of their new-found "tradition" of social democratic politics.

THE ANTI-TOCQUEVILLIAN TOCQUEVILLE

I have argued elsewhere that Bellah's frequent references to Tocqueville mischaracterize the Frenchman's thinking. Indeed, they stand Tocqueville's analysis of American individualism on its head.[1] Here I will provide only the heart of that argument.

To a large degree Bellah's status as a Tocquevillian analyst of American democracy rests on his self-conscious borrowing of Tocqueville's term "individualism."[2] Tocqueville defined individualism as that "calm and considered feeling which disposes each citizen to isolate himself from the mass of his fellows and withdraw into the circle of family and friends."[3] Bellah argues that individualism has become "cancerous" in American society and must be rooted out. Tocqueville also thought individualism on the whole destructive. In what way, then, does Bellah misuse the Frenchman's authority? He prescribes a "cure" for individualism that Tocqueville would not only reject but point to as the source of the malady.

Bellah finds the source of our individualism in our economic system. For him free market economics has made communities disposable in the name of increased salaries and so has reduced them, in most instances, to mere "lifestyle enclaves." Leaving home town, old friends, and even family in pursuit of wealth, Americans have become mere consumers and now can only "express their identity through shared patterns of appearance, consumption, and leisure activities."[4]

Individualism has triumphed in America. We have become too selfish to commit ourselves to our communities. What is more, because we no longer value family, religion, and local democratic politics, we are undermining them. Refusing to recognize the authority of these fundamental institutions, we no longer allow them to dictate which personality traits are legitimate and thereby prepare us to participate in a just public life. In particular, we have lost our commitment to social justice, defined as "an appropriate sharing of economic resources."[5]

To resuscitate our communities and our characters, Bellah prescribes social democracy. He claims, citing Tocqueville, that the American town was and should be a "moral grid" channeling "the energies of its enterprising citizens and their families into collective well-being."[6] Economic democracy—collective political control over the distribution of wealth and economic decision-making—is needed to form just and fulfilling communities. It also is necessary to combat the citizens' individualistic tendency to abandon their communities in pursuit of wealth.

According to Bellah, capitalism's essence is the destructive, individualistic pursuit of wealth. It must be fought through local democratic political action. He cites the leader of an activist group called the Institute for the Study of Civic Values, who "sees political organizing as more than a utilitarian means to the end of power. It is also a context in which to nurture a form of moral development on which democratic self-government depends: the practice of citizenship."[7]

The struggle for social justice creates citizenship. This struggle entails establishment of political control over the distribution of goods and opportunities.[8] Work itself "should be seen as 'a calling, contributing to the common good and responding to the needs of others as these needs become understood.' "[9] Bellah's community uses political means to understand needs and distribute work to meet them.

Bellah points to Tocqueville as authority for his claim that local associations are and must be primarily political.

Tocqueville argues that a variety of active civic organizations are the key to American democracy. Through active involvement in common concerns, the citizen can overcome the sense of relative isolation and powerlessness that results from the insecurity of life in an increasingly commercial society. Associations, along with decentralized, local administration, mediate between the individual and the centralized state, providing forums in which opinion can be publicly and intelligently shaped and the subtle habits of public initiative and responsibility learned and passed on. Associational life, in Tocqueville's thinking, is the best bulwark against the condition he feared most: the mass society of mutually antagonistic individuals, easy prey to despotism. These intermediate structures check, pressure, and restrain the tendencies of centralized government to assume more and more administrative control.[10]

Bellah presents associations as civic groups that provide forums in which public opinion can be shaped. Associations are inherently political, by nature intended to combat centralized government—the only form of despotism Bellah acknowledges to exist outside the sphere of commercial or private life. We interact and form communities only through *political* action.

It certainly is fair to point out Tocqueville's conviction that the individualistic pursuit of wealth undermines community and corrupts individual character. But

Bellah also argues that we must reduce public life to the political pursuit of material equality in order to avoid materialism. And this curious argument rests on an inverted reading of Tocqueville. Tocqueville encouraged us to nurture family, church, and voluntary associations because they bind individuals to their communities. Bellah asserts the importance of local institutions as well. But he chains them all to the political project of economic democracy. In the process he makes social institutions the pawns of political movements. Even the most primary socializing institution, the family, in Bellah's view must be the object of democratic experimentation.[11] The result, from a Tocquevillian perspective, is a loss of those forces which bring the individual out of himself and into the various activities constituting public life. The result is a mass of small, weak individuals terrified by and yet worshipful of the indistinct communal whole. The result, in a word, is individualism.

Like Bellah, Tocqueville feared centralization. But he also feared the tyranny of majorities within localities. And these tyrannies might well be instituted and upheld through democratic means. America remained free, according to Tocqueville, because political associations, of whatever geographical basis, "are only one small part of the immense number of different types of associations found there."[12] Associations varied from the local music society to political parties to the impromptu committee formed to remove an obstacle from the road. They were not formed by government and most of them had no overtly political goals. Instead each sought particular social, economic, and other ends and in the process taught its individual members how to care for their neighbors without recourse to government.[13]

Bellah sees politics at the heart of the community; Tocqueville sees the family. Bellah sees the traditional family structure and traditional property rights as bases of individualism. Tocqueville sees family and property rights as the very bases of community. For Tocqueville the father's authority in the family is natural. And it is in the family that we learn to respect authority, to fulfill our duties, and to love our neighbor. Political associations are proper only to the extent that they serve and protect the family.[14] And to the extent that the family loses its close, affectionate, and habitual character, society itself fragments.

Excessive politicization undermines habitual family relations, replacing them with necessarily impersonal political ones. They force man out of his family and into a political world made up of acquaintances and strangers. Lacking the links of family to connect him with society as a whole, man forms no strong attachments. Faced with the unmediated mass of the community, man sees himself as a small and weak creature confronting a powerful majority, and he withdraws from public life into his private world. The democratization of private life breeds individualism.[15] And individualism itself breeds the despotism of *local* political majorities which assume the functions of abandoned social institutions.

In his more recent works Bellah has strictly muted references to Tocqueville. *The Good Society* more reasonably claims a patrimony leading back to social democratic philosopher John Dewey. But then, as I will show below, Bellah deems the details of one's patrimony far from crucial.

TRADITION AS "VOICE"

Bellah's story of our patrimony is one of conflict and decline. Since before our founding, American public life has consisted of a number of modes of thought and behavior. "Along with biblical religion and republicanism, utilitarian individualism has been one of the strands of the American tradition since [Benjamin] Franklin's time."[16] Individualism was an American problem from the start. But there was a time when it did not dominate as it does now. Countervailing habits of thought and action once held individualism in check.

But biblical religion and republicanism did not last long as American traditions. Soon after our founding they lost their capacity to dictate proper conduct and character traits. Thus in the end Bellah is pointing us, not toward living traditions, but toward mere "voices" or mythical stories and exemplary individuals to use as models in constructing a fundamentally new tradition.

First in time was biblical religion. Bellah outlines this tradition through a description of Puritan leader John Winthrop. Winthrop came to America "determined to start life anew in the wilderness in company with those of like religious commitment." His "Model of Christian Charity" set forth the rules of this new communal life: "We must delight in each other, make others' conditions our own, rejoyce together, mourn together, labor and suffer together, always having before our eyes our community as members of the same body."

Bellah finds the Puritan body's hierarchical structure distasteful. But he praises the attempt to build "a genuinely ethical and spiritual life." He reserves his greatest praise for Winthrop's neglect of his own estate while rendering public service to the community.[17]

Likewise Bellah praises Thomas Jefferson, his chosen exemplar of the republican tradition, because Jefferson "left office much poorer than he entered it and faced bankruptcy in his later years." Sacrifice of one's personal wealth in pursuit of the public good is for Bellah a high virtue worthy of great praise.

Also worthy of praise was Jefferson's love of equality. Bellah glowingly reports that "the ideal of a self-governing society of relative equals in which all participate is what guided Jefferson all his life." Of course one could not establish perfect equality given the prejudices of the time, and Bellah notes Jefferson's moral dilemma as a slave-holder. But the ideal of equality was a great symbol to which Jefferson and all who followed him might aspire.

Unlike the biblical tradition, the republican tradition placed great emphasis on the virtue of patriotism. Where Winthrop, in Bellah's view, sought to make the Puritans a single body following God, Jefferson sought a nation in which all had learned to "Love your neighbor as yourself, and your country more than yourself." This patriotism, in Bellah's view, would be misused in America by imperialists and others not committed to the life of equality.[18]

But republicanism had its good side. Early on it fused with biblical religion, and this biblical/republican tradition bound the individual to his community. It produced the sacrifices of a revolution dedicated, in Bellah's view, to equality. In an earlier work, *The Broken Covenant*, Bellah argues that the remarkable coherence of the American revolutionary movement and its successful conclusion in the constitution of a new civil order are due in considerable part to the convergence of the Puritan covenant pattern and the Montesquieuan republican pattern. . . . Both patterns saw society resting on the deep inner commitment of its members, the former through conversion, the latter through republican virtue. Both saw government as resting on law, which, in its positive form, was created by the active participation of those subject to it, yet ultimately derives from some higher source, either God or Nature. When Jefferson evoked at the beginning of the Declaration of Independence the "laws of nature and of nature's God" he was able to fuse the ultimate legitimating principles of both traditions.[19]

During the Revolution, Americans successfully melded their traditions of service to God and service to nation. In effect the one became the other, as pursuit of equality came to be seen as a holy crusade worthy of great sacrifice. Our founders self-consciously emulated half-sacred mythical heroes from the early Roman republic. Cincinnatus, in Bellah's view, was a particularly influential and fitting model because of his self-sacrifice and voluntary poverty.[20]

But factionalism and commercialism set in. Politics became, by the time the Constitution was adopted, a matter of factional infighting over the spoils of government. Thus from our formal beginnings individualism has been on the ascendant. More than this, however, for Bellah individualism early on destroyed the republican tradition qua tradition and left in its stead a mere "voice" or "secondary language" urging us to public service.[21] The Constitution was justified as a mechanism balancing selfish interests against one another. Americans increasingly saw their nation as founded on individualism and ceased sacrificing for their communities as they pursued personal fulfillment.

Today we have no good tradition to look to in combating the corruptions of individualism. Instead of community Americans now seek individual satisfaction. Inevitably dissatisfied, they can only express their pain and loneliness in the "coping" language of a psychology focused solely on individual feelings. In interviews they conducted for *Habits of the Heart*, Bellah and his colleagues found Americans "on the defensive, struggling for biblical and republican language that could express their aspirations, often expressing themselves in the very therapeutic rhetoric that they consciously reject."[22]

In response to our dilemma Bellah recommends yet another tradition: "the tradition of democratic reform that arose in response to the emerging industrial capitalist order."

This reforming impulse flourished in various embodiments during the great transitional period at the beginning of the century. The motive force of these movements of democratic reform was a fundamentally similar, political understanding. It animated the agrarian populism of the Midwest and Southeast, the socialism of eastern industrial workers and western labor, some aspects of Progressivism, and the upsurge of industrial unionism in the 1930s. Suspicious both of the massive private power that was undercutting the basis for independent citizenship and of government without popular control, these movements sought to use government at all levels to bring a degree of public responsibility to the new technologies and the wealth they generated. They strove to adapt the old Jeffersonian republican sense of democratic citizenship to twentieth-century conditions. Politically, of course, the movements failed to do more than place limits, often fragile, on the exercise of private power. But they left a considerable legacy of experience, symbols, and the exemplary type of the movement organizer.[23]

The tradition, as Bellah calls it, of democratic reform has arisen only sporadically and has consistently failed to change significantly American values and behavior. Rather than a set of principles and actions that remain consistent and powerful over time, the reform tradition to which Bellah points is a source of examples of the kinds of character one ought to have. Much like our "second languages," this tradition does not have the consistency or force to determine what characters people should have. It serves only as one possible source of exemplary models.

Bellah does not really care whether we share an actual tradition of consistent values and behavior. He is searching our past for examples of conduct of which he approves. Historical rootedness, in the end, is not a critical criterion.

FORGETFUL COMMUNITIES

Communities, in the sense in which we are using the term, have a history—in an important sense they are constituted by their past. . . . In order not to forget that past, a community is involved in retelling its story, its constitutive narrative, and in so doing, it offers examples of the men and women who have embodied and exemplified the meaning of the community. . . . But the stories are not all exemplary, not all about successes and achievements. . . . And if the community is completely honest, it will remember stories not only of suffering received but of suffering inflicted—dangerous memories, for they call the community to alter ancient evils. The communities of memory that tie us to the past also turn us toward the future as communities of hope. They carry a context of meaning that can allow us to connect our aspirations for ourselves and those closest to us with the aspirations of a larger whole and see our own efforts as being, in part, contributions to a common good.[24]

Bellah seeks to re-connect Americans to one another through communities of memory. Concern for one another, in his view, rests on common feelings growing out of common memories concerning shared events, pains, and joys. But Bellah's communities are amorphous and malleable, with little basis in history or even memory. Communities, for Bellah, need not in fact share a history. They are merely cohesive groups pursuing common projects—preferably social democracy.

Writing in the 1970s, Bellah expressed hope that the counterculture would produce political innovation furthering his communal values.

In the great welter of urban and rural communes, political and religious collectives, sects, cults, and churches that have sprung up in recent years, there are many interesting developments. A new balance of manual and mental labor, work and celebration, male and female traits have been experimented with. Harmony with nature and one's own body, a more "feminine" and less dominating attitude toward one's self and others, an ability to accept feelings and emotions—including feelings of weakness and despair—a willingness to accept personal variety, have all been valued and tried in practice.[25]

In expressing his limited hope for the future, Bellah looks to experimental collectives and the "innovative way of life" there being lived. In the process he calls into question his own commitment to memory as an objective communal bond.

Bellah seeks to allay his readers' fears that the community he advocates will stifle innovation. This will not happen because neither communities nor the traditions that make up a large part of them are backward-looking. A "living tradition is never a program for automatic moral judgments. It is always in a continuous process of reinterpretation and reappropriation. Such a process assumes, however, that tradition has enough authority for the search for its present meaning to be publicly pursued as a common project."[26]

Our traditions' contents are subject to constant reinterpretation. Our communal memory serves only to tell us that we have and should continue to value certain things. We have an American Way and, it being our way, we should maintain it. This is the essence of civil religion or the sanctification of politics. Civil religion allows us to maintain public service as a constantly valued good while changing radically the goods we as a people pursue.

Tradition provides only abstract principles like equality and mythical exemplars like Cincinnatus to which we can look for guidance. The actual shape and content of our community—its distribution of honor and wealth, the very shape of its families—must be subject to constant reinterpretation. Only in this way can we move toward the kind of community Bellah genuinely values—social democracy, in which the community decides, through political means, who shall receive what goods and on what grounds.

Bellah's communities are based, not on a shared past, but on a subjective memory that is accepted as true. This memory of the community's values, sins, and accomplishments determines how members should act and the goals the community should serve. Of course, the proper goal is social democracy.

THE RETURN OF CLASS ANALYSIS

Even myths such as that of Cincinnatus for Bellah are just tools in the pursuit of social justice. Cincinnatus was good, for Bellah, because he served his nation without seeking rewards, instead returning to a life of poverty. But Cincinnatus also was a dictator committed to the strength, glory, and military might of Rome. Of this Bellah says nothing.

Indeed, as shown by the new introduction to *Habits of the Heart*, Bellah relies on an ahistorical analysis that reduces our roles in civic life to ones in which we play out the interests of our economic class. In all the world America's is the society most trapped by economic necessity and inequality. The root of our prob-lem is economic individualism or "the belief that economic success or misfortune is the individual's responsibility, and his or hers alone."[27]

According to Bellah our individualist ideology has produced excessive eco-nomic inequality and deprivation. And our other traditions have contributed their own problems. The biblical tradition or voice "encourages secession from public life rather than civic engagements, and is even tempted to condemn the most vulnerable as morally unworthy." And the republican tradition, in addition to justifying an intolerant patriotism, gave birth to "a paranoid fear of the state."[28] Our "individualist focus on adolescent independence . . . involves enduring fears of a meddling, powerful father who might push one back to childish dependence, fears easily transferred to a paternalistic state seen as threatening to reduce free citizens to helpless subjects." Our fear of the state keeps us from embracing the cure for what ails us—social democracy. Thus even our "good" traditions stand in need of radical reformation.

Bellah now must engage in "an explicit treatment of class" to determine how to combat our new and disturbing "knowledge/power elite." This economic class hurts society by withdrawing from civic life and by seeking its own interests without regard to the interests of others. This elite has produced poverty for millions of Americans by taking more than its share. And "poverty breeds drugs, violence, and unstable families."[29]

Increasing income inequality constitutes a "war against the poor." By decreas-ing their income, the upper classes in America have effectively disenfranchised the poor. "Poverty—income insufficient to maintain an acceptable level of liv-ing—operates to deprive the poor not only of material capital but of social capital as well." In Bellah's view poverty lowers self-esteem and causes individuals to reduce "social capital" by withdrawing from the associations of public life. "By reducing social capital, chronic poverty blocks economic and political partici-pation, and consequently weakens the capacity to develop moral character and sustain family life."[30]

Throughout the new introduction Bellah blames economic inequality and pov-erty for America's problems. He dismisses moralistic talk of a crisis in family values on the grounds that those who divorce or fail to marry are "unemployed and thus unable to get married or [do not have] enough income to support an existing family" due to economic pressures. Moral arguments are useless, even counterproductive, without material security.

Likewise, to talk of the need for renewed commitment to traditional family loyalties "only increases the level of individual guilt, it also distracts attention from larger failures of collective responsibility." Not personal morals but collec-tive economics holds the answer to our families' decline.

We must look to political action for solutions. To talk of the need for more individual involvement in the community is to ignore the fact that "the vol-untary sector is disproportionately run by our better-off citizens and a good many voluntary activities do more to protect the well-to-do than the needy." Emphasis

on volunteerism partakes of individualism's "hostility to the role of government."[31]

According to Bellah economics determines behavior. Thus only social democracy can make community possible today. Neocapitalist ideology keeps us
from recognizing our need to establish social democracy. But the true way lies
not in resuscitating any American tradition or even in returning to local communities. It lies rather in augmenting the role of the state (through democratic
means) in organizing our economic and civic lives.[32]

In the end Bellah's is a universalist conception of the good community. He
does not want us tied to any particular, substantive tradition. He does not want
us tied only to our neighbors or even our local community. As he puts it, "Any
community short of the universal community is not the beloved community."
We must embrace all mankind in universal benevolence. And such an embrace
cannot be motivated by common experience. The lives of an American and a
Bengali are radically different, so any community formed between the two must
grow up over time, be based on a necessarily loose natural law–based affection
for other human beings, or have its basis in Bellah's materialistic ideology.

CONCLUSION

Bellah's ideology must be inculcated in differing ways. It requires a "turning
away from preoccupation with the self and toward some larger identity." This
conversion experience "is characteristic of most of the great religions and philosophies of mankind." Yet for each religion and people conversion must be
motivated through the familiar "stories and symbols in whose terms it makes
sense."[33]

Bellah must use our traditional stories and experiences to convince us to abandon our traditional way of life. Committed to universal benevolence, equality
and above all social democracy, he sees his job as that of convincing us that we
should join him in his program of innovation. The most effective way to do so
in his view is to convince most people that the innovation is minor and in
keeping with the spirit of our civil religion. But the innovation entails a radical
restructuring of political and economic institutions, breaking with tradition in
pursuit of equality.

In one form or another, Bellah throughout his career has called for social
democracy. And he has been willing to use varied tools in that pursuit—from
economic to moralistic argument, from historical to religious myth. This willingness to change tactics seems to stem, not from an explicit desire to mislead,
but from the conviction that truth, whether about history or God, is subjective.
Whether historical or religious, for Bellah we create our own truths. So it is best
to create truths that support good communities.

For example, Bellah sees religion's proper role as that of aiding the process of
"communal recreation through public worship." From his earliest to his most
recent work, Bellah has insisted that only a public church calling "for sweeping

cultural and institutional transformation," can foster community and spiritual fulfillment. From Zen Buddhism to New Age-ism to feminist theology, all proper religions share hostility toward neocapitalist America's economic individualism. As to those who believe in the more traditional notion that God's will is revealed in the Bible, such believers must recognize that the "Bible is the collection of texts that Jews and Christians have used through history to make meaning."[34]

Religion is a means by which we decide what we shall value and how we shall pursue these things. It is a means by which we determine what is right and what is wrong, and so create morality. Likewise, history is a means by which we create our past. In reinterpreting our past and our understanding of God we reconstruct models of proper conduct and principles on which to build our community. Thus democratic participation itself becomes the highest good because it makes one a participant in the process of communal self-creation. A community has no past beyond the time of its creation. Thus a persistently re-created community effectively has no past at all, save that which it gives to itself. Lacking a God or transcendent order that is beyond our ability to re-create, we lack constraints on our desire to change our past and ourselves. We lack any need for objective history, and any basis on which to believe it exists.

NOTES

1. See my "Robert Bellah and the Politics of Civil Religion" in *Political Science Reviewer* 14 (1992): 148–218.

2. Of course, Bellah's claims in this area at one time reached much further. The title *Habits of the Heart* is a literal translation of Tocqueville's term "mores," and in this work Bellah purports to present a Tocquevillian analysis of the habits of belief and action constituting contemporary America's disjointed character or way of life. Indeed, Bellah's work, a series of interviews with individuals—including a Vietnam war deserter, an environmental activist, and a nurse who has named her "faith" after herself—"not unrepresentative" of active Americans, is seen by its authors as "a detailed reading of, and commentary on, Tocqueville" (Robert Bellah, Richard Madsen, William M. Sullivan, Ann Swidler, and Steven M. Tipton, *Habits of the Heart*, updated edition [Berkeley: University of California Press, 1996], 306). I have argued elsewhere (see note 1) that such claims are indefensible. Apparently Bellah and his co-authors agree. The readings in *Individualism and Commitment in American Life* (New York: Harper and Row, 1987) contain only one selection from Tocqueville's two-volume work on *Democracy in America*—three pages on individualism. And in their more recent works, including *The Good Society* (New York: Knopf, 1991) and the new introduction to *Habits of the Heart*, the claims to be Tocqueville's heirs are much more muted and narrow in scope.

3. Alexis de Tocqueville, *Democracy in America*, translated by George Lawrence (Garden City, NY: Doubleday, 1969), 506.

4. Bellah et al., *Habits*, 335.

5. Bellah et al., *Individualism and Commitment*, 6; Bellah et al., *Habits*, viii.

6. Bellah et al., *Habits*, 39.

7. Ibid., 216.

8. See ibid., 217–218, for Bellah's use of Schwartz to argue that " 'people's political

development—their capacity to organize their common life—is both an end and a means. It fundamentally conditions their ability to participate in other development, including economic development. Job creation should take place through locally based, cooperative organizations such as community development corporations . . . 'to create jobs to meet the neighborhood's needs and to help neighborhoods to meet society's needs. It is a matter of justice.' "

9. Ibid., 218.

10. Ibid., 38.

11. Ibid., 110–111.

12. Tocqueville, *Democracy in America*, 513.

13. Ibid., 511.

14. Ibid., 167.

15. Ibid., 167, 507–508.

16. Bellah et al., *Habits*, 33.

17. Ibid., 28–29.

18. Ibid., 30, 31.

19. Robert Bellah, *The Broken Covenant: American Civil Religion in Time of Trial* (New York: Seabury Press, 1975), 27.

20. Bellah et al., *Habits*, 30.

21. See especially Bellah, *Broken Covenant*, 31–32.

22. Bellah et al., *Habits*, 83–84.

23. Ibid., 212–213.

24. Ibid., 153.

25. Bellah, *Broken Covenant*, 159.

26. Bellah et al., *Habits*, 140–141.

27. Ibid., viii.

28. Ibid., x.

29. Ibid., xii, xiv.

30. Ibid., xiii, xiv.

31. Ibid., xxiii, xxiv, xxv.

32. See especially ibid., xxviii–xxix, for Bellah's rejection of face-to-face communities as a substitute for social democracy. See also the comment at xxxiii: "subsidiarity is not a substitute for public provision but makes sense only when public provision is adequate." That is, the tradition of leaving public tasks at the lowest level of public involvement possible will work only if the central state guarantees that the lower level's actions will be superfluous.

33. Ibid., xxx–xxxi.

34. Robert Bellah et al., *The Good Society* 183, 209.

5

Universal Benevolence, Adjective Justice, and the Rousseauean Way

BRAD LOWELL STONE

The introduction to the recently published "updated edition" of *Habits of the Heart* displays the humane spirit of the original work.[1] Robert Bellah and his co-authors make several concessions to their critics but mainly inspect American life over the ten years since the publication of *Habits of the Heart* for additional evidence of what the book called an American individualism "grown cancerous."[2] The approach of the new introduction, however, is quite different from the book itself. For whereas the analysis contained in *Habits of the Heart* is more "cultural" than "institutional," the approach of the new introduction, like that of *The Good Society*—the sequel to *Habits of the Heart*—is more "institutional" than "cultural."[3] The new introduction analyzes American individualism in light of changes in the American class structure. The analysis conveys certain insights but it is, alas, far from entirely successful or enlightening.

The introduction informs us that individualism today is promoted by, and most visibly expressed in, a "neocapitalist ideology more impervious to discomformation than the most dogmatic Marxism."[4] The evidence provided in the introduction, however, suggests that the materialist republicanism of Bellah and his co-authors is an ideology as impervious to discomformation as any form of neo-capitalism or Marxism. I say this because the new introduction is replete with false or distorted claims.

These claims are hardly accidental or random. They issue from a tenaciously held and largely misconceived world view that has been at the center of Robert Bellah's work since at least the mid-1960s.[5] (Indeed, this is so clearly true that one is tempted to relieve Bellah's co-authors of any responsibility for misstatements.) The main features of this world view are a Rousseauean-styled belief in political participation as an end in itself; a deep fear of egoism and economic inequality; a belief in the need to submit the natural inclinations of individuals to a socially constructed "common good"; the conviction that the American problems associated with individualism result exclusively from the misarrangement of "the large structures of the economy and state"; and a fervent belief in the unifying, equalizing and redemptive powers of the state. Coterminous with these beliefs is an animus toward liberal thinking, especially classical liberal thought, and toward the liberal public order of unregulated markets and rights-based, limited government. The empirical distortions of Bellah and his co-authors, needless to say, follow these theoretical contours perfectly; each sustains the authors' egalitarian materialist view and/or defames the liberal public order and liberal thinking. Yet I believe a brief analysis of these claims points to the true sources of "cancerous" individualism and other American problems—the failings of the character-forming and culture-purveying institutions of civil society, especially the family. Moreover, this analysis points to the rich resources contained within classical liberal thinking. For contrary to the assertions made by Bellah and other anti-liberal thinkers, the classical liberals did not espouse an "ontological individualism."[6] They believed, rather, that humans are by nature social or communal. In this view, the political order is artificial but the particularistic and parochial institutions of what is today called civil society—the institutions of kinship, friendship, conscience and locale—are natural and essential to human flourishing.

BELLAH'S AMERICA

The new introduction's survey of the last ten years emphasizes several American trends including the globalization of the economy, the stagnating wages of the majority of men, the widening gap between the "haves" and "have nots," the middle-class exit from the cities, and the geographic and institutional secession of the richest Americans. Although these trends have been discussed by a variety of authors, Bellah and his co-authors draw chiefly from Robert Reich and Michael Lind.[7] Following Reich and Lind, the authors organize most of their comments around a distinction among three American social classes: the "underclass," the poorest 10 percent of Americans; the "anxious class," the majority of Americans "trapped in the frenzy of effort it takes to preserve their standing"; and the "overclass," America's wealthiest fifth. This organization may be carried over here because both the expression and the consequences of "radical individualism" differ, we are told, according to class location.

Taking the underclass first, let me begin with an egregious but representative sentence. Bellah and his co-authors state, "It is worth noting that five of six poor people in America are white and that poverty breeds drugs, violence and unstable families without regard to race."[8] I must confess to having a difficult time imagining how a social scientist could have written the first of the two propositions contained in this sentence. The proposition is demonstrably false. According to the Census Bureau, 38,059,000 Americans (14.5 percent) lived in poverty in 1994 (down from 39,265,000 or 15.1 percent in 1993).[9] Of these, 47 percent (18,110,000) were non-hispanic whites, and 9.4 percent of whites lived in poverty. This is a far cry from the 5/6 or 83 percent of the poor who are white, according to Bellah et al. Indeed, even if one defined "white" to include all hispanics and considered all of the 8,416,000 poor hispanics (30.7 percent of all hispanics) as poor whites, only 66 percent of the poor would be "white" and 11.7 percent of whites would be poor. Yet, 30.6 percent of blacks, 14.6 percent of Asians and Pacific Islanders, and 21 percent of "other races" (mainly native Americans) live in poverty. No matter what definition of white is used, every other group has a significantly higher poverty rate, and if one employs the most commonly used definition of white as non-hispanic white, then the two largest non-white groups—blacks and hispanics—are more than three times as likely to be poor as are whites.

The sentence's second proposition is at the very least grossly misleading, but it is far more significant than the first proposition because of all the ideological baggage it portrays. According to this proposition, poverty breeds drugs, violence, and unstable families. Such a materialistic and mechanistic view is common enough. This view, however, is at least problematic and probably false. For example, to maintain this view one would have to also maintain a furious rate of blinking when comparing contemporary America with America in 1960. In 1960, 22 percent of Americans (55 percent of black Americans) lived in poverty.[10] Yet the percentage of all American births that were out-of-wedlock in 1960 was one-sixth its current percentage[11]; the divorce rate was less than half its current rate[12]; the rate of violent crime was a third what it is today[13]; and, of course, in 1960 drug use was highly localized and by today's standards rare.

Because of discrimination, "structural" causes of poverty clearly existed in 1960. Just as clearly, however, the United States is far more meritocratic today than it was in 1960. For example, black women have achieved income parity with white women; the income of black males is on par with that of white men when adjusted for age, experience, and education; and black intact households have virtual income parity with comparable white households. (Thus, in 1994 the median household income for black dual-earner families was $49,692; for comparable white families, it was $56,468.) Within this more meritocratic context, the evidence does not indicate that poverty or any other structural factor produces unstable families. Rather, it is unstable, that is, fatherless, families that produce poverty, in addition to producing drug use and violence. Families headed by females are five to six times as likely to be poor as male-headed families, and although poor children are more likely to be poor adults than are other children, this is chiefly a function of fatherlessness.[14] Similarly, children in fatherless households are at least twice as likely as two-parent children to use drugs.[15] And the relationship between fatherlessness and violence is so strong that if one controls for the effect of fatherlessness, the relationship between poverty and crime and between race and crime disappears.[16] Seventy percent of all juveniles in state reform institutions, 70 percent of long-term prison inmates, 60 percent of rapists, and 72 percent of adolescent murderers are from fatherless homes.[17] Regarding violence, it is also worth noting—given the media misrepresentations of the issue—that the decline in marriage is the root cause of increased violence against women. Generally, unmarried and divorced women are four times more likely to be victims of violent crime than are married women.[18] Regarding domestic violence specifically, The National Crime Victimization Survey reveals that unmarried and divorced women suffer much more abuse than married women. As David Blankenhorn observes: "For example from 1979 through 1987, about 57,000 women per year were violently assaulted by their husbands. But 200,000 women per year were assaulted by boyfriends and 216,000 by ex-husbands."[19]

Consistent with their structural conception of poverty, Bellah and his co-authors refer to the work of William Julius Wilson and others who argue that the increases in crime, out-of-wedlock births, welfare dependency, and the like result from changes in the American economy.[20] According to this argument, since the mid-1960s changes in the American economy that are bound up with global changes have created a socially and economically isolated underclass. Jobs, especially manufacturing jobs, have gone overseas or to the suburbs, and the middle-class has followed the jobs to the suburbs. Urban males, according to the theory, have been especially hard hit by these changes because their educational and skill levels do not allow them to take the high-paying jobs in the city's financial towers, and manufacturing jobs—the traditional first-generation ticket to middle-class incomes—are not available. Consequently, idle and dispirited males forego marriage, women bear children without benefit of marriage, welfare and poverty increase, and crime rises.

This argument highlights American trends that must be acknowledged by any comprehensive theory of the American underclass. The problem is that Bellah and his co-authors mistake the theory for a comprehensive explanation of the American underclass, which it most decidedly is not. At best the theory explains what I would put at about 25 percent of the changes in the lives of the urban underclass over the last thirty years or so. The theory has many problems. For instance, it offers no explanation for the doubling in black out-of-wedlock births between 1950 and 1965 or for why one-third of all current out-of-wedlock births are to members of the middle-class (phenomena, by the by, that Charles Murray and his cohorts can not explain either).[21] But even more fundamental facts contradict the theory. For example, the population losses of American cities *preceded* the job losses, probably because of the dramatic increases in crime during the prosperous 1960s, and these losses accelerated in the 1970s in those cities under mandatory busing orders.[22] In the 1960s, the poverty rate fell by half but the number of people on welfare more than doubled.[23] Between 1982 and 1989, the unemployment rate fell by 50 percent but the number of people on welfare hardly budged.[24] The increased social pathology in cities such as Atlanta and Washington, D.C., that have never been manufacturing centers, rivals or exceeds the increased pathology of traditional manufacturing cities like St. Louis and Chicago. And most significantly, the marriage rates for employed males and highly educated males have plummeted. Regarding blacks specifically, for example, between 1960 and 1980 the decline in marriage among 35- to 44-year-old black men employed year-round full-time differed very little from the decline among all black men[25]; and between 1970 and 1980 the proportion of college-educated black males at age 29 who were unmarried rose from 19 percent to 29 percent, while it rose from 19 to 30 percent among high school graduates and from 24 to 38 percent among high school dropouts.[26] Employment and education make a difference, but very little difference.

In the eyes of Bellah et al., the underclass suffers because the "predatory" overclass has abandoned its civic obligations. "Educated in the highly competitive atmosphere of excellent universities and graduate schools," the overclass has withdrawn to its gated communities, becoming tight-fisted, tax-hating oligarchs.[27] Similarly, the anxious class—both black and white—has fled the cities as well. "Those left behind," we are told, "were then subjected to the systemic withdrawal of institutional support, both private and public. . . . Cities under increasing fiscal pressures closed schools, libraries, and clinics, and even police and fire stations in ghetto areas. The most vulnerable left behind have to fend for themselves in a Hobbesian world."[28] "The money that would have been required to provide an infrastructure of education and economic opportunity for those in chronic poverty was never spent."[29]

The images here of a "predatory" overclass and a "vulnerable" underclass speak volumes about the nature and extent of Bellah's pristine ideology—an ideology devoid of subtlety or complexity. Rather than focus upon this, though, let me pay attention to something concrete within these images and close to the heart of Bellah's world view: namely, that material resources determine the quality of educational opportunities. In fact, whether one consults international, national, or local data, there is no evidence confirming a causal relationship between material resources and educational achievement. On a per-student basis the United States outspends virtually every other advanced industrialized nation, and in constant dollars we are spending almost three times as much today as we were in 1960.[30] Yet our students typically are at the bottom of the barrel on achievement tests administered internationally, and their average SAT scores are much lower today than in 1960. Similarly, there is no systematic relationship between money spent and educational achievement among the fifty states and the District of Columbia.[31] National data reveal that several states—the Dakotas, Idaho, Iowa, New Hampshire, and Utah—rank among the lowest in per-pupil expenditures but among the very highest on standardized test performance. Meanwhile, Minnesota ranks fairly high on each indicator, Mississippi ranks low on each, and Washington, D.C., is near the top in per-pupil expenditures but outperforms only Mississippi on standardized tests. Correlation is not sufficient for proving causation, but it is necessary, and on a national level there is no correlation between material resources and student achievement. To take one example of local data, among the eight Atlanta area school districts, per-pupil expenditures have a negative association (−.70) with standardized test scores and a positive relationship (.90) with student attrition.[32] Thus, for example, the city of Atlanta outspends Cobb and Gwinnett counties per student by 50 percent. Yet anxious parents recognize the insignificance of material resources and have beaten a path in the direction of Cobb and Gwinnett from Atlanta, not the other way around. Indeed, since the Coleman report in the mid-1960s, not one of the 200 plus studies of the topic has found that material resources affect educational outcomes.[33]

So, what does account for the variation in educational achievement in the United States? Two deeply related sets of things: characterological and family variables. Regarding the characterological variables, what psychologists call "self-efficacy"—the belief that what happens to one is a function of one's actions, not external forces—is what most strongly correlates with educational success, and high self-efficacy is strongly associated with the stability and environmental predictability of intact households. In fact, the variable that best predicts educational achievement among the fifty states and the District of Columbia is the percentage of children in these different locations who live in two-parent households. Every study of this relationship has found that children from intact households are at least twice as likely to be educational high achievers as single-parent children, and that single-parent children are more that twice as likely to give up on school altogether.[34]

To their credit, when countering the claims of those such as Charles Murray who maintain that the material inducements of welfare account for increases in out-of-wedlock births and welfare dependency, Bellah and his co-authors recognize the limits of materialistic explanations. They observe, "The facts that welfare payments, including Aid to Families with Dependent Children, have systematically declined in real dollars over the last twenty years and that they have fallen by half during the 1980s alone are ignored by those who tell this story." Still, the tenacity of the authors' intellectual posture is revealed in what remains of this sentence—"as is the fact that over 70 percent of those on welfare stay on it for less than two years, and over 90 percent for less than eight years."[35] Bellah et al. do not cite their source for this information, but the source is recognizable to most sociologists as Greg J. Duncan's *Years of Poverty, Years of Plenty*.[36] This work is based upon longitudinal data (1969–1978) provided by what is known as the Michigan Panel Study of Income Dynamics. This is an excellent study, but several problems with Duncan's original conclusions—those cited by Bellah—have been revealed by Duncan and others through subsequent analyses of the data. In a source cited by Bellah et al., William Julius Wilson observes that based upon revised methodology "it was found that, although most people who became poor during some point in their lives experience poverty for only one or two years, a substantial sub-population remains in poverty for a very long time. Indeed, these long-term poor constitute about 60 percent of those in poverty at any given point in time and are in a poverty spell that will last eight or more years."[37] Moreover, these two groups—the temporarily poor and persistently poor—are quite different in ways Bellah et al. fail to acknowledge. For as Andrew Cherlin records, Duncan found that "most temporarily poor families had an adult male in the household, but 61 percent of the persistently poor were female-headed." And, of course, the latter percentage has increased dramatically since 1978. According to one report, a child born out-of-wedlock today is thirty times more likely to live in persistent poverty than a child from an intact household. Indeed, according to three Census Bureau researchers, if we consider the effects of illegitimacy and divorce, the increase in the number of female-headed households (the number tripled between 1960 and 1993) has been the chief cause of the widening gap in household incomes. They assert, for example, that had household composition been the same in 1989 as it had been in 1969, the median income for *all* American families would have risen 11 percent in those twenty years.[38]

The underclass, according to Bellah and his co-authors, is significant to the self-definitions of the overclass and the anxious middle-class. They say, "The underclass story, which involves blaming the victims rather than recognizing a catastrophic economic and political failure of American society serves to soothe the conscience of the affluent, and it even allows them to wax indignant at the cost of welfare in a time of expanding deficits."[39] Similarly, "the shrinking middle-class, shorn of its postwar job security by the pressure of global competitiveness, is tempted to look down at those worse off as the source of our national problems."[40]

Middle-class fears, we are told, are great. The middle or "anxious" class fears "downsizing, re-engineered jobs and the pink slip of dismissal." They have a "gnawing uncertainty" about the future of their jobs and adequate income.[41] And all of this is justified, according to Bellah et al., in that Americans have "significantly higher rates of economic deprivation" than citizens of the industrial nations of East Asia and Europe.[42] "Yet," Bellah and his co-authors observe, "through all these wrenching threats to prosperity there has been curiously little public protest about the changing rules of the economic game."[43] At its best, in the eyes of Bellah and his co-authors, the middle-class is stoic in its resignation. Anxious middle Americans quietly suffer job insecurity, stagnant wages, and declining unions, the latter stemming "from legislative changes in the last twenty years that have deprived unions of much of their power and influence."[44] Instead of protest, "More and more families are trying to patch together two and sometimes more paychecks to meet the widening income, health-care, and pension gaps that are spurring the 'disintegration' of the middle-class as it has historically been defined."[45] At its worst, though, the anxious middle-class submits to "the hegemony" of neocapitalist ideology and criticizes our "pitifully inadequate welfare system" and "welfare liberalism."[46]

There is perhaps some merit to this analysis but it is also filled with blind spots and false claims. It is, frankly, more a mixture of nostalgia, fantasy and hyperbole than it is social science. Regarding job security, the American unemployment rate has been below 6 percent for several years and though the recession of the early 1980s pushed unemployment to 10.8 percent in 1982, unemployment in the 1980s averaged 7.2.[47] As I write (October 1996), the unemployment rate is 5.1, about where it was in January of this year when the new introduction to *Habits of the Heart* was completed. This means, among other things, that our unemployment rate is less than half the European Union's rate (11 percent), that we have enjoyed what amounts to full employment—given inevitable job turnover—for several years, and that we have dipped below what economists call "the natural rate of unemployment"—the rate below which inflation is supposed to escalate—with as yet no increases in inflation.[48] (Our inflation rate is at 3 percent. The fears of the Federal Reserve are real, however, and we *do not want* a lower unemployment rate). In 1995, only 2 percent of American workers were fired from their jobs.[49] We enjoy job stability the like of which is unprecedented in the postwar era. For example in 1991, men aged 45 to 54 had typically been at their jobs 12.2 years; in 1978, the figure was 11 years, and in 1966, it was 8.8 years.[50]

The false images created by Bellah and his co-authors mirror those of the American media and probably have the same origin. Lay-offs have hit the overclass, the class to which many professors and media people belong and from which these people typically draw their friends. Increasingly, households in the upper fifth of incomes are comprised of two professionals or managers, and while professionals and managers were more immune to lay-offs than were blue-collar workers twenty years ago, they are no longer immune. For example, unemployment among managers rose 55 percent in 1991.[51] Now, again, given that professionals and managers are pairing off two-by-two in greater and greater numbers—what Barbara Ehrenreich calls "class consolidation" and what Mickey Kaus and Christopher Lasch call "assortative mating"[52]—overclass families have far more reason to be anxious than was the case twenty years ago. The debt load of such people is often staggering, and the loss of one job can mean foreclosure.

Still, one should not cry too long or hard for these overclass households. In 1987 the median male salary for all families in which only the male worked and was employed full-time, year round was $29,556. The median income for all families with two earners employed full-time, year round was $44,536.[53] And the gap has grown over time. In constant dollars, single-earner families saw an 8 percent decline in their household incomes between 1977 and 1987, while dual-earner families saw a 10 percent increase between 1980 and 1987.[54] The trend toward dual-earner families, like the increase in single-parent households, has contributed to the shrinkage of the American middle class, but this trend makes its contribution by elevating the class standing of certain households. Increasingly, the rich in the United States are dual-earner families. Nonetheless, it should be noted that the widening gap between single-earner and dual-earner families has not restrained the overclass's pursuit of their interest. Overclass families, for example, typically invoke "collective responsibility" and support efforts to federalize day care. In reality, however, what such a program would do is tax the lower middle-class—traditional, single-earner families—in order to support the often debt-ridden, gaudy life styles of the overclass. "If we only truly loved our children," the justification invariably begins, as if any type of day care is as good as "traditional" arrangements for the care of children.

The principal reason for the widening gap between single-earner and dual-earner families is the decline in male wages over the last twenty years. As the authors of *Habits of the Heart* report, "The average income for a white male has slowly drifted down from an all time high in 1992 dollars of $34,231 in 1973 to $31,012 in 1992"—a 9.4 percent decline.[55] Bellah et al. note that many households have responded to this decline by sending a second family member into the labor force. What they fail to note, however, is that in addition to being an effect of the decline in male wages, the increase in women's labor force participation is a cause of this decline (and, I am compelled to note, it is *the chief cause* of increases in the age of marriage, the decline in birth rates, and the increase in divorce rates over the last twenty or thirty years[56]). Additionally, the competition for jobs that has suppressed wages has come from the sheer numbers of baby boom workers, from high school students, the majority of whom work during the school year (compared to 5 percent working in 1950), and from the 25 million new American immigrants over the last thirty years (18 million of whom immigrated legally). No doubt more is involved in the decline in male wages than these sources of increased domestic competition for jobs, but just as certainly Bellah et al. greatly mislead their readers on this count by focusing exclusively upon the globalization of the economy and upon dwindling union membership "stemming from legislative changes in the last twenty years."[57] Regarding the latter, union membership, as Bellah et al. note, peaked in "the middle 1950s" (1958, actually). What the authors fail to say, however, is that it declined as much as or more between 1958 and 1976 (a period in which real male wages increased by over 50 percent) than it has since 1976.[58] The causes of this decline clearly are not legislative or political.

I can with some relief say that I am perfectly sympathetic with the authors' sentiments on one point, but it is not a point of dramatic convergence—that is that, given our levels of government expenditure, the typical American anti-tax posture is irresponsible. If we lack the resolve to cut government programs, we must increase taxes. We cannot continue to mortgage our children's future. This noted, I would like to make four points related to the apparent meanness of the lower-echelon overclass and the middle-class, before turning briefly to possible solutions to our problems and to more theoretical issues. First, despite the decline in tax rates for the very richest, federal tax rates in the Reagan years averaged 18.9 percent of GDP, compared to 18.5 percent in the 1970s.[59] Second, Americans have not abandoned the "social infrastructure," as Bellah and his co-authors suggest. In 1965, entitlement programs (including Social Security and Medicare) were 31 percent of non-interest federal spending, but they were 61 percent in 1995.[60] Currently, a majority of American families (51.7 percent in 1992) receive payments from at least one source of federal benefits (not including agricultural subsidies).[61] Such income transfers may be good things on balance, but we must be mindful of their ill effects if these entitlements are to be analyzed rationally. For example, payroll taxes relieve the baby boom generation of money they could be spending on their own children in order to provide Social Security to their parents—a generation who because of the wage increases they enjoyed, their meager mortgages, and their massive equity, is the richest generation in American history. Third, regarding families with children, the inflationary 1960s and 1970s were far worse than the Reagan, Bush, and Clinton years in terms of what happened to family budgets because of taxation. I say this because inflation eroded the value of the dependent exemption. Thanks to the 1948 Revenue Act, the dependent exemption was tripled from $200 to $600 dollars.[62] For a family of four at the median family income this meant that 75 percent or more of their household income was shielded from federal taxes through the late 1940s and the 1950s. Because increases in the dependent exemption lagged far behind the rate of inflation between 1961 and 1980, however, only about 20 percent of such a family's income was shielded from taxation in 1980. Fourth, finally and in sum, our national expenditures and tax policy are focused on the wrong generation. Bellah et al. defend Social Security and Medicare on the grounds of "generational justice," but as a percentage of their income, young parents are paying much more in income taxes, payroll taxes, state taxes, local taxes, and on rent and mortgages, than previous generations.[63] The anemic growth in household incomes over the last twenty years in fact hides dramatic declines in the after-tax income and standard of living for young families today when compared, for example, to the after-tax income and standard of living that the postwar generation (Bellah's own) enjoyed as young parents. At the very least, some of the complaints of the middle-class and the lower-echelon overclass have much more merit than Bellah and his co-authors acknowledge. The authors may love humanity in the abstract, but they occasionally seem indifferent to the real problems of real people.

REPUBLICAN DREAMS AND CLASSICAL LIBERAL SOLUTIONS

The sources of American problems for Bellah et al., as we have seen, are structural. They lie with the "large structures" of the economy and state, and to get at these sources, we are told, requires a form of "republicanism or nationalism," the center of which is "national consensus and national action."[64] Individuals must "seek the common good."[65] In this view, to focus upon the family or upon face-to-face communities is "sadly mistaken" because "the deep structural problems" our society faces cannot be alleviated with such a narrow focus.[66] Our problems are rooted in "failures of collective responsibility."[67] Indeed, the health of smaller communities depends ultimately "upon the well-being of the whole."[68] Accordingly, Bellah and his co-authors affirm an idea of community developed in *Habits of the Heart* that calls us "to wider and wider circles of loyalty ultimately embracing that universal community of all beings."[69] Such loyalty is the essence of what the authors call "civic membership." Civic membership ennobles the individual while leading to the betterment of society.[70] It also combats "class crucification," the very opposite of universal community. Thus, the authors say of the overclass specifically, "They may come to see that civic engagement—a concern for the common good, a belief that we are all members of the same body—will not only contribute to the good of the larger society but will contribute to the salvation of their own souls as well. Only some larger engagement can overcome the devastating cultural and psychological narcissism of our current overclass."[71] As things are, however, our "civic life is a shambles." Our "crisis in civic membership" has depleted our "social capital" and even threatens our personal identity.

Following Robert Putnam, the authors define "social capital" as "features of social organization, such as networks, norms and trust, that facilitate coordination and cooperation for mutual benefits."[72] The two most important indices of social capital are associational memberships and trust in public institutions, both of which have declined in recent years for what the authors call "structural reasons," especially those stemming from "changes in the economy."[73] It is primarily for structural reasons that the overclass has fled to its gated communities, the middle class is suspicious of the government, and the underclass finds itself segregated in " 'reservations' that are effectively outside the environing society." Personal identity is threatened by these changes because within our society personal identity "is conferred primarily by one's relationship to the economy, by one's work and the income derived from one's work."[74]

I suppose we can allow Putnam and Bellah et al. to define terms in any way they want. Nonetheless, this conception of "social capital" differs greatly from the idea as originally developed by Glenn Loury and James Coleman, and I believe the original idea—now employed by many social scientists—is a much more useful concept.[75] It is explicitly not directly concerned with economic and political structures or with extended notions of community. Specifically, Loury and Coleman define social capital as "the set of resources that inhere in family relations and in community social organization and that are useful for the cognitive and social development of a child or young person."[76]

For Loury and Coleman, social capital is a matter of the resources provided by those with whom one has immediate contact, especially one's family, and personal identity is a matter of the character one has developed before entering the adult world of work—although these resources and this identity ultimately affect adult behavior. The empirical grounds for my preferring this conception of social capital to that of Bellah et al. should be clear enough at this point. Loury's and Coleman's conception of social capital helps us diagnose our problems, and it points us in directions that could actually be fruitful when considering possible solutions to our problems. These problems, the evidence suggests, do not inhere within the large structures of the economy and state. They do not, by comparison, plague the Japanese, who in the postwar era have enjoyed limited, representative government and free markets but whose divorce rate today is as low as it was thirty years ago, whose 1 percent illegitimacy rate is where it was in 1965, and who have not suffered dramatic increases in other types of social pathology. (For example, in Japan the rate of adolescent suicide has been declining since 1955, but since 1955 the American rate has quadrupled, mainly because of divorce.[77]) Our problems, including the decline in our social capital, are cultural. They are chiefly problems of the heart. Ours is a culture in which the natural end of marriage, the rearing of children to maturity, has been replaced by the emotional and sexual gratification of adults; in which a natural division of labor and gender complementarity have been replaced by an androgynous ideal buoyed by avarice; in which we have somehow convinced ourselves of a women's exclusive right to choose but in which we are surprised to find that men often refuse to shoulder responsibility for women's choices. Ours is a culture in which marriage is deemed just one among many equal "lifestyle options" and in which volitional father-lessness has become routine. Our manners and morals have led to laws by which shucking one's spouse and children is easier than firing an employee, and under which violators of the marital covenant suffer fewer consequences than someone who breaches a business contract involving the sale of kiwis. Most generally, ours is a culture in which individuals are alienated from natural sentiments, natural attachments, natural duties, and natural institutions.

On more theoretical grounds, I believe the evidence suggests the truthfulness of many Old Whig or classical liberal views. The classical liberals considered certain attachments and responsibilities natural but considered the idea of a national or universal "community" faulty. Nations exist, but they are not com-munities; and love of nation, as Adam Smith and Edmund Burke maintained, arises only from one's love of family, friends, neighbors and other intimates—what Burke called "little platoons."[78] Loyalty to nation cannot exist without more local and parochial attachments. Moreover, as Smith and Burke argued, without local grounding, the sort of universal loyalty or benevolence recom-mended by Bellah and his co-authors is at best impotent and is potentially dan-gerous. Benevolence, Smith and Burke believed, is a natural sentiment; we are naturally inclined toward generosity and selflessness directed at our intimates. By its nature, however, salutary benevolence is particularistic. Thus, universal be-nevolence, for Smith, is the source of "no solid happiness." The "administration of the great system of the universe . . . the core of the happiness of all rational and sensible beings," he says, "is the business of God and not of man." Our lot is a humble one. Our duties lie close to home: genuine benevolence looks its object in the eye. As Smith observes, "The most sublime speculation of the contemplative philosopher can scarce compensate the neglect of the smallest active duty." And as Burke observed concerning Jean-Jacques Rousseau, who deposited his bastard children in foundling homes, Rousseau exhibited constantly "the stores of his powerful rhetoric in the expression of universal benevolence, whilst his heart was incapable of harboring one spark of common parental affec-tion. . . . He melts with tenderness for those only who touch him by the remotest relation, and then, without one natural pang, casts away, as a sort of offal and excrement, the spawn of his disgustful amours and sends his children to the hospital of foundlings."[79] The danger of universal benevolence is that it can mask smug and indolent self-love while distracting one from natural and tangible duties.

Contrary to suggestions made by Bellah over several decades, views such as these are at the center of classical liberal thinking. They are maintained by thinkers such as John Locke, the Baron de Montesquieu, Adam Ferguson, and David Hume, in addition to Smith and Burke, and each of these thinkers exerted some influence over the American founding generation.[80] By nature, humans are social or communal, for these thinkers. Our natural circumstance is conjugal, familial, tribal, or communal. According to these thinkers, within our original tribal condition, humans were naturally devoted to each other but distrustful or hateful of strangers. Political society, in this view, is not natural but is rather the human solution to the problem of innate human partiality and to the related problem of conflict over accumulated property. Within political societies, as in our original condition, however, the reach of communal affection and obligation is naturally limited, and because of the social and geographic extent of nation-states, the classical liberals distinguished between two realms within civil society (in the nonpolitical sense of the term)—a communal, private realm and a public, primarily commercial, realm. These two realms are arranged on very different principles, according to the original liberals. Within the realm of kinship, religious congregation, friendship and neighborhood, character is formed, benevolence toward intimates displayed, and common aims undertaken; within the public realm of commerce, on the other hand, personal identity is irrelevant, impartial laws of justice regulate encounters among strangers, and self-interest is pursued.

For the classical liberals, the natural communal realm and the public realm of commerce and the state are intertwined but they are different and distinguishable. Whereas the intimate or communal realm is founded upon particularistic regard for the few, the public realm is universalistic and is founded upon calculating self-interest. Whereas the first relies upon our original and natural benevolent sentiments, the second relies upon conventional forms of justice produced by utilitarian reason. Whereas one's status in the first is largely ascribed and one's relationships are beyond contracts and codified rules, in the second, one's status is achieved and one's relationships are contractual and rule-governed (one's rights are "imperfect" in the private realm and one's rights are "perfect" in the public realm). And, whereas the intimate or communal realm is sustained incrementally by exceptional acts of benevolence, justice sustains public encounters systemically; exceptional or particularistic treatment is vicious.

By contrast, in addition to making love, loyalty, and benevolence universal, Bellah and his co-authors tend to modify justice in ways that seem to imply that justice is particularistic. In any event, the term "justice" is almost always preceded by an adjective. In their different works, Bellah and his co-authors speak of "participatory justice," "generational justice," "distributive justice," "substantive justice," "economic justice," "social justice," and "global justice"—anything but just justice.[81] Now, I must confess that I am not certain what each of these terms means, but each clearly is used to refer to an unrealized ideal and seems to impute to society deficiencies that exist above and beyond the deficiencies of individuals. Thus it seems, for example, that in a society wherein each individual is equitably treated according to universal rules, the aggregate itself can somehow be unjust according to an ideal of "social justice." Unequal results are taken not as evidence of the equitable treatment of unequals but as breaches of justice. Such usages make me sympathetic with Friedrich Hayek's characterization of terms like social justice as "weasel words."[82] They are used with almost religious fervor, but they typically create a verbal haze and seem to invite breaches of justice while pretending to invoke it.

For the classical liberals, the distinction between the familiar or communal realm of particularistic benevolence and the public realm of universalistic justice is essential to the modern social order. Similitude of conscience, dedication to the common good, and equal devotion to all might be possible in some measure within tribes or within city-states, but they cannot be achieved within modern nation-states. Accordingly, I would suggest, Bellah suffers from an elementary but profound miscomprehension of the nature and ends of modern institutions. Simply stated, Bellah's communitarian vision is a romantic vision that conceives public institutions as familiar ones, just as they had been in the era of tribes and city-states. Stated otherwise, it is a vision that depends upon a confusion of the communal and public realms, as conceived by classical liberalism. In the context of contemporary American realities, Bellah's statist communitarianism is relatively benign; but, at the risk of sounding heavy-handed, it must be recorded that the confusion of realms at the heart of Bellah's work has not been so benign in every context: it has been the centerpiece of all totalitarian regimes in this century. All twentieth-century totalitarian regimes have made elaborate use of communal imagery and have justified the purging of millions of their own people as efforts to purify community, especially of those representing bourgeois individualism. All such regimes have depended upon the impulse toward familial solidarity writ large and upon the subordination of individuals to a supposed greater good. Additionally, of course, while such regimes have relied upon familial imagery in their efforts to reconstruct the public realm, they have also typically worked to minimize the influence of actual communal institutions. Genuine communal institutions become superfluous or dangerous in the eyes of a state founded upon communitarian principles. Yet it is precisely these institutions, the institutions of civil society, that require rehabilitation if we are going to address our most pressing problems.

NOTES

1. Robert Bellah, Richard Madsen, William M. Sullivan, Ann Swidler, and Steven Tipton, *Habits of the Heart*, updated edition (Berkeley: University of California Press,

1996). Cited in the notes as HH. After the introduction and preface the pagination of this edition is identical to earlier editions.

2. HH, xlii.

3. Robert Bellah et al., *The Good Society* (New York: Knopf, 1991).

4. HH, xxvii.

5. For example, see Robert Bellah, "Civil Religion in America," in his *Beyond Belief* (New York: Harper and Row, 1970); "The Revolution and the Civil Religion," in *Religion and the American Revolution*, edited by Jerald C. Brauer (Philadelphia: Fortress Press, 1976).

6. HH, 143.

7. Barbara Ehrenreich, *Fear of Falling* (New York: Pantheon, 1989); Christopher Lasch, *The Revolt of the Elites* (New York: Norton, 1995); Mickey Kaus, *The End of Equality* (New York: Basic Books, 1992); Kevin Phillips, *Boiling Point* (New York: Harper, 1993); Richard Herrnstein and Charles Murray, *The Bell Curve* (New York: Free Press, 1994); Robert Reich, *The Work of Nations* (New York: Knopf, 1991); Michael Lind, *The Next American Nation* (New York: Free Press, 1995).

8. HH, xiv.

9. Bureau of the Census, "Income and Poverty: 1994 Poverty Summary," Table F, World Wide Web (April 1996).

10. Christopher Jencks, *Rethinking Social Policy* (New York: Harper, 1992), 76; Lawrence Mead, *The New Politics of Poverty* (New York: Basic Books, 1992), 31.

11. Jencks, *Rethinking*, 77.

12. Andrew Cherlin, *Marriage, Divorce and Remarriage* (Cambridge, MA: Harvard University Press, 1992), 21.

13. Charles Murray, *Losing Ground* (New York: Basic Books, 1984), 114.

14. For the comparisons of black and white incomes, see Bureau of the Census, "Annual Report on African-American Incomes," World Wide Web (June 1996). For the effects of fatherlessness on income, see Sara McLanahan and Gary Sandefur, *Growing Up with a Single Parent* (Cambridge, MA: Harvard University Press, 1994).

15. Sylvia Ann Hewlett, *When the Bough Breaks* (New York: Basic Books, 1991), 92.

16. James Collier, *The Rise of Selfishness in America* (New York: Oxford University Press, 1991), 255.

17. Barbara Defoe Whitehead, "Dan Quayle Was Right," *Atlantic Monthly* (April 1993): 77; David Popenoe, *Life Without Father* (New York: Free Press, 1996), 63.

18. David Blankenhorn, *Fatherless America* (New York: Basic Books, 1995), 55–56.

19. Ibid., 35. Blankenhorn estimates that only 9 percent of all male domestic violence (including the violence of boys) is committed by husbands. Another Justice Department report estimates that 29 percent of adult male domestic violence is committed by husbands. See David Popenoe, *Life Without Father*, 73–74. Those feminists who attack marriage as the cause of domestic violence are attacking the most important institutional hedge against domestic violence. Popenoe (ibid., 64–73) also discusses the increases in the physical and sexual abuse of children attributable to the increased numbers of single-parent households, live-in boyfriends, and step-parents. Such abuse is rare in households with both biological parents but common in these other contexts.

20. William Julius Wilson, *The Truly Disadvantaged* (Chicago: University of Chicago Press, 1987).

21. The figure for middle-class births comes from Blankenhorn, *Fatherless*, 81.

22. Mead, *New Politics*, 99–109.

23. Ibid.

24. Ibid., 76–84.

25. Jencks, *Rethinking*, 133.

26. Cherlin, *Marriage*, 104–105.

27. HH, xii.

28. HH, xiv.

29. HH, xxvii.

30. William Bennett, *De-Valuing of America* (New York: Summit, 1992), 55.

31. This relationship can be analyzed using numerous sources. See, for example, Marion Cetron and Margaret Gayle, *Educational Renaissance* (New York: St. Martin's Press, 1991), 240–325.

32. Gary Orfield and Carole Ashkinaze, *The Closing Door* (Chicago: University of Chicago Press, 1991), 140–141.

33. Regarding studies of material resources, see Bennett, *De-Valuing America*, 55. Bennett discusses 150 reports but the figure is more like 200.

34. Regarding the characterological virtues, a summary is provided by William Donohue, *The New Freedom* (New Brunswick, NJ: Transaction, 1990), 168–169. The studies of one-parent and two-parent children are discussed in Daniel Patrick Moynihan, *Family and Nation* (San Diego: Harcourt Brace Jovanovich, 1986), 92–93.

35. HH, xv.

36. Greg J. Duncan, *Years of Poverty, Years of Plenty* (Ann Arbor: Institute for Social Research, University of Michigan, 1984).

37. Wilson, *Truly Disadvantaged*, 10.

38. Cherlin, *Marriage*, 92. See National Center for Children in Poverty, *Five Million Children* (New York: Columbia University Press, 1992), 29, for the study of children in persistent poverty. The Census Bureau findings are discussed in Ben Wattenberg, *Values Matter Most* (New York: Free Press, 1995), 93–95.

39. HH, xv.

40. HH, xv.

41. HH, vii.

42. HH, viii.

43. HH, vii.

44. HH, xx.

45. HH, xv.

46. HH, xxv–xxix.

47. Kaus, *End of Equality*, 142.

48. Robert Samuelson, *The Good Life and Its Discontents* (New York: Times Books, 1995), 91, 127.

49. Robert Samuelson, "Capitalism Under Siege," *Newsweek* (May 6, 1996), 51.

50. Samuelson, *Good Life*, 80.

51. Lind, *The Next American Nation*, 202.

52. Ehrenreich, *Fear of Falling*, 213–220; Kaus, *End of Equality*, 31; Lasch, *Revolt*, 33.

53. The figure of $29,556 comes from the Census Bureau. The other figures are drawn from Phillips, *Boiling Point*, 48–49. The median income for all single earner families in 1987 was $28,230.

54. Phillips, *Boiling Point*, 48–49.

55. HH, xxxii.

56. Cherlin, *Marriage*, 52.

57. HH, xx. The figures on high school students who work come from Laurence Steinberg, *Beyond the Classroom* (New York: Simon and Schuster, 1996), 164–182.

58. Thomas Kohler, "Civic Virtue at Work," in *The Seedbeds of Virtue*, edited by Mary Ann Glendon and David Blankenhorn (Lanham, MD: Madison Books, 1995), 158–159.

59. Samuelson, *The Good Life*, 160.

60. Ibid., 157.

61. Ibid., 158.

62. See Eugene Steuerle, "The Tax Treatment of Households of Different Size," in *Taxing the Family*, edited by Rudolph Penner (Washington, DC: American Enterprise Institute, 1983), 75.

63. HH, xxvii.

64. HH, xxviii.

65. HH, xxix.

66. HH, xxii–xxiii.

67. HH, xxiii.

68. HH, xxix.

69. HH, xxx.

70. HH, xxxi.

71. HH, xxxviii, xxxi.

72. HH, xvi; Robert Putnam, "The Prosperous Community: Social Capital and Public Life," *American Prospect* 13 (Spring 1993): 35.

73. HH, xvii.

74. HH, xix, xviii–xix.

75. See, for example, McLanahan and Sandefur, *Growing Up with a Single Parent*.

76. James Coleman, *Foundations of Social Theory* (Cambridge, MA: Harvard University Press, 1990), 300. Coleman is quoting Glenn Loury, "Why Should We Care About Group Inequality," *Social Philosophy and Policy* 5 (1987): 249–271.

77. See Steinberg, *Beyond the Classroom*, 94–96.

78. Adam Smith, *The Theory of Moral Sentiments* (Indianapolis: Liberty Press, 1982), 227–234; Edmund Burke, *Reflections on the Revolution in France* (London: J. M. Dent, 1960), 44.

79. Edmund Burke, "Letter to a Member of the French National Assembly," *Works*, Vol. 4 (London: John C. Nimmo, 1899), 26.

80. See, for example, John Locke, *Two Treatises of Government* (Cambridge: Cambridge University Press, 1960); Montesquieu, *The Spirit of the Laws*, trans. Anne Cohler, Basia Miller, and Harold Stone (Cambridge: Cambridge University Press, 1989); Adam Ferguson, *A History of Civil Society* (New Brunswick, NJ: Transaction, 1980); David Hume, *An Inquiry Concerning the Principles of Morals* (Indianapolis: Bobbs-Merrill, 1957).

81. HH, xxvii, xxxiii, 25–26; Bellah et al., *The Good Society*, 88, 188–189, 245.

82. Friedrich Heyek, *The Fatal Conceit* (Chicago: University of Chicago Press, 1988), 114.

6

Communitarianism and the Federal Idea

WILFRED M. McCLAY

The communitarian "movement" has arisen as an effort to address the evident deficiencies of modern liberalism, and to push our political thinking beyond its fixation on the sovereign autonomy of rights-bearing individuals.[1] There is much that is commendable in such an effort. But the communitarianism we have been getting so far suffers from a fatal defect: it is much too closely bound to the very liberalism it would correct. As a result, it tends to use the language of "community" as a form of mood music, a pleasingly imprecise way to soften our image of all organizations, including those that are decidedly not families or communities, such as universities, business corporations, or nation-states. The problem with such discourse, as was brilliantly explained in the late Robert Nisbet's 1953 classic *The Quest for Community*, is that it is not only inaccurate but pernicious. It serves to dismiss or devalue the elements of genuine community where they exist, while distorting our speech about other kinds of organizations with imprecision, sentimentality, and coercive unctuousness.[2] Hillary Rodham Clinton's celebrated effort to endow the national social-services bureaucracy with the attributes of a cozy "village" is a case in point.[3] Such rhetoric simply claims the wrong territory for community, and in so doing, makes it harder to reckon that term's proper limits. It merely repackages, rather than challenges, the shortcomings of liberalism as now practiced.

Much more promising, however, is the work of Harvard political scientist Michael J. Sandel, whose *Democracy's Discontent: America in Search of a Public Philosophy* is one of the most accessible and thoughtful explorations of the communitarian alternative yet to appear.[4] Sandel argues that today's public philosophy is the liberalism of "the procedural republic": a liberalism that makes government the referee of fair procedure and guarantor of individual rights, but insists that government be scrupulously, antiseptically neutral when it comes to passing judgment upon the substantive ends individuals elect to pursue. This is the liberalism of what Richard John Neuhaus has called "the naked public square," a liberalism that eschews any attempt to identify and uphold public goods, since there can never be any agreement about such goods anyway, and besides, rights always trump goods.[5] This liberal-neutralist philosophy, Sandel asserts, has proven inadequate to the needs of a democratic republic, since it fails to inculcate the personal and civic virtues needed to sustain liberty and self-governance. Its failure lies at the root of our current troubles.

So far, so good. It is also encouraging that Sandel looks to a revitalized conception of citizenship as a starting place for a more adequate public philosophy, drawing on the republican political theory that so greatly influenced the generation of the American Founders. The liberalism of the "procedural" republic, he argues emphatically, does *not* represent an inevitable elaboration of American political ideals. Instead, its current predominance represents a dramatic and relatively recent departure from the spirit of the Founding, and of most of the nineteenth century, which still sought to balance liberal conceptions against republican ones. Unlike liberals, republicans did not exalt the ideal of the freely choosing, unconditioned, unencumbered, autonomous individual, and the "negative liberty" he enjoyed. Rather, they exalted public life, involvement in the process of self-rule, participation in the civic life of the *res publica*, deliberation with one's fellow citizens on matters of the common good. The republican conception of freedom, Sandel asserts, implies a "formative politics," which takes responsibility for shaping the qualities of character that self-government requires. It takes a republic to make a citizen—and vice versa. Therefore, republican politics will entail the dispersion of power, so that the responsibilities of governing can be kept within reach of the individual citizen. But by the same token, the "republican self" is more than a "consumer of citizenship," free to pick and choose the obligations it will honor. Instead, its choices are limited. It is a "situated" and "encumbered" self, which acknowledges its embeddedness in a particular social order—an order to which it is accountable, but without whose constraints it could never aspire to the good life.

Sandel's historical chapters offer an especially compelling challenge to liberal assumptions. He envisions the evolution of American public philosophy as a tale of two traditions, liberal and republican, and of how the former gradually crowded out the latter, in legal, social, economic, and political thought, and eventually in the very texture of our lives. In instance after instance, the centripetal requirements of the self-governing, soul-forming republic came to be displaced by the primacy of the rights-bearing unencumbered individual, dwelling in the neutral liberal state. Though one can quibble with some elements of his account, what emerges is a generally persuasive argument that, in nearly every important sector of American life, the normative standard of public life used to be very different. In conceptions of the economy, the family, church-state relations, free speech, Constitutional law, privacy, productive labor, consumerism—to name a few of the topics Sandel explores—there was once an assumption that the polity had a formative, prescriptive, "soulcraft" function to perform, an assumption that has been so completely undone by the procedural republic that we have forgotten it was ever there.

In light of such an argument, it is strange that Sandel has so little to say about federalism, and most of that unfavorable. Does this represent precisely the sort of practical boundary that liberal communitarians will never be able, or willing, to cross? It is one thing to protest against the building of Wal-Marts (a cause about which Sandel feels passionately), for that is merely a variation on the familiar liberal theme of antagonism to concentrated corporate power. But it is quite another to protest against government gigantism, and against the lost political independence of states, localities, and cities. Yet a revitalized federalism is the single most feasible and logical step in the direction Sandel advocates. He seems not to have noticed that the nation has for several years been engaged in the most serious reconsideration of the federal idea it has undertaken in a century. Admittedly, that reconsideration has won only a few political victories so far; but some of those (e.g., the transformation of welfare provision) have been dramatic and far-reaching. What may be even more telling, however, is the striking contrast between the uniformly unimpressive quality of our national political leaders, of both parties, and the increasingly thoughtful and impressive performance of so many of the nation's governors, both individually and in the context of organizations like the National Governors' Association. There are probably many reasons for this state of affairs. But one surely is the fact that states and localities are slowly but surely regaining some of their viability, as venues of effective political action—even as Washington seems to be losing its.

These are remarkable developments, and they may reflect a growing disenchantment not only with big government but also with the very same pathologies of the unencumbered self that lead many communitarians to take a renewed interest in *citizenship*. But hortatory talk of reviving citizenship is only a beginning. The current mood of reform needs an institutional component if it is to enjoy any success. It will not be enough to emphasize the need for "civic virtue," that is, for a restoration of the beliefs, habits, and behaviors that make citizenship and ordered liberty possible. It will also be necessary to give serious attention to what is being called "devolution," to the extent that devolution is dedicated to the re-creation or preservation of the kind of proximate contexts within which the public virtues of citizens can be exercised.

This is where the concept of federalism enters into the picture, and why it is an essential element in a proper answer to communitarians' concerns.[6] But I think it is important to entertain a fairly expansive view of what federalism means. If we tie our understanding of federalism too closely to a single constitutional formula, we may miss the fertility and dynamism inherent in the federal idea. At its heart, federalism is an attempt to reconcile opposites, to find a balance between the considerable advantages of large-scale combination and the equally considerable virtues of autonomy and small-scale organization, without having to choose finally between one and the other. The specific terms in which that balance can be struck have varied widely in time and space. In its modern and American incarnation, it is used to denote a government that James Madison accurately presented in *Federalist* 39 as a "composition" of federal and national elements.[7] One could argue, as some did, that this government was not "federal" at all. Certainly such an arrangement differs dramatically from the minimalist federalism of the premodern world, in which the federal entity was not even regarded as a true unit of government, since it did not deal directly with the internal character of the polity or the governing of its citizenry, those jobs being reserved for the federation's sovereign constituent states. It may be more accurate to call the American system a form of "decentralist-federalism," as Martin Diamond suggested, as a way of indicating the independent dignity, and ultimate primacy, it accords to the national union.[8]

Nevertheless, the ambiguities that complicate our understanding of the word "federalism" have their uses. The new regime did not, and could not, entirely erase an older conviction that the small, autonomous community is the proper seedbed of republican virtue, and that the cultivation of such virtue was indispensable to the nation's moral and political health. Such concerns were aired repeatedly in the debates over ratification of the U.S. Constitution. That document was born in the crossfire of fundamental political debate, and its final form showed the influences of the very contending factions it was designed to reconcile. Indeed, as Herbert Storing has rightly emphasized, the views of the Constitution's opponents, and their successors, lived on as an active part of the dialogue that defines American political principles, faithfully trailing the Constitution's historical path like the tail of a comet.[9] The opposition worried that the Constitution was inattentive to questions of virtue and religious piety, and that moral declension would surely befall any community that based itself solely upon the pursuit of self-interest, however cleverly channeled and controlled. They believed, as Storing put it, that "the American polity had to be a moral community if it was to be anything," and feared that the Constitution took the perpetuation of a virtuous citizenry for granted.[10]

The persistence of the very classical republicanism they so doggedly represented has made it impossible to maintain that American political institutions were born exclusively liberal and modern. For a generation now, historians and political scientists have contended that American political thought of the eighteenth and nineteenth centuries was significantly influenced (the precise extent and character of the influence remaining a matter of intense debate) by classical ideas about the meaning of political life.[11] For classical republicans, independence meant, not the anomic pleasures of *Leaves of Grass*, but the rigors of self-governance. Republican institutions required virtuous citizens, with the capacity for individual and collective self-governance. In republican discourse the word "virtue" retained its classical and pre-Victorian meanings, emphasizing the values of excellence, economic independence, manliness—and dedication to civic life. The *vita activa* was incompatible with the "unencumbered" premises of modern American individualism. Indeed, it seems inappropriate to speak of the "individual" or the "self" at all in this context. The republican ideal was, as J.G.A. Pocock has expressed it, "a civic and patriot ideal in which the personality was founded in property, perfected in citizenship but perpetually threatened by corruption." Civic life was not only a worthy end, but also a means of instructing the soul in its higher nature.[12]

Such are the appealing features of classical republicanism. But before getting too carried away with enthusiasm, it is well to remember some less pleasant things about it, aside from the problem of its chronic instability. Pocock himself has observed that the ideal of virtue is highly compulsive, for it demands that the individual participate in the *res publica*. Hence, this ideal makes serious claims upon our liberty. Once we tune in and turn on, there is no dropping out. Indeed, the quest for civic virtue, taken to its extreme, makes virtuous political activity the acme of existence. There is something thoroughly unappealing, even vaguely totalitarian, about such a vision, for it seems to deny that there is a legitimate need for private reflection or individual enterprise. Bad as it is to assert that human beings are by nature unencumbered individuals, it may be even worse to assert that their life in the polity exhausts who and what they are.[13]

The proper federal settlement, then, seeks to avoid this either/or. It proposes to give scope to individual ambition, to economic dynamism, to the "bourgeois" virtues of a liberal democracy, while respecting and upholding the formative role that acts of citizenship, and public life in general, play in the deepening and elevation of the soul. This connects the federal idea's central concerns with those of Tocqueville, who acknowledged that self-interest, not virtue, would be the engine driving modern democracies—but who feared that its ascendancy would lead individuals to withdraw from public life.

Such a prospect was in Tocqueville's view an even more ominous threat to a civilized and self-governing polity than was the tyranny of the majority. For he too saw public life as an indispensable school of the soul, wherein individuals would be gradually drawn out of themselves, to grow into more enriching and elevating connection with their fellows. The habit of virtuous behavior, even if initiated for entirely self-interested reasons, could give rise to something like the original virtue itself. But he did not make the mistake of thinking that such behaviors and attitudes could be cultivated or compelled by exhortation alone. There had to be an *institutional* framework within which such exhortation would be rewarded, reinforced, and perpetuated. There had, in short, to be proximate opportunities for meaningful acts of citizenship. Fortunately, he believed, the American framers understood this too, and did not fall prey to the idea that a *national* community could provide such an arena. Instead, they took care to infuse political life into each portion of the territory in order to multiply citizens' opportunities to act in concert. They sought to provide infinite opportunities, that is, for Americans to develop as citizens.

In other words, Tocqueville saw in the federal idea a way that Americans could retain the spirit of republican citizenship, even as they were embracing the self-interested dynamism of liberal individualism. In so doing, American federalism was in effect attempting to reconcile the central principles of both classical and modern political thought. This did not mean that Tocqueville specified how political authority should be subdivided; nor did it mean that he opposed an energetic national government. But he did understand that political communities must spur their inhabitants to exercise their highest natures, and provide them public spaces in which to do so. It must allow them—and require them—to be citizens. They will be drawn into public life by being given a palpable stake in it.

Hence the importance of experiments in devolution being undertaken in our time. The issue of size has not lost its importance. Writers on republicanism from Aristotle to Montesquieu insisted that a republic had to stay relatively small, because only a small polity could possess sufficient social and moral commonality to be self-governing. And even James Madison, despite his celebrated argument for an "extended republic" as a brake on faction, did not assume that a large and diverse nation could offer the same sense of moral community as a small and relatively homogeneous republic. Rather, he assumed that a judicious modification and mixture of "the *federal principle*" could combine the advantages of both.

This is an admirable goal: sustaining the sense of accountability and belonging offered by smaller, more human-scale institutions, institutions that can serve as schools of citizenship, while retaining the considerable benefits of national government. And that is precisely what the federal idea claims to do. Contrary to the familiar claims of its polemical opponents, it does not require us to renounce a national government. It only requires that we specify and enforce that national government's limits. And those limits are imposed not only as a protection against the excessive concentration of power, but to preserve certain kinds of association that are beyond the power of a "national community" to sustain.

Still, one cannot deny that the federal idea presents us with an immensely complicated task. By attempting to accommodate within a single overarching structure what are in fact different principles of government, traceable ultimately to different views of human nature, a federal system demands a great deal of its adherents. They will need a highly developed ability to distinguish what laws and actions are appropriate to each given sphere; an ability to distinguish between and among different spheres of possible activity—and in so doing, to grasp and distinguish the different principles appropriate to each. Federalism requires us to be forever balancing not only contending external interests, but competing understandings of what it means to be most fully human. And there is every reason to believe that these balances will always be unstable and shifting, rather than resting once and for all in a serene equilibrium.

American federalism is often caricatured as a kind of inert legalism, but in fact its structure serves to underwrite something very different: the tensions and ambivalences at the heart of American political life. Martin Diamond, one of the most thoughtful students of American federalism, observed that "any given federal structure is always the institutional expression of the contradiction or tension between the particular reasons the member units have for remaining small and autonomous but not wholly, and large and consolidated but not quite."[14] This puts it exactly right, and makes it clear why we should never wish to see these tensions finally resolved. To leave them unresolved, and thereby leave institutional space for the very kinds of associations that today's communitarians claim to cherish, is precisely the genius of federalism, properly understood. Hence it behooves our communitarians, and everyone else besides, to give the federal idea a fresh look.

NOTES

1. See, for example, Michael J. Sandel, *Liberalism and the Limits of Justice* (New York: Cambridge University Press, 1982); and *Liberalism and Its Critics* (New York: New York University Press, 1984).

2. Robert Nisbet, *The Quest for Community: A Study in the Ethics of Order and Freedom* (New York: Oxford University Press, 1953).

3. Hillary Rodham Clinton, *It Takes a Village; and Other Lessons Children Teach Us* (New York: Simon and Schuster, 1996).

4. Michael J. Sandel, *Democracy's Discontent: America in Search of a Public Philosophy* (Cambridge, MA: Harvard University Press, 1996).

5. Richard John Neuhaus, *The Naked Public Square: Religion and Democracy in America*, 2d ed. (Grand Rapids: Eerdmans, 1984).

6. See Wilfred M. McClay, "A More Perfect Union? Toward a New Federalism," *Commentary* 100 (September 1995): 28–33; and "The Soul of Man Under Federalism," *First Things*, No. 64 (June/July 1996): 21–26.

7. Clinton Rossiter, ed., *The Federalist Papers* (New York: Mentor, 1961), 246.

8. Martin Diamond, "The Ends of Federalism," *As Far as Republican Principles Will Admit: Essays by Martin Diamond*, edited by W. Schambra (Washington, DC: AEI Press, 1992), 152–166.

9. Herbert Storing, *What the Anti-Federalists Were For* (Chicago: University of Chicago Press, 1981), 3–6.

10. Ibid., 76.

11. There is an immense literature on republicanism in early America. A sampling of some of the more useful essays, by way of introduction, would include: Willi Paul Adams, "Republicanism in Political Rhetoric before 1776," *Political Science Quarterly* 85 (1970): 397–421; Joyce Appleby, ed., "Republicanism in the History and Historiography of the United States," *American Quarterly* 37 (1985): 461–598; James Kloppenberg, "The Virtues of Liberalism: Christianity, Republicanism, and Ethics in Early American Political Discourse," *Journal of American History* 74 (1987): 9–33; and Daniel T. Rodgers, "Republicanism: The Career of a Concept," *Journal of American History* 79 (1992): 11–39. In addition to the classic works of Bernard Bailyn, Gordon Wood, and J.G.A. Pocock, one should consult Paul Rahe, *Republics Ancient and Modern: Classical Republicanism and the American Revolution* (Chapel Hill: University of North Carolina Press, 1992).

12. J.G.A. Pocock, *The Machiavellian Moment: Florentine Political Thought and the Atlantic Republican Tradition* (Princeton, NJ: Princeton University Press, 1975).

13. Glenn Tinder, "Alone for Others," *First Things* No. 62 (April 1996): 8–10.

14. Diamond, "The Ends of Federalism," 145.

7

Readings of Therapeutic Culture: From Philip Rieff to Robert Bellah

ALAN WOOLFOLK

> To reserve the capacity for neutrality between choices, even while making them, as required by this new science of moral management, produces a strain no less great than choosing itself. The analytic capacity demands a rare skill: to entertain multiple perspectives upon oneself, and even upon beloved others. A high level of control is necessary in order to shift from one perspective to another, so to soften the demands upon oneself in all the major situations of life—love, parenthood, friendship, work, and citizenship. Such conscious fluidity of commitment is not easily acquired. In fact, the attainment of psychological manhood is more difficult than any of the older versions of maturity; that manhood is no longer protected by a fantasy of having arrived at some resting place where security, reassurance, and trust reside, like gods in their heavens. The best that one can say for oneself in life is that one has not been taken in, even by that "normal psychosis," love.
>
> —Philip Rieff, *The Triumph of the Therapeutic*

In the past several years, a growing body of scholarly work has added theoretical and empirical weight to the original case made by sociologist Philip Rieff in *The Triumph of the Therapeutic: Uses of Faith After Freud*[1] for the rise of a revolutionary personality type in western culture. Rieff first sketched the skeletal structure of this new personality type in an earlier work, *Freud: The Mind of the Moralist*,[2] under the rubric of "psychological man," and then proceeded to flesh out the implications of his theoretical intimations with the ideal type of "the therapeutic" in the former and subsequent works. The ideal type of the therapeutic has, in turn, figured prominently in the calculus of a variety of scholarly efforts to understand late twentieth-century culture, perhaps the three leading examples being Christopher Lasch, *The Culture of Narcissism*,[3] Alasdair MacIntyre, *After Virtue: A Study of Moral Theory*,[4] and Robert Bellah et al., *Habits of the Heart: Individualism and Commitment in American Life*.[5]

The influence of Rieff's vision upon these three widely acclaimed works has gone largely uncommented upon, perhaps most significantly in the case of *Habits of the Heart*, which stands more squarely within Rieff's own discipline of sociology than the other two (professionally, the late Christopher Lasch was a historian; Alasdair MacIntyre is a philosopher). Although one may question, for a variety of reasons, whether disciplinary boundaries neatly hold in these cases, it is nonetheless within the scholarly community of sociologists that one might expect the theoretical ties between Rieff and those indebted to him to be widely recognized. Yet, this is not the case. Furthermore, although the work of both Rieff and Bellah has been widely studied and commented upon outside the field of sociology, their names have rarely been linked. In a widely read anthology on *Habits of the Heart* contributed to by non-sociologists, *Community in America*,[6] for instance, Rieff's name is only mentioned twice in passing. This chapter aims to clarify the theoretical links between Rieff and Bellah, and in so doing to see in a very preliminary way what their respective theories can illuminate.

THERAPEUTIC HABITS OF THE AMERICAN HEART?

Prior to the publication of *Habits of the Heart*, little reason existed for linking Bellah's work to that of Rieff, although both had repeatedly emphasized the moral implications of sociological theory and its pejorative readings of religion. In *Habits of the Heart*, however, Bellah's work underwent an apparent transformation with the introduction of Rieff's ideal type of the therapeutic and MacIntyre's concept of practices, and the absence of Bellah's concept of civil religion. Yet, for those not familiar with Rieff's work, the origin of the concept of the therapeutic may escape the reader's attention because no explicit reference is made to Rieff in the main text of *Habits of the Heart*. Nonetheless, the centrality of the therapeutic personality type is clear enough: for Bellah contends in the pivotal second chapter that the "representative character" of American culture has undergone repeated transitions, beginning with the "independent citizen" of the nineteenth century, passing through "the entrepreneur" of the early industrial era, and culminating in "the manager" and, finally, "the therapist" of the late twentieth century.[7]

In earlier work, Bellah identified the original and primary source of corruption in American culture as the "utilitarian individualism" of the entrepreneur and the manager.[8] *Habits of the Heart* both amplifies and modifies this thesis. As an original corruptive source, utilitarian individualism is traced back to the calculated pursuit of economic self-interest present from the beginnings of the American republic, exemplified in the maxims of Benjamin Franklin and later commented upon by Tocqueville. For Bellah, the living Franklin was a public-spirited republican and the ethical capitalist of Weber's imagination, but the utilitarianism that Weber also identified became Franklin's cultural legacy. Although Bellah does not say so, it is what Van Wyck Brooks called the "infinite flexibility" and "accommodating wisdom" of Franklin as "lowbrow" that has lived in the American imagination. As the quintessential lowbrow, Franklin exemplifies an American adaptability of mind and spirit that routinely bends reason more to the common interests of the self than to those of the community. According to the vision of Habits of the Heart, however, utilitarian individualism, which has been successively represented in the character types of the entrepreneur and the manager, is no longer the only source of corruption.

As the primary source of American cultural corruption, utilitarian individualism has been complemented and transformed by what Bellah, drawing upon the work of his coauthor Steven Tipton, calls an "expressive ethic" of individualism.[9] This second type of individualism is explicitly discussed in terms of Rieff's concept of therapy. Habits of the Heart argues that the managerial ethic of efficiency in public and economic life has been given powerful support from the emergence of a therapeutic ethic in private life that has encouraged a self-conscious cultivation of the self and freedom of expression. This therapeutic ethic has carried the instrumental rationality of utilitarian individualism to its logical conclusion by defining the life worth living as one rich in experience rather than merely rich in material goods and other measures of worldly success, not to mention the moral commitments of private life. "Moral standards" in private and public have given way respectively "to the aesthetic tastes and technical skills of the achievement-oriented upper middle class."[10] "Self-realization" or "actualization" has become the new gospel of private life, just as "self-improvement" was, and still is, the old gospel of public life.

The therapeutic ethic of "self-realization," according to Bellah, arose from expressive, not utilitarian, individualism, but he does not stipulate the origins of the former individualism. Nonetheless, the implications of his analysis are clear enough: for in his choice of the American artist Walt Whitman as an archetypal example, Bellah implies that expressive individualism originated in the early modern artist's aesthetic acceptance of all experiences. Following Rieff, Bellah assumes that it was the Nietzschean denial of the distinction between art and life by early modern artists that helped to prepare for the popular recognition in the late twentieth century that psychic rewards are to be "valued" more than economic rewards.[11] The emergent therapeutic ethic, in any case, has directed the growth of a new brand of individualism that has proven even more impervious than the old economic, utilitarian brand to appeals for unconditional moral commitments. Expressive individualism, according to Bellah, has come close to ending the American cultural "conversation." But in Bellah's view that "conversation" has not quite ended, because the therapeutic character type has not triumphed, although the implications of Bellah's model of culture as "conversation" would seem, if anything, to push one even further toward pessimistic conclusions.

One key passage in *Habits of the Heart*, for instance, reads "cultures are dramatic conversations about things that matter to their participants."[12] American culture, Bellah continues, is "no exception." Individualism, as Tocqueville told us, is the dominant motif of the American conversation, defining a common "moral vocabulary" or "first language" for understanding the world and ourselves. Today, as explained above, there are dual varieties of this language made up of utilitarian and expressive individualism that must be listened for and distinguished if one is to understand the inner lives of Americans. Each of these types of individualism has, in turn, been shaped by a more intermittent, bivalent "second language" of communal commitment composed of the biblical and republican "strands" of American tradition, which have been the mainstays, at least until recently, of our culture and character. Not surprisingly, Bellah points to the Puritan tradition as central to what he means by the "biblical strand" of American culture, identifying John Winthrop as its exemplar, while founding fathers such as Washington, Adams, and Jefferson exemplify for him the republican tradition of American public commitment. What ties these respective, diverse strands of our "second language" together for Bellah, giving them a common ground of self-understanding, is the shared assumption that the self can only realize itself in commitments that are not to the self alone.

Bellah identifies the prevailing condition of American culture as one of impoverishment in which symbolic resources have failed precisely because this second language of commitment and tradition has waned in the twentieth century. Individualism is not new; it has simply become stronger and more dominant as the second language of our inherited culture has been undermined and forgotten. Increasingly, the language of individual rights and individual autonomy has invaded realms of life formerly defined by the first language of tradition—relations between husbands and wives, masters and servants, leaders and followers, rich and poor.[13] We are no longer truly bilingual and therefore unable to carry on the "dramatic conversations" necessary for culture with ourselves and others. If one word had to be applied to Bellah's description of American culture in *Habits of the Heart*, that word would have to be "inarticulate."

THE RECALCITRANT INDIVIDUALISM OF PSYCHOLOGICAL MAN

Much of what Bellah and his colleagues have to say about American culture parallels Rieff's analysis of the "symbolic impoverishment" of western culture.[14] Indeed, Bellah's characterization of the four "strands" of American culture— republican, biblical, utilitarian, and expressive—follows Rieff's earlier identification of four character ideals that have successively dominated western culture—the classical Greek ideal of political man, the Christian and Judaic ideal of religious man, the Enlightenment ideal of economic man, and the twentieth-century ideal of psychological man.[15] However, Rieff emphasizes the importance of the expressive ideal of psychological man for understanding the essential dynamic of American culture, whereas Bellah accentuates the psychohistorical significance of the republican and biblical for defining the integrity of American identity.

According to Rieff, the definitive characteristic of Americans may be located in the individualism endemic to democracy described by Tocqueville. That individualism helped to define and to corrupt the eighteenth-century ideal of an enlightened economic man pursuing his own self-interest to the benefit of the community, which dominated during Tocqueville's day, and it also contributed to the rise of the twentieth-century ideal of a self-informed psychological man scrutinizing his own and other's motives to the detriment of the community.[16] Indeed, Rieff assumes, unlike Bellah, that neither the republicanism of the founding fathers nor the faith of Protestant forbears defined the American character because the inner detachment and withdrawal of affections from the community that Tocqueville noted was present from the beginning. Even economic man proved to be a transitional personality type. According to Rieff's theory, the ideal of psychological man is not simply material or physical well-being but primarily psychological well-being. While Tocqueville feared that the quest for individual well-being might become detached from superordinate cultural demands, Rieff argues that today that quest has become *the* dominant demand of an "impossible culture." Psychology, Rieff contends, has replaced religion, morality, and custom as a source of symbolic guidance. Freud has become the dominant theorist of the twentieth century in a way that is little understood and that he never anticipated; for Freud's advocacy of a limited and private therapeutic release from cultural restrictions has led to a public culture of unchecked therapeutic demands. Psychological scrutiny about the self and society, the suspicion of all cultural ideals as an ideal, has gradually dissolved our inherited criteria of good and evil, right and wrong, into new criteria of well and ill, exciting and boring.

There are, according to Rieff, explicit hints of psychological man in Tocqueville's description of "individualism," which he defined in psychological rather than economic or political terms. "Individualism," Tocqueville stated, "is a mature and calm feeling, which disposes each member of the community to sever himself from the mass of his fellows and to draw apart with his family and friends, so that after he has thus formed a little circle of his own, he willingly leaves society at large to itself."[17] As Rieff describes this private circle, it has gradually receded to the inner circle of the self. Not only the public commitments of citizenship, but also the private demands of love, parenthood, friendship, and work have been eased by an intellectual and emotional retreat from binding communal attachments.

"Positive communities," in Rieff's theory, no longer exist because "therapies of commitment," in which the individual submits to a range of self-limitations in return for some sort of salvation achieved through symbolic integration into the community, have grown dysfunctional. Identification with communal purposes no longer works. The community is "no longer able to supply a system of symbolic integration."[18] Furthermore, the individual's sense of well-being has

ceased to depend upon larger and saving commitments. Therapeutic enhance-
ment of one's sense of self has become an end in itself, detached from any communal purpose, with "nothing at stake beyond a manipulable sense of
well-being."[19]

The rise of the therapeutic culture of psychological man constitutes a cultural
revolution that transforms the traditional link between belief and action, creed
and conduct. "Our cultural revolution does not aim," Rieff contends, "like its
predecessors, at victory for some rival commitment, but rather at a way of using
all commitments which amounts to loyalty towards none."[20] Therapeutic culture
is "anticredal" because no particular symbolic of moral demands, of militant
ideals, can penetrate the self deeply enough to mandate what is and is not to be
done. All creeds—whether they be Christian, Marxist, or otherwise—grow shallow in such soil. There is a rapid turnover of all commitments, and those who
do not explicitly reject militant ideals and absolute truths wittingly and unwittingly tend to use the language of credal culture in the service of therapeutic
ends.

THE DUBIOUS GOD-TERM OF CIVIL RELIGION

Bellah maintains, in apparent contradiction to his own analysis and to that of
Rieff presented above, that utilitarian and expressive individualism have not won
the American kulturkampf—that "the cultural hegemony of the managerial and
therapeutic ethos is far from complete."[21] Philip Rieff, he writes, in a footnote
of Habits of the Heart, "has developed a typology similar to ours. He speaks of
'religious man, political man, economic man, and psychological man.' He tends
to believe, however, that his 'psychological man' (our expressive individualist)
has 'triumphed' more completely than we believe."[22] Given the thrust of Bellah's
own analysis, how does he support such contentions?

The answer is located in the especially strong emphasis that Bellah places on
the differences between belief and action, language and practice; for he, like
Rieff, has long emphasized the anticredal characteristics of American culture (see,
for instance, one of Bellah's earlier works, Beyond Belief[23]). However, Bellah turns
his analysis of anticredal culture in a different direction from Rieff. Indeed, Alasdair MacIntyre's conception of "practices" is central to his analysis because he
maintains that Americans continue to engage in activities that belie their "inarticulate" language of individualism. With the term practices, Bellah follows
MacIntyre in defining cooperative activities in which the participants strive to
conform to established standards of excellence as essential to the moral life—
specifically the cultivation and sustenance of virtues. "The tensions of our lives
would be even greater," reads one passage in Habits of the Heart, "if we did not,
in fact, engage in practices that constantly limit the effects of an isolating individualism, even though we cannot articulate those practices nearly as well as we
can the quest for autonomy."[24] Likewise, in a follow-up essay entitled "The Idea
of Practices in Habits: A Response," Bellah writes that "practices necessarily

persist in our lives even when we find it difficult to articulate them." He continues: "We locate these persistent practices in those spheres of our lives where biblical religion and civic republicanism still survive."[25] Although Bellah argues that many Americans have retreated into "lifestyle enclaves" in pursuit of expressive individualism, he maintains that "concrete commitments" have persisted in "communities of memory," especially in the lower and upper reaches of the class structure. What he calls "practices of commitment"[26] still *embody* the definitive, second language of American culture in contemporary society, even if that language is poorly spoken.

Bellah places such a heavy emphasis on MacIntyre's concept of practice because social practices constitute, as Christopher Lasch has pointed out, the discipline of character formation.[27] Under MacIntyre's rubric of practices, Bellah is able to make a theoretical distinction between traditional American culture and character and to reintroduce effectively his controversial concept of civil religion in new guise. Our traditional character persists—even though the members of our public culture frequently speak a self-serving, modern language that values the "external goods" of money, status, and power—because the "internal goods" of true practices continue beneath the managerial-therapeutic surface of American culture. The traditional American character of our biblical and republican heritage persists within ethnic, racial, religious, and national communities that have retained a historical memory—what Bellah calls "communities of memory."[28]

At the heart of such communities are the cultural residues of Christianity and what Bellah in earlier writings has called American "civil religion"—the religiously influenced republican strand of American culture that has been regularly articulated by public leaders since the founding fathers. In these earlier writings, Bellah argued for the definitive importance of "a collection of beliefs, symbols, and rituals with respect to sacred things and institutionalized in a collectivity" that served the American people "as a genuine vehicle of national religious self-understanding."[29] Vital to this "in God we trust" language of civil religion "at its best," Bellah maintained, has been "a genuine apprehension of universal and transcendent religious reality as seen in or, one could almost say, as revealed through the experience of the American people."[30] By the time he wrote *Habits of the Heart*, Bellah clearly understood that the language of civil religion had become divisive and uncivil, even corrupt. Consequently, he appeals directly to the "experience" of Americans: it is through "practices of commitment" embedded in "communities of memory" that a higher authority is revealed. Although the term civil religion is not used in *Habits of the Heart*, the hold of the concept on the theory of the book is clearly evident. In fact, the authors' faith in the recuperative powers of American civil religion helps to account for the insistent optimism and voluntaristic idealism of their study, in the face of their own evidence to the contrary.

Rieff's answer to Bellah is barely concealed. Rieff *both* acknowledges *Habits of the Heart* as a "leading example" of scholarly work confirming the existence of therapeutic culture *and* throws into question its sanguine conclusions by characterizing "communities of memories" as "a therapeutic and professional abstraction without doxologies of observance." In what is clearly a critical comment about the concept of civil religion, Rieff states that even "the mythic hero of my boyhood, Lincoln, no longer has a birthday to celebrate publicly." He continues: "as surely as residual faiths recur as present neurosis, the notional religion of the cultivated American classes, 'civility,' becomes a quaint Anglo myth, circulated by some sociologists and by all travel agents specializing in 'ye olde England.' "[31] For Rieff, Bellah's "practices of commitment" are not sustained within "communities of memory" because such communities are no longer culturally "positive," demanding a variety of self-renunciations in return for the salvation of the individual achieved through symbolic integration into and participation in the community.

According to Rieff's theory, Bellah's concept of civil religion is not the God-term that he imagines it to be. Genuine God-terms are interdictory, stipulating "values that forbid certain actions and thereby encourage others."[32] Nothing in Bellah's analysis explains how the "practices of commitment" embedded in "communities of memory" can resist the therapeutic culture of what MacIntyre calls "emotive values." Indeed, when Bellah approvingly states in *Habits of the Heart* that for ecologist Marra James the " 'whole world' is a community of memory and hope and entails practices of commitment,"[33] or that labor activist Cecelia Dougherty "describes her solidarity with working people and 'the have-nots' as an expression of concern for human dignity,"[34] one must question how much Bellah's own theory has absorbed the self-deceptive therapeutic language that Rieff and MacIntyre condemn. What Bellah elides, according to Charles Taylor, is "the search for moral sources *outside* the subject through languages which resonate *within* him or her, the grasping of an order which is inseparably indexed to a personal vision."[35] Rieff, in contrast, has undertaken precisely this search.

THE INSENSIBILITIES OF ANTICREDAL CULTURE

Rieff does not completely deny the continued presence of the earlier ideals of political man and religious man in contemporary western culture. In a passage that Bellah would approve as evidence of the continuance of the American republican tradition and civil religion, Rieff states in an early article that "President Kennedy's Inaugural Address aimed at the American 'individual' in the Tocquevillean sense of the word, in order to bring him back to an essential classical ideal of public service."[36] Yet, Rieff emphasizes that all such ideals mandating saving commitments are emptied of imperative meaning under the regime of therapeutic culture. His analysis agrees with that of Thomas Pangle who contends that what Bellah calls the republican tradition cannot be assimilated to the classical model of political man.[37] Indeed, Rieff suggests that there has long been a separation between ideals and experience, belief and action, in American society. Like Tocqueville, he contends that democratic ideals are often off on the horizon, bearing little relation to the realities of everyday life. In the language of Rieff's later theory, such ideals are "remissive" because they lack the militant, interdictory characteristics that Tocqueville found in aristocratic cultures.

Interdictory forms, in Rieff's theory, perform the chief function of every culture. That function is the limitation of possibilities, the restriction of experience, at such depths within the personality that individuals find there are certain possibilities they "cannot perform; more precisely, would dread to perform."[38] Remissions, on the other hand, define permissions and exceptions with respect to the interdicts that make other possibilities of thought and action acceptable. These interdictory-remissive complexes define and organize human action to varying degrees, establishing the learned capacity of acceptance and rejection within the personality. A culture that has grown more and more remissive, as Rieff argues that therapeutic culture has, performs the interdictory function less and less effectively. Interdicts decline in number and become less compelling, as what constitutes acceptable experience expands within various spheres of human activity, whether political, economic, sexual, or otherwise. Therapeutic culture, in particular, is remissive on principle, opposing the interdictory form itself, except insofar as the interdicts too can further enhance one's sense of well-being. In fact, Rieff contends that therapeutic culture may have veered permanently away from a repressive-inhibitory organization of the personality toward a more expressive-impulsive order. Ideals may continue to exist in this new type of culture, but they are no longer militant. Personality ceases to be identified with an idealized image of itself.

A personality that no longer identifies with an idealized image of itself can only do so at the cost of losing what Rieff calls in his revision of Freud a "sense of guilt." Guilt, Rieff maintains in his later writings, is humanity's most precious asset. Indeed, it is the atrophy of a "true" sense of guilt that Rieff takes as the definitive sign of the failure of Western culture in modernity; for a genuine sense of guilt not only prevents remissions from subverting the interdictory structure of high culture but also warns the personality away from direct violations of the interdicts. Rieff has termed such violations "transgressions," thereby enabling one to analyze cultures in terms of particular complexes of interdicts, remissions, and transgressions (see especially *Fellow Teachers*[39]). Rieff's deeper aim, however, is to relate theoretically the deepest sensibilities and insensibilities of the self to the very structure of culturally defined existences.

Through his theory, Rieff has attempted to link individual sensibilities to moral, even sacred, orders that transcend the self, as in the following passage:

The opposition to the Vietnam war, even crossed as it was by various transgressive protest movements, gave reasons for hope. I have said many times over that there can be no culture without guilt; Vietnam rekindled our sense of guilt, not widely or deeply; nevertheless, that indispensable and true sensibility seemed alive again. But I fear that true guilt for which I hope was crossed by false, creating predicates which mixed criticism of warmongers, professionals of state-abstracted violence, with amplifications of transgressive behavior among anti-culturemongers.[40]

The references to "true" and "false" guilt are the most telling in this passage. Whether Rieff has indeed succeeded in transcending therapeutic culture and answering Taylor's criticism of Bellah raises some very unorthodox questions for sociologists.

NOTES

1. Philip Rieff, *The Triumph of the Therapeutic: Uses of Faith After Freud* (New York: Harper and Row, 1987 [1966]).

2. Philip Rieff, *Freud: The Mind of the Moralist*, 3rd ed. (Chicago: University of Chicago Press, 1979 [1959]).

3. Christopher Lasch, *The Culture of Narcissism* (New York: Warner Books, 1978).

4. Alasdair MacIntyre, *After Virtue: A Study of Moral Theory*, 2d ed. (Notre Dame, IN: University of Notre Dame Press, 1984 [1981]).

5. Robert Bellah, Richard Madsen, William M. Sullivan, Ann Swidler, and Steven Tipton, *Habits of the Heart: Individualism and Commitment in American Life*, updated edition (Berkeley: University of California Press, 1996 [1985]).

6. Charles Reynolds and Ralph Norman, eds., *Community in America* (Berkeley: University of California Press, 1988).

7. Bellah et al., *Habits of the Heart*, 27–51.

8. Robert Bellah and Charles Glock, ed., *The New Religious Consciousness* (Berkeley: University of California Press, 1976), 335–337; Robert Bellah and Philip Hammond, *Varieties of Civil Religion* (New York: Harper and Row, 1980), 169–171.

9. Steven Tipton, *Getting Saved from the Sixties* (Berkeley: University of California Press, 1982), 232–233.

10. Bellah et al., *Habits of the Heart*, 60.

11. Philip Rieff, "The Impossible Culture: Wilde as Modern Prophet" (1982–1983), in *The Feeling Intellect*, ed. Jonathan Imber (Chicago: University of Chicago Press, 1990), 273–290.

12. Bellah et al., *Habits of the Heart*, 27.

13. Ibid., 143–144.

14. Rieff, *The Triumph of the Therapeutic*, 48–65.

15. Philip Rieff, Introduction in *Therapy and Technique* (New York: Collier Books, 1963), 7–24; *The Triumph of the Therapeutic*, 58; *Freud: The Mind of the Moralist*, 356–357.

16. Rieff, *The Triumph of the Therapeutic*, 52–78.

17. Alexis de Tocqueville, *Democracy in America*, Vol. 2, edited by Phillip Bradley (New York: Alfred A. Knopf, 1945), 98.

18. Rieff, *The Triumph of the Therapeutic*, 69.

19. Ibid., 13.

20. Ibid., 21.

21. Bellah et al., *Habits of the Heart*, 50.

22. Ibid., 311.

23. Robert Bellah, *Beyond Belief: Essays on Religion in a Post-Traditional World* (New York: Harper and Row, 1970).

24. Bellah et al., *Habits of the Heart*, 151.

25. Robert Bellah, "The Idea of Practices in *Habits*," in Reynolds and Norman, eds., *Community in America*, 271.

26. Bellah et al., *Habits of the Heart*, 154.

27. Christopher Lasch, "The Communitarian Critique of Liberalism," in Reynolds and Norman, eds., *Community in America*, 179.

28. Bellah et al., *Habits of the Heart*, 152–155.

29. Bellah, *Beyond Belief*, 173–174.

30. Ibid., 179.

31. Philip Rieff, "For the Last Time Psychology" (1987), in Imber, *The Feeling Intellect*, 354.

32. Rieff, "The Impossible Culture," 280.

33. Bellah et al., *Habits of the Heart*, 159.

34. Ibid., 162.

35. Charles Taylor, *Sources of the Self: The Making of Modern Identity* (Cambridge, MA: Harvard University Press, 1989), 510.

36. Rieff, *Therapy and Technique*, 11.

37. Thomas Pangle, *The Spirit of Modern Republicanism* (Chicago: University of Chicago Press, 1988).

38. Philip Rieff, "Toward a Theory of Culture" (1972), in Imber, *The Feeling of Intellect*, 323.

39. Philip Rieff, *Fellow Teachers*, 2d ed. (Chicago: University of Chicago Press, 1985 [1973]).

40. Ibid., 155.

8

Advice from a Tocquevillian Liberal: Arendt, Tocqueville, and the Liberal-Communitarian Debate

BARRY SHARPE

Perhaps no single idea has attracted more attention in recent years in academic political theory and political rhetoric than community. While Republicans and Democrats alike scramble to see who can successfully highlight the role of community in their political rhetoric, many scholars in academic political theory remain engaged in a "debate" over the value and meaning of community in liberalism. The so-called debate between liberals and communitarians, a series of exchanges inspired by John Rawls's *A Theory of Justice* and largely framed by Michael Sandel's critical response, *Liberalism and the Limits of Justice*, was a driving force in academic political theory in the 1980s (and continues intermittently today). The central issues surrounding the communitarian critique have revolved around presumed defects of liberal political theory: an inadequate, "flattened" conception of the self that failed to capture the social "embeddedness" of individuals, its inherent inability to protect and maintain the necessary foundations for liberal theory and practice, its thoroughly flawed ahistorical model of the individual and community, and its damaging advancement of the priority of the right over the good.[1] A debate dominated by conflict over ontology (e.g., atomism versus holism) and claims and counterclaims about what community is and is not ultimately gave way to a variety of exchanges that made it very difficult to differentiate so-called liberals from communitarians. More to the point, the liberal-communitarian debate, conceived as a singular exchange between identifiable camps, "ended" as liberals and communitarians alike moved on to exchanges on various forms of community and tradition, including liberal traditions and communities.

Recently a number of observers of and participants in the liberal-communitarian debate have offered assessments of its value and merit. The assessments of Charles Taylor and Alan Ryan are notable because they rate the terms of the debate as unhelpful and confused. Taylor argues that from its inception the debate operated at "cross-purposes," that is, the terms of the debate worked against one another because the language of the debate was underdeveloped and confused many issues important for liberals and so-called advocates of community.[2] For example, he indicates that the use of the terms liberal and communitarian presumed that there was only one issue at stake, or at least, the differences between the two was obvious and carried distinctive implications about ontology, methodology, and advocacy. To support this claim, he pairs off two possible ranges of positions—atomism-holism and individualist-collectivist. If liberals and communitarians were easily distinguishable, he argues, then they consistently would be identified on separate ends of these pairs. Recognizing how the labels liberal and communitarian do not subsume these frameworks, but are in fact confused by them, highlights, according to Taylor, how the debate was at "cross-purposes."

Similarly, Alan Ryan argues that the debate was so "muddled" from the very beginning that it was a "figment of our imagination."[3] Recognizing the difficulty of identifying many thinkers simply as liberals or communitarians, he advises that we reconsider the example of John Stuart Mill. Mill, the quintessential modern liberal, in his struggle to accommodate Bentham's utilitarianism, Tocqueville's sociology, and Coleridge's romanticism highlights the extent to which many of the issues and concerns alleged to separate liberal and communitarians were present already in Mill's mature theory.

What I propose is an examination of two authors whose works preceded the liberal-communitarian debate and cut across categories and defy easy labeling: Alexis de Tocqueville and Hannah Arendt. Tocqueville and Arendt have been the source of inspiration and support for a wide range of thinkers different in temperament and political persuasion: liberals and conservatives, elitists and radical democrats, champions of tradition and critics of modernity. Moreover, viewing Tocqueville and Arendt together—that is, identifying the debt Arendt owed to Tocqueville (so much so that we might call her a Tocquevillian liberal)— offers an effective perspective from which to assess important connections and tensions between individuals, tradition, and community.[4]

Although I present this discussion of Tocqueville and Arendt as a useful way of thinking about the liberal-communitarian debate, I do not confront directly the individual arguments associated with communitarians and liberals. Instead, I compare Tocqueville and Arendt on history, tradition, political liberty, and public space as useful reminders of the deficiencies associated with simple dichotomies like liberal and communitarian, individual and community, tradition and change.

I begin with Tocqueville and Arendt on history and historical vision. Tocqueville's famous distinction between the writing of history in aristocratic and dem-

ocratic ages is useful here because of the contrast it draws between the individual
as a subject of history and the individual as an object of history.

Historians who write in aristocratic ages generally attribute everything that happens to
the will and character of particular men, and they will unhesitantingly suppose slight
accidents to be the cause of the greatest revolutions. . . . Historians who live in democratic
ages show contrary tendencies. Most of them attribute hardly any influence over the
destinies of mankind to individuals, or over the fate of a people to the citizens. But they
make the great general causes responsible for the smallest particular events. . . . [W]hen
all the citizens are independent of one another and each is weak, no one can be found
exercising very great or, more particularly, very lasting influence over the masses. At first
sight individuals appear to have no influence at all over them, and society would seem to
progress on its own by the free and spontaneous action of all its members. That naturally
prompts the mind to look for the general reason which acts on so many men's faculties
at once and turns them all simultaneously in the same direction.[5]

For Tocqueville, a proper understanding of history requires due attention to "general causes" and "particular influences." His concern is that in a democratic age
there is a tendency to emphasize the role of general forces and to impart to them
a power and initiative like that of human beings. In such an environment, the
doctrines of necessity and fatalism take root and the perceived power and role
of the individual fade away. The obvious weaknesses individuals suffer in the
face of mass society is thus reinforced. As Tocqueville says elsewhere, "one must
not despise man, if one wants to obtain great efforts from others and oneself."[6]
In other words, such claims about the impotence of individuals in the face of
general forces (e.g., modernity, individualism, "the market," etc.) could become
self-fulfilling prophecies. Tocqueville's fear of democratic despotism—that the
individual will be subsumed under the weight of mass society and self-rule will
become impossible—leads him to counsel against the tendency within democratic societies to make such claims on behalf of general forces. "The need is to
preserve the credibility of and the connection between self-mastery and self-
government because we need to raise men's souls, not to complete their prostra-
tion" (496). This is why he is willing to "surrender" the virtue of humility for
the vice of pride. Enervation of spirit and abdication of judgment become defining features of a mass society and therefore the dangers associated with the individual energy and assertion linked with pride are more than outweighed by the
dangers of stagnation and indifference characteristic of a society defined by "petty
virtues" (632).

Arendt was taken by Tocqueville's remarks about the writing of history in
democratic ages. "Tocqueville . . . was the first to wonder why the 'doctrine of
necessity . . . is so attractive in democratic ages.' "[7] The novelty that Tocqueville
ascribed to democracy and the potential despotism represented by democracy was
also a concern for Arendt. She too worried about the extent to which the tendency to concentrate on general forces and talk about historical developments

as if they were inevitable would obscure our understanding of and faith in choice and action. "It is true that in retrospect—that is, in historical perspective—every sequence of events looks as though it could not have happened otherwise, but this is an optical, or, rather, an existential illusion: nothing could ever happen if reality did not kill, by definition, all the other potentialities originally inherent in any given situation."[8] In the extended passage cited from Tocqueville and this passage from Arendt, there is a common concern for the predominance of general causes and the retreat of the individual. In fact, such a perspective on the past and its connection to the present not only obscures what happened in the past but offers a distorted model of the nature of anxiety, choice, and individual responsibility in the present. We need to rediscover, though not overestimate, choice and variability in the past. It is not unusual to believe that the world in which one is currently living is witnessing the death of a tradition/world and the birth of another. On a trivial level, this is what the present means for the past and future. On a more important level, connecting our understanding of the past to one of choice and variability and the promise and limits of individual action establishes the basis for a more desirable and robust understanding of individual and communal responsibility. However, an acknowledgment that every genera-tion laments the loss of tradition and is anxious about the future should not slip into a complacency about the makeup or character of the future. This historical sense of the pervasiveness of anxiety over the condition of the present should focus our attention on what is possible, not on what is inevitable.

This concern with the possible as distinguished from the inevitable is a defense of human dignity. Attention to human dignity, that humans are subjects and not objects, is at the same time a commitment to responsibility: to acknowledge that individuals can and should have some control over their lives is to accept that individuals bear some responsibility for their choices and actions. When Arendt in *The Origins of Totalitarianism* identifies the target of totalitarianism as "human dignity," she shares Tocqueville's fear that individuals in mass society would be engulfed by the oppressive power and moral suasion of the majority. "For respect for human dignity implies the recognition of my fellow-men or our fellow-nations as subjects, as builders of worlds or co-builders of a common world. No ideology which aims at the explanation of all historical events of the past and at mapping out the course of events of the future can bear the unpredictability which springs from the fact that men are creative, that they can bring forward something so new that nobody ever foresaw it."[9]

Part of Tocqueville's optimism about our ability to direct, control, or, at the very least, step out of the overwhelming forces of change is contained in his observations about the promise of each new generation. "[N]ations do not grow old as men do. Each fresh generation is new material for the lawgiver to mold" (95). Tocqueville's observation about the potentiality contained in subsequent generations becomes "the central category of political thought" in the work of Hannah Arendt. "[T]he human condition of natality; the new beginning inher-ent in birth can make itself felt in the world only because the newcomer possesses the capacity of beginning something anew, that is, of acting. . . . [S]ince action is the political activity par excellence, natality, and not mortality, may be the central category of political, as distinguished from metaphysical thought."[10] Natality guarantees the promise of a new beginning, but it also guarantees the promise of change. The best and the worst of human artifice are equally threatened by natality. What we as human beings create is fragile for a variety of reasons, not the least of which is the future encroaching on the present. Discussing the prospects of protecting what has been handed down from the past and what has been erected and maintained in the present, Arendt, nonetheless, admits the fundamental fragility of the present under the weight of the new. "Limitations and boundaries exist within the realm of human affairs, but they never offer a framework that can reliably withstand the onslaught with which each new generation must insert itself."[11]

To leave our understanding of the threat the future poses to the present simply in terms of the "here and now" as opposed to the "unborn" would terribly simplify the process of change, the transmission of tradition and experience, and the crucial importance of education and socialization. Arendt in an essay entitled "No Longer and Not Yet" picks up on this theme but admits there are periods when there is a "break" between the old and new.

Hume once remarked that the whole of human civilization depends upon the fact that "one generation does not go off the stage at once and succeed, as is the case with silkworms and butterflies." At some points of history, however, at some heights of crisis, a fate similar to that of silkworms and butterflies may befall a generation of men. For the decline of the old, and the birth of the new, is not necessarily an affair of continuity. . . . [T]he chain is broken and an "empty space," a kind of historical no man's land, comes to the surface which can be described only in terms of "no longer and not yet."[12]

Because Tocqueville's life was marked by the bloody period of the French Revolution and his observations of the "New World's" experiment with democracy, Tocqueville was quite attuned to the promise and danger represented by starting anew. Indeed, he described himself as "nicely balanced between past and future" with a view to a dying world and the birth of another. "I came into the world at the end of a long revolution which, after having destroyed the old order, created nothing that could last. When I began my life aristocracy was already dead and democracy was still unborn. Therefore my instinct could not lead me blindly toward one or the other. . . . I was so nicely balanced between past and future that I did not feel instinctively drawn toward the one over the other."[13]

In this transitional period between past and future, Tocqueville saw himself as offering counsel to those blindly holding on to the past, aristocracy, and those naively embracing the future, democracy. Tocqueville was writing to democrats who thought the past was easily forgotten and aristocrats who thought the present easily ignored in favor of the past. In both cases, an act of forgetting became a political principle. As Bruce Smith describes it, democrats and aristocrats alike "overestimated the possibilities of oblivion."[14] Tocqueville knew it was impossible for any man to wholly "detach himself from the past" (48), and it would be wise to remember, as Arendt advises, that tradition, even a dying or dead tradition, exerts influence on the minds and habits of the living.[15]

This sentiment about following the past is clearly expressed in Tocqueville's call for a "new political science . . . for a world itself quite new." Just after making this call, he warns of the danger of remaining transfixed by the images and categories of the past: "Carried away by a rapid current, we obstinately keep our eyes fixed on the ruins still in sight on the bank, while the stream hurls us backward—facing toward the abyss" (13). Stagnation is a recurring theme in Tocqueville's work and it is by following the form rather than the experience of the past that individuals and society may suffer its effects. He cites Chinese civilization as an example of the dangers of stagnation.

The Chinese, following in their fathers' steps, had forgotten the reasons which had guided them. . . . They had to copy their ancestors the whole time in everything for fear of straying into impenetrable darkness if they deviated for a moment from their tracks. Human knowledge had almost dried up at the fount, and the stream still flowed, it could neither increase nor change its course. (464)

Just as there is a struggle to separate oneself from the ruins of the past, Tocqueville struggles to understand the novelty of democracy, and, in particular, the novelty of democratic despotism. The alternative to holding one's gaze on the ruins on the shore is not an easy understanding and acceptance of the future, in this case of democracy. This transitional "space" fills Tocqueville with dread because the "past throws no light on the future, and the spirit of man walks through the night" (703). In particular, the past offers no guidance for understanding democratic despotism. What Tocqueville struggles to label is the condition where individuals, through the enervation of spirit that comes from the pursuit of petty pleasures and the substitution of citizenship for material comfort and safety, either place the chains of tyranny on themselves or are too weak to resist another's imposition.

Arendt struggles with the same kind of break in tradition described by Tocqueville—"the past throws no light on the future"—and the novelty of a form of tyranny, totalitarianism, not too dissimilar to Tocqueville's fears about democratic despotism. She believes that totalitarianism and genocide have "exploded our traditional categories of political thought (totalitarian domination is unlike all forms of tyranny and despotism we know of) and the standards of our moral judgment (totalitarian crimes are very inadequately described as 'murder' and totalitarian criminals can hardly be punished as 'murderers')."[16]

When Tocqueville described himself as "balanced between past and future," he was at the same time describing the transitional period between aristocracy and democracy. His counsel to aristocrats was that they not fight the inevitable; helped or hindered, democracy would win the day. The question was how democratic momentum was to be directed. To this task, he advised that the past not be forgotten until it was little more than the dead relics of a lost civilization, but that the better features of the aristocratic past be incorporated into a democratic future. Like Tocqueville's view of a world ending and a world coming of age, today we stand at the end of the modern age and await the "maturation" of our postmodern world. We can highlight, as Hannah Arendt does, the rupture of a tradition of political thought in the aftermath of Auschwitz and Hiroshima. By announcing a "break in tradition," a kind of transitional period not unlike Tocqueville's own, we can fight the loss of tradition and try to recreate a past that is no longer achievable (a kind of political action based on nostalgia); or, we can see the break in tradition as a kind of opportunity, like Arendt, and we can struggle, like Tocqueville, with forms and categories of our "new" political experience. A "break in tradition" provides a "great chance to look upon the past with eyes undistracted by tradition, with a directness which had disappeared from Occidental reading and hearing ever since Roman civilization submitted to the authority of Greek thought."[17]

After introducing his readers to the fortunate bequest of nature to America and the importance of its Protestant heritage, Tocqueville turns to the preeminent place of political experience in the formation of American mores. He is struck by the absence of administrative centralization and the strength and vitality of its local institutions and voluntary associations. Local institutions and voluntary associations thrive in America because they are allowed the chance to live and breathe. One of the strongest contrasts that Tocqueville draws between America and his country is the level of administrative centralization in France and the level of administrative decentralization in America. He admired American administrative decentralization not for its administrative, but for its political, effect (95). The difference between administration and politics corresponds to the difference between being a subject and being a citizen. "No doubt he is less successful than the state would have been in his place, but in the long run the sum of all private undertakings far surpasses anything the government might have done" (95). In fact, too much administration undermines the formative role that local institutions play in the education and development of citizens. Increasingly centralized administration saps the resources and serves as a dampening agent on a fundamental vehicle for the expression of public liberty, associations.[18] According to Tocqueville, we should resist the tendency that as individuals become comparatively weaker in a mass society of equal conditions that the "government must become more skillful and active, so that society should do what is no longer possible for individuals." As government intervenes to take the place of associations, a vicious cycle of need and dependency is created that depletes vital public resources. Through the "art of pursuing in common," "[f]eelings are renewed, the heart enlarged, and the understanding developed only by the reciprocal action of men upon another" (515). As he puts it in volume one of *Democracy*: "Local institutions are to liberty what primary schools are to science; they put it within the people's reach; they teach people to appreciate its peaceful enjoyment and accustom them to make use of it. Without local institutions a nation may give itself a free government, but it has not got the spirit of liberty" (63).

This classic expression of civic republicanism's emphasis on the importance of public spaces for the exercise of public liberty is also found in Arendt. "Whatever the administrative advantages and disadvantages may be, its political result is always the same: monopolization of power causes the drying up or oozing away of all authentic powers sources in the country."[19] Current claims on behalf of decentralization of government are based largely on perceived inefficiencies of the administrative apparatus (red tape, bloated work forces, etc.). Tocqueville and Arendt remind us that the truly important political reasons for decentralization need to be rediscovered, or at least, better appreciated. If the established criterion is efficiency, then the likely movement back and forth between claims for more and less centralized administration will obscure important political effects, and the political capital of public knowledge, interest, support, commitment, responsibility, and efficacy will continue to be depleted.

Just as an emphasis on the inexorable movement of general forces in democratic ages raised fears for Tocqueville concerning individual faith in the capacity for judgment and action, Arendt, drawing on Jefferson's ideas about the need for "small republics," feared that without proper attention to accessible public spaces for the exercise of political liberty, no opportunities would exist for "*being* republicans" and "*acting* as citizens."

Jefferson, though the secret vote was still unknown at the time, had at least a foreboding of how dangerous it might be to allow the people a share in public power without providing them at the same time with more public space than the ballot box and with more opportunity to make their voices heard in public than election day. What he perceived to be the mortal danger to the republic was that the Constitution had given all power to the citizens, without giving them the opportunity of *being* republicans and *acting* as citizens. In other words, the danger was that all power had been given to the people in their private capacity and that there was no space established for them in their capacity of being citizens."[20]

Where Tocqueville claimed that associations were the source of the reciprocal action crucial for the development of attachments to others and an enlargement of "heart," Arendt claimed that faith in and commitment to republican institutions required a "living presence in the midst of its citizens" only possible through the public, not the private, realm.

We might respond to Tocqueville's fears of a despotism of conformity and stagnation and Arendt's parallel fears in *The Human Condition* that the rise of the social over the political signals the threat of a new kind of tyranny by claiming that their fears are not our fears. In other words, it is plausible to suggest that a more likely threat to democracy today does not rest with the specter of conformity; rather, the more likely threat is that the "center won't hold." It may be the case as Tocqueville suggests that there is a logic to democracy and equality that may lead to isolation, indifference to the fate of others, and despotism. As Tocqueville himself makes quite clear, we should consider the formative connections between institutions and culture. To suggest a variation on Tocqueville's theme of the march of democracy, fragmented political institutions and the primacy of individual rights (may) have debased the idea of "the people" and attenuated its appeal. The consequence of this is not the disappearance of the individual into a complacent mob, but the victory of partial identification (e.g., "identity politics") in the form of group identification. The difficult balance between public sentiment and individual liberty, in other words, has been upset by the forces of democratization, but its consequences pose different sorts of problems for a liberal democratic order than the pressures of mass society.

In Tocqueville and Arendt the fear of conformity begins with the assumption that isolated and equally powerless individuals will in time lose faith in their judgment and defer to others and to perceived external forces. Disaffection, indifference, loss of freedom, and the sacrifice of liberty for security and material comfort become the defining features of democratic despotism for Tocqueville. One of the great advantages possessed by America according to Tocqueville was a relative lack of administrative centralization. If we read much of what he had to say about democracy in America as advice for France about the important links between character and institutions, the temporal separation between Tocqueville's America and America today may place us in a similar position regarding the dangers of centralized administration. Tocqueville speaks to us today in a way that is quite like what he was saying to his French contemporaries. If we consider Arendt's *The Human Condition* as an update of sorts on Tocquevillian themes, her story picks up at a point when administrative centralization is a defining element of democracy in America. The independence and political liberty cherished by Tocqueville in the townships of New England and the newly created municipalities of Ohio and Illinois is, for Arendt, exemplified in the Greek *polis*. The classical Greek model of politics becomes a standard for courage and excellence that stands in sharp relief to the norm of twentieth-century mass society. The ascendancy of "the social" is a victory of administration over politics and an indication that behavior, rather than action, is the central category of political life. Arendt's "update" of Tocqueville's themes concerning public space and liberty thus becomes an investigation of the conditions for politics in a mass society.

Arendt has a two-fold characterization of the *polis* that captures both the limits to and the possibilities for politics today. She describes the *polis* as the actual space for deliberation and action, a space that secures the relative permanence of memory and protects against its futility. "The organization of the *polis*, physically secured by the wall around the city and physiognomically guaranteed by its laws—lest the succeeding generations change its identity beyond recognition—space is an essential component in promoting and protecting political speech and action. Seen from another perspective, the *polis* is less an actual physical place crucial for the maintenance of political activity, rather it is an idea generated through political speech and activity. "The *polis*, properly speaking, is not the city-state in its physical location; it is the organization of the people as it arises out of acting and speaking together for this purpose, no matter where they happen to be."[21] Seen together, these two perspectives on the *polis* help to explain Arendt's admiration for the Greek city-state and public space and liberty generated by revolutionary activity. In addition, her characterization of the *polis* as a physical space *as well as* the potential space created whenever people come together to meet and discuss "things of the public," illustrates how public spaces are always potentially there, but that some care and concern for the conditions conducive for their appearance is vital as well. Just as a house left untended will deteriorate from within and without, the public realm, if neglected or taken for granted, will deteriorate as well.[22] Although Tocqueville discusses the importance of nature and the physical environment for the formation of American political culture and institutions, he, like Arendt, stresses the importance of the artificial world, the human artifice, and is not nostalgic for a "lost Eden." Arendt's, like Tocqueville's, model of political community does not bemoan the loss of an alleged communal harmony or togetherness. In both thinkers, "common" is as much a description of separateness and individuality as it is a reference to togetherness. To hold something in common, according to Arendt, is not to obliterate the differences between individuals, but to provide the basis for plurality and individuality to be expressed. One of the greatest dangers of a mass society is the loss of a vital "in-between" that "relates and separates at the same time."[23] Mass society is unbearable not because of the number of people involved, or at least not primarily, but the fact that the world between them has lost its power to gather them together, to relate and separate them."[24] This final image, the world losing its power to gather together, is a theme that guides much of Tocqueville's and Arendt's work. This image also contributes to their fears about the increasing impotence of the individual in the modern age.

The kind of political advantages Tocqueville and Arendt associated with decentralization are not likely to be present in simple wholesale movement of governmental authority and decision-making to the state and local level. As Richard Dagger notes in "Metropolis, Memory, and Citizenship," urban political life is not well suited to the kind of association and reciprocal action so admired by Tocqueville and Arendt. Because of overwhelming size, administrative focus, political fragmentation, and the mobility of people, cities no longer function as incubators or "free schools" of citizenship. Because our cities do not have a "civic memory," according to Dagger, they are poor public spaces for the exercise of political liberty. Poorly situated "between past and future," cities become interest-oriented battlegrounds that do more to separate people than bring them together. The theme of "between past and future" is explicit in his rendering of civic memory: "the memory which by tying its residents to the past of a city, enables them to play a part in its present and to help shape its future."[25] To understand our position with regard to the past and to view ourselves as individuals participating in the shape of the future is to take seriously the idea of human dignity where authorship, participation, and responsibility are key components. Tocqueville's fears about the diminution of the individual in the writing of history in democratic ages and the retreat of the individual in the face of mass society, as well as Arendt's concern about the "existential illusion" associated with historical vision and the victory of administration over politics, echo this commitment to human dignity. Seen in this perspective, Dagger's claim for the function of memory—"without memory there is no personality, no sense of self. Indeed, we can think of and act as selves only because we can *recollect* the experiences which constitute our selves"—is less a characteristic statement demonstrating the divide between the "unencumbered" liberal self and the "situated" or "socially constituted" communitarian self, and more a reflection on the interdependence, promise, and fragility of individual *and* public action and memory.

It is possible to argue that the "democratic moment" captured by Tocqueville and Arendt's exemplary model of the Greek city-state is not relevant for today's mass political life. In other words, to hold Tocqueville and Arendt up as possible "remedies" for current political problems or use them as models for a possible politics is simply engaging in nostalgia. Perhaps. Even if there is some element of nostalgia in valuing Tocqueville's and Arendt's work as standards for contemporary politics, however, their fears about mass society and the importance they place on public space for the exercise of political liberty are worth our attention. Because of their emphasis on the importance of beginnings, their warning about holding to broken or dead traditions, their call for individual action and responsibility while maintaining the need for vital public spaces, and their stress on the art of "associating together" as the touchstone for the formation of political habits and the cultivation of public space, reading Tocqueville and Arendt, perhaps even reading Tocqueville and Arendt together, may not be simply a nostalgic exercise but a hopeful and sober statement on the health and possibility of politics today.

NOTES

1. Allen Buchanan provides a nice summary of major communitarian criticisms of liberal theory in "Assessing the Communitarian Critique of Liberalism," *Ethics* 99 (July 1989): 852–882.

2. Charles Taylor, "Cross-Purposes: The Liberal-Communitarian Debate," in *Liberalism and the Moral Life*, edited by Nancy L. Rosenblum (Cambridge, MA: Harvard University Press, 1989).

3. Alan Ryan, "The Liberal Community," in *Democratic Community*, edited by John W. Chapman and Ian Shapiro (New York: New York University Press, 1993), 91.

4. Even scholars who have explicitly linked Tocqueville and Arendt draw different conclusions concerning shared themes, concerns, and prescriptions. See Margie Lloyd, "In Tocqueville's Shadow: Hannah Arendt's Liberal Republicanism," *Review of Politics* 57 (Winter 1995): 31–58; Suzanne D. Jacobitti, "Individualism and Political Community:

Arendt and Tocqueville on the Current Debate in Liberalism," *Polity* 22 (Summer 1991): 585–604.

5. Alexis de Tocqueville, *Democracy in America*, translated by George Lawrence, edited by J. P. Mayer (Garden City, NY: Doubleday, 1969), 493–494. Subsequent references to the book are by page numbers in the text.

6. Ralph Lerner, *Revolutions Revisited: Two Faces of the Politics of the Enlightenment* (Chapel Hill: University of North Carolina Press, 1994), 117.

7. Hannah Arendt, *On Revolution* (New York: Viking Press, 1965), 113.

8. Hannah Arendt, *Between Past and Future: Eight Exercises in Political Thought* (New York: Viking Press, 1968), 243.

9. Hannah Arendt, *The Origins of Totalitarianism*, rev. ed. (New York: Harcourt, Brace and World, 1966), 458.

10. Hannah Arendt, *The Human Condition* (Chicago: University of Chicago Press, 1958), 9.

11. Arendt, *Between Past and Future*, 191.

12. Hannah Arendt, *Essays in Understanding 1930–1954*, edited by Jerome Kohn (New York: Harcourt Brace, 1994), 158.

13. Cited in Sheldon Wolin, *The Presence of the Past: Essays on the State and the Constitution* (Baltimore: Johns Hopkins University Press, 1989), 66.

14. Bruce James Smith, *Politics and Remembrance: Republican Themes in Machiavelli, Burke, and Tocqueville* (Princeton, NJ: Princeton University Press, 1985), 182.

15. Arendt, *Between Past and Future*, 26.

16. Arendt, *Essays*, 405.

17. Arendt, *Between Past and Future*, 28–29.

18. Theda Skocpol offers an interesting account of the positive role of centralized institutions in the promotion and maintenance of voluntary associations. See Theda Skocpol, "Unravelling from Above," *The American Prospect* no. 25 (March–April 1996): 20–25. Skocpol also seeks to counter what she perceives to be a distorted reading of Tocqueville offered by many conservatives who present market-based images of local voluntarism with a more politicized reading of independence, freedom, and voluntary associations. See her "The Tocqueville Problem: Civic Engagement in American Democracy," Presidential Address, Annual Meeting of the Social Science History Association (October 12, 1996).

19. Hannah Arendt, *Crises of the Republic* (New York: Harcourt Brace Jovanovich, 1972), 182.

20. Arendt, *On Revolution*, 253.

21. Arendt, *The Human Condition*, 198.

22. Arendt, *Essays*, 74.

23. Ibid., 52.

24. Ibid., 52–53.

25. Richard Dagger, "Metropolis, Memory, and Citizenship," *American Journal of Political Science* 25 (November 1981): 729.

9

Liberal Ironism and the Decay of Citizenship

JOSEPH KNIPPENBERG

THE POSTMODERN CONDITION

It is common nowadays to describe our time as postmodern. Postmodernity is everywhere, from art and architecture to literature to philosophy and social science. In Richard Rorty's words, it has achieved "cultural hegemony."[1] While such a fashionable term runs the risk of being so overused and over-applied as to become virtually meaningless—at least in more or less popular discourse—it has been and can be used with a certain amount of precision to denote the critique and abandonment of the modern project of enlightenment. Because postmodernists display "an incredulity towards metanarratives,"[2] they cannot support a project whose purpose is to discover, popularize, and universally apply rationally discernible principles. Unlike enlightenment rationalists, who have confidence in the power of human reason, postmodernists mistrust reason and the universalism they associate with it. Rather than speaking in categories applicable to all human beings as human beings, they attend to the unique habits, ways, and cultures of particular peoples. In Richard Rorty's words, postmodernists believe that "there is nothing 'beneath' socialization or prior to history which is definatory of the human."[3] For postmodernists, it does not make sense to speak of a natural order or of human nature.[4]

Some find this understanding of our situation quite liberating. If identities and moral and cultural truths are "made, not found," then we are free to make and remake ourselves and our "values" as often as we wish, borrowing from the plethora of sources that the pluralistic life of the postmodern world makes available.[5] Individual ways of life come to resemble the menu offerings we find in fashionable restaurants: a meat, a starch, some vegetables, and some spices, all from different parts of the world and all "fused" in the same dish. As one observer has put it, postmodernism "involves seeing cultural 'mongrelization' as a positive and enriching thing."[6] Once we become bored with the one identity or once it has outlived its usefulness, we move on to something else. We tell a story about ourselves that changes as our intentions, aims, and perspectives change.

The premise that underlies this approach to life is that every perspective, every way of life, is culturally conditioned or, if you will, tribal and, as such, should be taken "a bit less seriously."[7] The truths that the authors of the Declaration of Independence regarded as self-evident to all human beings as human beings, the "facts of reason" that Kant thought intelligible, not merely to all human beings, but indeed to all rational beings, are all cultural constructs. When we speak carefully and precisely as postmoderns, we should perhaps refer to ourselves as "postmodernist bourgeois liberals" who are the contingent products and beneficiaries of a prosperous North Atlantic liberal tradition.[8] We do not have any peculiar access to the truth about the human condition because there is no human condition as such.

What I propose to investigate in this chapter is whether this postmodern attitude toward the character and source of our political and moral principles is as politically salutary as some of its advocates seem to believe. I take as my point of departure a question Thomas Jefferson once asked: "[C]an the liberties of a nation be thought secure when we have removed their only firm basis, a conviction in the minds of the people that these liberties are of the gift of God?"[9] Jefferson had in mind, I think, the notion that the commitment to respecting the rights of individuals required in most people at least some sort of cosmic support.[10] In the somewhat more technical language of postmodern philosophy, Jefferson thought that liberal political principles required "metaphysical" foundations. Whatever may the case for those whose minds are "of a peculiar structure,"[11] the belief that one's way of life is arbitrary or contingent, that it has no significant support from either God or nature, would go a long way toward undermining one's willingness to make any genuine sacrifices on its behalf.[12] If one "life-style" becomes inconvenient, why not simply find another that better serves one's current needs? From the Jeffersonian point of view, it is hard to imagine a postmodernist bourgeois liberal who would be willing to pledge his or her "life, fortune, and sacred honor" in support of any set of political and moral principles.[13] Postmodernism and patriotic citizenship would seem to be antithetical.

But before rendering summary judgment against postmodernism on this ground, I would like to examine the best case that can be made on its behalf. To that end, I shall consider Richard Rorty's "liberal ironism" as the characteristic stance of the postmodern liberal. Having permitted the postmodernists to speak for themselves, I shall conclude with some brief remarks about the requisites of healthy political community.

INTELLECTUAL IRONISTS AND PRAGMATIC CITIZENS

In *Contingency, Irony, and Solidarity* Rorty claims that the recognition of the contingency of one's political beliefs should be "the chief virtue of the members of a liberal society" and furthermore that "the culture of such a society should aim at curing us of our 'deep metaphysical need' " to ground our beliefs in something prior or higher.[14] We would, he argues, be better off as a community if we were able to dispense with the need for foundations. Indeed, the insistence upon foundations, upon nonnegotiable "self-evident truths," is, according to him, ultimately antithetical to a genuine liberal society: "It is central to the idea of a liberal society that, in respect to words as opposed to deeds, persuasion as opposed to force, anything goes."[15] While once upon a time liberals may have sought for rhetorical reasons to adopt the pseudo-religious scientific pose of foundationalism, it is no longer necessary, for the religious opponents of liberalism who provided the context and audience for these efforts have long since been vanquished.[16] The self-avowed purpose of contemporary liberalism ought to be the fostering of human inventiveness and creativity, "the creation of ever more various and multicolored artifacts."[17] In the more traditional language of the Declaration of Independence, a Rortian liberal society would be devoted above all to the pursuit of happiness (understood as whatever pleased anyone and did not lead to cruelty and violence). Such a society would facilitate "the free and open encounters of present linguistic and other practices with suggestions for new practices" and would have "no goal except a willingness to see how such encounters go and abide by the outcome."[18]

The "ideal citizen" of Rorty's liberal utopia is someone who eschews the need for foundations and is fully conscious of the contingency of his or her "language, . . . conscience, . . . morality, and . . . highest hopes."[19] While such a citizen may be privately Nietzschean,[20] he or she is publicly committed to a political order that fosters individual creativity while at the same time minimizing cruelty. Now, Rorty is often (but not always) careful to distinguish this simple awareness of the contingency of one's condition from ironism, liberal or otherwise.[21] In his ideal liberal society, ordinary citizens would be "commonsensically nominalist and historicist," but not ironic about their situations; that is, they would not feel "any particular doubts about the contingencies they happen to be."[22] Ordinary citizens would not look to nature or reason to justify or test their allegiance to their community; for them, their community and its "values" would provide their lives with meaning. To this extent, postmodern non- or anti-foundationalism would seem to support a kind of ethnocentricity that supports citizenship.[23] On the other hand, ironism is and would continue to be reserved for intellectuals, who have "continuing doubts about the final vocabulary [they] currently [use]," realize "that argument phrased in [their] present vocabulary can neither underwrite nor dissolve those doubts," and do not think "that [their] vocabulary is closer to reality than others."[24] In short, in Rorty's ideal liberal society no one—not citizens, not political leaders, not public or private intellectuals—would seek to make an appeal to the "laws of nature and nature's God," to justify in universal or transhistorical terms the principles or habits in accordance with which they happened to live.[25] What does and should move ordinary citizens of liberal societies, however, is the concrete "hope that life will be freer, less cruel, more leisured, richer in goods and experiences, not just for our descendants but for everybody's descendants."[26]

In other words, a Rortian liberal society will apparently for most of its citizens be justified, not by some reference to God or nature, but by a pragmatic and progressive "philosophy of history" (if that is not a contradiction in terms).[27] Such a "story" can be buttressed and, needless to say, undermined only by "facts," or, if you will, references to the events of history.[28] To the extent, however, that recent history does not seem to support our hopes, to the extent that life does not seem to be getting better and better for all of us, we may well come to regard "the last few hundred years of European and American history . . . as an island in time, surrounded by misery, tyranny, and chaos."[29] The hope that grounds the allegiance of ordinary people to liberalism would thus seem to be at the mercy of "contingencies." If Rorty's bleak vision of our age is plausible, then the very century in which for the first time a liberal utopia might be possible (because of the allegedly growing nominalism and historicism of the general population and the growing ironism of the intelligentsia) is also the one in which the devotion of most people to the principles of liberalism is most at risk.

There are two ways out of this apparent political conundrum. The first is to depend upon the intelligentsia to "redescribe" our circumstances so as to sustain hope. The question here is whether ironists who are so full of doubts would be willing or able to do so. A second avenue is to reject Rorty's description of the political psychology of liberal hope. Let us briefly consider the second before returning to the first.

Rorty's claim that ordinary allegiance to liberalism depends upon a progressive account of history that may be subject to "factual" refutation turns on the argument that for most contemporary liberal citizens hopes for the afterlife have been replaced by hopes for the this-worldly future. We care now more for the happiness of our grandchildren than for the salvation of our souls.[30] In Rorty's world, religious faith has declined, probably irretrievably and certainly for the better. By most other accounts, however, "American religion today is thriving, activist, and diverse," with 94 percent of Americans professing "a belief in God or a universal spirit" and about 70 percent believing in life after death.[31] Now, these "metaphysical" commitments are not necessarily inconsistent with belief in a progressive account of this-worldly history. Indeed, I have suggested elsewhere that Kant's philosophy of history requires some sort of faith in an extra-historical guarantor of the hoped-for outcome.[32] It is possible to argue, in other words, that hope for this world as well as for the next depends upon faith in a Supreme Being. From the point of view of perpetuating liberalism, the advantage of religiously grounded hope over a purely secular account of historical progress is that it is more resistant to apparently contrary facts. It enlists the inscrutability or "semi-scrutability" of God's will and the confidence in divine beneficence on behalf of our temporal hopes, even against the best available "empirical" evidence. Needless to say, it is also possible to offer a variety of other religiously derived "metaphysical" arguments on behalf of liberalism.[33]

Of course, the work it would take to appropriate religion on behalf of liberalism will have to be undertaken, if at all, by intellectuals. That Rorty himself is not about to take on this task is abundantly clear; for him, a "postreligious culture" is as desirable as a "postmetaphysical culture."[34] He further implies that there is no necessary connection between ironism—the current stance of most intellectuals—and liberalism.[35] The kinds of doubts that ironists entertain do not arise only in liberal societies, nor are only those who begin as liberals subject to them.[36] In addition, he assumes that ironists have a certain kind of intellectual integrity. They cannot be " 'progressive' and 'dynamic' liberals" because they "cannot offer the same sort of social hope as metaphysicians offer." In their view, the ability "to conquer the forces which are marshaled against you . . . is a matter of weapons and luck, not a matter of having truth on your side, or having detected the 'movement of history.' "[37] Just as ironists cannot believe, wholeheartedly or otherwise, in God or nature, so also can they not believe in any sort of providential history.[38] Indeed, for Rorty a philosophy of history is merely "a large blurry object around which to weave our concrete local fantasies."[39] What, then, is the current connection between ironism and liberalism? Why might ironists wish to support liberalism? And, finally, how would they offer their support?

Rorty's answer to the first question is that some ironists like himself happen to have been born in liberal societies and raised as liberals. A liberal ironist is an ironist who happens to be a liberal, but who apparently also is not convinced by or satisfied with the principles upon which his or her society is supposed to be based. The question of why in the face of this dissatisfaction the liberal ironist remains a liberal or conditions the pursuit of personal perfection on the limits imposed by liberalism is not one that Rorty explicitly addresses. Part of the answer may, however, be constructed from the following consideration. According to Rorty, ironism is essentially privatistic; for ironists, "theory has become a means to private perfection rather than to human solidarity."[40] Because the ironist cannot wholly invest him- or herself in any common project, because the ironist will always have doubts about the "final vocabulary" in accordance with which the project is justified, he or she will always keep a certain distance from his or her fellows. The ironist's goal is autonomy understood as self-creation.[41] To the extent that this is a genuinely private goal, it probably can most easily be pursued in a society that is tolerant, makes minimal public demands on its citizens, and offers as great as possible a range of opportunities for individual self-fulfillment.[42] Thus there is an essentially selfish strategic ground for ironists to make common cause with liberalism, so long, presumably, as their attempts to promote or perpetuate liberalism do not overburden their efforts at self-perfection.[43]

Now, Rorty denies that the hope that moves ordinary citizens must be grounded in a philosophy of history. "There are," he says, "a lot of fantasies that can stand on their own, without being twined around some large conceptually graspable object."[44] Every day, we hope for all sorts of concrete small things and work toward their realization without grounding our efforts in any "philosophy of history." We simply and pragmatically try to work things out. Thus instead of offering us a philosophy of history, Rorty appears to proffer a "groundless hope" as the motivation for our efforts to sustain and improve liberalism.[45] If, in effect, we do not care about history, we will never give up our efforts at improving our lot, regardless of what "the facts" seem to suggest.

Rorty's approach to the inconvenient import of certain historical trends stands in striking contrast to that of Kant, who deals with a similar issue in "Theory and Practice." What is certain, Kant says, is our duty. The facts of history may seem to undermine our capacity for remaking the world in the light of our duty, but "so long as they cannot be made entirely certain, I cannot exchange my duty (as a liquidum) for a rule of expediency which says that I ought not to attempt the impracticable."[46] Our duty gives rise to hope, which in turn gives rise to a comforting account of history. The duty does not depend upon the reassuring history, but nevertheless inevitably engenders it.[47] Now, even if we abstract from the "ontological" status of history, Kant is making an important "anthropological" observation: human beings cannot have hope without presuming that something—history, God, or both—supports or gives substance to that hope. It is precisely this contention that Rorty denies. In place of historically grounded hope, he proposes that we experiment with groundless hope. But if Kant is correct, then the position Rorty favors is untenable. People cannot be narrowly pragmatic in the manner that he suggests. They will not give up their belief in God or history (or both). Still, without any responsible leadership in the formation of historical and theological opinions, there is no guarantee that what comes forth will in any way support liberal citizenship.[48] Indeed, much of the rhetoric of classical liberalism was directed at this end.[49] In short, Rorty's pragmatic eschewal of historical or theological supports for liberalism may well pave the way for its popular abandonment.[50]

Of course, one could respond on Rorty's behalf that the small things for which we hope—a job that pays well enough, a roof over our heads, a comfortable retirement, and happy, beautiful grandchildren—do not in fact require a full-blown philosophy of history. People work toward and hope for these sorts of things all the time without imagining that they are participating in some large historical project. The pursuit of these essentially private aims seems not to involve many people and certainly not world history. There are, however, three points that can be made against this contention. The first is a sociological "fact." These small private goals are precisely the sorts of things for which many Americans do indeed quite literally pray. They work to the best of their ability and trust that God will provide for them. Whether they would act in quite the same way without a trust in God's providential care is a question that cannot be answered on the basis of the available evidence. Second, these aims and hopes are not quite as private as they seem, for they all depend on the continued existence of a liberal regime that at the very least protects life, liberty, and property. We may often take this regime for granted, but we cannot have these sorts of private hopes without it. Thus our private hopes have to be supplemented by one big public hope: for the continued existence of the regime that facilitates the attainment of these private goals. This big public hope requires the mastery of circumstances beyond the control of any particular individual and hence may well implicate "impersonal" forces like history. The third point is connected with the second. Rorty himself makes an effort to defend liberalism against its contemporary adversaries. He offers a strategy that would lead to its perpetuation. What he pursues in the pages of his book is not some small, private fantasy, but rather a large public project. If he is simply screaming into a maelstrom that is totally beyond his capacity to influence, then he has to acknowledge that his efforts are, strictly speaking, vain. His only defense for writing as much as he does about these subjects is that it is a pleasant way to make a living.[51] The rest of us need not, however, bother to read any further than the claim that human events are simply beyond our control. In order to avoid regarding his writings on liberalism as nothing more than the scribblings of a sophist who cynically preys on our love of a regime that we ultimately can do nothing to protect, we are compelled to discount his claims about history and nature. The "groundless hope" must have a hidden ground.

Rorty's own efforts to show how liberalism can be buttressed pursue an essentially Rousseauean strategy.[52] Like Rousseau, he insists that much of liberal morality can be constructed out of sympathy for the suffering of others.[53] He further suggests that "our sense of solidarity is strongest when those with whom solidarity is expressed are thought of as 'one of us,' where 'us' means something smaller and more local than the human race."[54] The perpetuation of liberalism thus depends on the education of imagination in sympathetic identification, a project carried out much more effectively by literary than by philosophical means.[55]

Of course, there are also instructive differences between Rorty and Rousseau. For the purposes of this chapter, I shall focus on two: the contrast between the patriotic narrowness of Rousseau's citizens and the ever-broadening sympathetic imaginations of Rorty's liberals; and the central role that religion plays in Rousseau's political scheme.

Like Rorty, Rousseau believes that the intensity of one's affection for a community varies inversely with its scope: in large communities, attachments are lukewarm, while in smaller ones, attachments are intense. As Rousseau puts it, "Interest and commiseration must in some way be confined and compressed to be activated."[56] Like Rorty, Rousseau also believes that these patriotic ties are the conventional products of cultivation.[57] Unlike Rorty, however, Rousseau does not appear to hold out the prospect that these ties can gradually be widened to include a larger and larger portion of the human race.[58] What keeps Rousseau from drawing Rorty's conclusion is his understanding of the foundation of patriotism. To the extent that a patriot is supposed "to love [the homeland] with that delicate sentiment that any isolated man feels only for himself," he is able "to transform into a sublime virtue this dangerous disposition [self-love] from which all our vices arise."[59] For Rousseau, community grows out of the imaginative enlargement of self-love, not out of compassion. Because love is always bound up with making comparisons,[60] patriotic solidarity is absolutely dependent upon the distinction between "us" and "them." Furthermore, when self-love—enlarged or otherwise—and compassion compete, the former will almost inevitably defeat the latter. Genuine cosmopolitanism is rare.[61]

Now, Rorty might respond to this line of argument by insisting that it makes no sense to speak—as, on Rousseau's behalf, I do—about human nature, but his claim of complete human plasticity and consequently of an—in principle—ever wider circle of solidarity is as much a claim about human nature as is Rousseau's argument. When Rorty says that for the liberal ironist "human solidarity is not a matter of sharing a common truth or a common goal but of sharing a common selfish hope, the hope that one's world . . . will not be destroyed," and that human beings have the capacity for a special kind of pain—humiliation—it is virtually impossible not to take these as descriptions of human nature.[62] Of course, Rorty may respond by saying that the identification of this particular feature of human beings as the salient one has no warrant beyond the culturally cultivated inclinations of our contemporaries, that people in other times and places may well not focus on our common capacities to feel pain and particularly humiliation.[63] This is undeniable. Nevertheless, he is also making a contestable claim about what will work now and in the future to perpetuate liberalism. There has to be some way of adjudicating the claim. What would Rorty say if his insight proved to be wrong and Rousseau's right? I am tempted to say that we may have found something that is not readily susceptible to socialization.

In cultivating the civic solidarity of which human beings are capable, Rousseau regards religion as an indispensable instrument. There are, he says, a few "sentiments of sociability without which it is impossible to be a good citizen or a faithful subject." All citizens must believe in the "existence of a powerful, intelligent, beneficent, foresighted, and providential divinity; the afterlife; the happiness of the just; the punishment of the wicked; the sanctity of the social contract and laws."[64] Patriotism, founded on the imaginative transformation of a powerful individual passion, requires a "supernatural" supplement. What these "dogmas" provide are assurances that the world will ultimately sanction the actions and intentions of the good and that the bad will be punished. In other words, to the extent that the imaginative transformation is successful, the good will have hopes that cannot evidently and immediately be satisfied by means of their efforts in this world. And to the extent that private passion continues to manifest itself, there may be need for a vision of the future that is both beautiful and fearful to serve as the basis of self-restraint.[65]

Of course, Rorty proudly announces that his liberal utopia can do without religion. At the same time, however, he concedes that the widening of the sphere of solidarity may well depend upon the "Jewish and Christian element in our tradition" that clothes even strangers with human dignity.[66] If the popular antidote to narrowness is the Judeo-Christian tradition, then Rorty cannot have it both ways. He must either eschew religion and accept that, for the most part, cosmopolitanism will be the preserve of the liberal ironist elite or he must concede religion a role in the popular culture of liberal regimes. The question is whether religion and postmodernism can coexist.

RELIGION AND POSTMODERNISM

I cannot in this chapter definitively address the question of the relationship between religion and postmodernism, but I can offer a few preliminary reflections. First, to the extent that modern rationalism is (or was) hostile to revealed religion, it might seem that the postmodern critics of modernity are the natural allies of the religious. The enemy of my enemy must be my friend. It certainly is true that the postmodernists are friendlier to particularity, ineffability, and mystery than were their modern predecessors.[67] Postmodernity may then create a space for religion.

But what I have granted with this first observation I will take back with my second. Postmodernists may criticize enlightenment rationalism, but they are also its legitimate (albeit unacknowledged) heirs.[68] What they have inherited are the individualism and humanism born of the modern critique of premodern religiosity. The particularity, ineffability, and mystery of which they are fond owe more to Freud than to Pascal. In other words, for many postmodernists the "religious sensibility" is just another private, humanly created experience, not really distinguishable in quality from other inner or creative experiences. Religion is a human artifact, not a way of approaching or appreciating something superhuman.[69] If I am correct about postmodernism, then I am compelled to conclude that it is genuinely open only to an essentially trivialized religious sensibility, but not to the real thing.

Let me go even further. The "anti-foundationalist" or "anti-metaphysical" character of postmodernism is ultimately hostile to human inquiry into the most serious questions of our existence. We are not permitted to ask the big questions. We are encouraged to be either shallow and smug (like Rorty's ordinary liberals) or shallow and ironic (like Rorty's intellectuals).[70]

I shall conclude by returning to the ostensible theme of this chapter—postmodernism and liberal citizenship. It is perhaps correct to say that postmodernists and classical liberals have in common a rejection of premodern "metaphysical" religion. But the classical liberals were compelled by their situation to take seriously the human urges and questions to which religion appealed. They had to offer their own answers to these big questions. Or they had to make prudent rhetorical use of the answers that religion provided. In both cases, the human longing for meaning was—one way or another—met. There was an ultimate ground or measure for or of the temporal allegiances human beings formed. There was something at stake when commitments and choices were made. Once made, a choice or commitment could not lightly be cast aside. I cannot find this kind of depth in much of postmodernism and, as a practical matter, I worry that the casual approach it encourages will ultimately rob us of genuine citizens. The shallow and thoughtless progeny of postmodernism will indeed get going when the going gets tough. But they will go their own way.

NOTES

1. Richard Rorty, *Contingency, Irony, and Solidarity* (Cambridge: Cambridge University Press, 1989), 3.

2. The quotation comes from Jean-François Lyotard's *The Postmodern Condition: A Report on Knowledge*, translated by Geoff Bennington and Brian Massumi (Minneapolis: University of Minnesota Press, 1984), xxiii. In general, I follow Catherine Zuckert's usage in *Postmodern Platos* (Chicago: University of Chicago Press, 1996), 1–2, and Peter A. Lawler, "Political Correctness and the End of History," *College Teaching* 44 (Winter 1996): 21.

3. Rorty, *Contingency*, xiii.

4. See Richard Rorty, "Cosmopolitanism Without Emancipation: A Reply to Jean-François Lyotard," in Rorty, *Objectivity, Relativism, and Truth* (Cambridge: Cambridge University Press, 1991), 213.

5. This happy view of the postmodern condition can be found in Walter Truett Anderson, ed., *The Truth About the Truth: De-confusing and Re-constructing the Postmodern World* (New York: G. P. Putnam's Sons, 1995), 8.

6. Ronald Beiner, "Introduction: Why Citizenship Constitutes a Theoretical Problem in the Last Decade of the Twentieth Century," in Beiner, ed., *Theorizing Citizenship* (Albany: State University of New York Press, 1995), 9.

7. Anderson, *The Truth About the Truth*, 11. A somewhat different view, which emphasizes the importance of rootedness within a cultural horizon, is described in Thomas L. Pangle's *The Ennobling of Democracy* (Baltimore: Johns Hopkins University Press, 1992), 34–47.

8. See Richard Rorty's "Postmodernist Bourgeois Liberalism," reprinted in his *Objectivity*, 197–202. Since the 1980s, John Rawls has adopted a similar stance, which is especially evident in his *Political Liberalism* (New York: Columbia University Press, 1993). I disagree with Lawler's contention in "Political Correctness" that Rorty "emphatically" rejects the "postmodern" label for himself. On the contrary, Rorty explicitly includes himself among the "postmodernist bourgeois liberals" (see his *Objectivity*, 199).

9. Thomas Jefferson, *Notes on the State of Virginia*, in Adrienne Koch and William Peden, *The Life and Selected Writings of Thomas Jefferson* (New York: Random House, 1994), 278 (Query XVIII). For Rorty's attempt to appropriate Jefferson on behalf of his "postmetaphysical" liberalism, see "The Priority of Democracy to Philosophy," in his *Objectivity*, 175–196.

10. For a concise rehearsal of the argument, see Michael W. McConnell, "Accommodation of Religion," in *Supreme Court Review, 1985* (Chicago: University of Chicago Press, 1985), 16–18.

11. This phrase comes from Alexander Hamilton's draft of George Washington's "Farewell Address," in Morton J. Frisch, ed., *Selected Writings and Speeches of Alexander Hamilton* (Washington, DC: American Enterprise Institute, 1985), 444.

12. Peter A. Lawler has explored this issue very well in "James Madison and the Metaphysics of Modern Politics," *Review of Politics* 47 (Winter 1986): 92–115. For a somewhat different view that arrives at virtually the same conclusion about the problematic character of postmodernism, see J.G.A. Pocock, "The Ideal of Citizenship Since Classical Times," in Beiner, ed., *Theorizing Citizenship*, 47–48.

13. I paraphrase the peroration of the Declaration of Independence.

14. Rorty, *Contingency*, 46.

15. Ibid., 51–52.

16. On this point, see, for example, Thomas Bridges, *The Culture of Citizenship: Inventing Postmodern Civic Culture* (Albany: State University of New York Press, 1994), 8–11.

17. Rorty, *Contingency*, 54.

18. Ibid., 60.

19. Ibid., 61.

20. See ibid., 65, 68.

21. In the "Introduction" to *Contingency*, he says that "[o]ne of my aims in this book is to suggest the possibility of a liberal utopia: one in which ironism, in the relevant sense, is universal" (xv).

22. Rorty, *Contingency*, 87.

23. I am indebted to Steven Kautz for emphasizing this aspect of Rorty's thought. See Kautz, *Liberalism and Community* (Ithaca, NY: Cornell University, 1995), 84–86.

24. Rorty, *Contingency*, 73.

25. See Rorty, *Objectivity*, 199.

26. Rorty, *Contingency*, 86.

27. That such a "philosophy of history" may well be a contradiction in terms is implied by Rorty's argument in "The End of Leninism and History as a Comic Frame," in Arthur M. Melzer, Jerry Weinberger, and M. Richard Zinman, eds., *History and the Idea of Progress* (Ithaca, NY: Cornell University Press, 1995), 215. In "Cosmopolitanism Without Emancipation," written some years earlier, Rorty was more sanguine about the possibility of a pragmatic philosophy of history, at least as an "edifying first-order [narrative]" or a "utopian fantasy" (*Objectivity*, 211, 212).

28. In his more optimistic phase, Rorty averred that "[n]o event—not even Auschwitz—can show that we should cease to work for a given utopia" (*Objectivity*, 220).

29. Rorty, *Contingency*, 86; see also 93.

30. See ibid., 85.

31. Robert Booth Fowler and Allen D. Hertzke, *Religion and Politics in America: Faith, Culture, and Strategic Choices* (Boulder, CO: Westview Press, 1995), 28.

32. See my "The Politics of Kant's Philosophy," in Ronald Beiner and William James Booth, eds., *Kant and Political Philosophy: The Contemporary Legacy* (New Haven, CT: Yale University Press, 1993), 155–172; "From Kant to Marx: The Perils of Liberal Idealism," *Political Science Reviewer* 20 (1991): 101–143; and "The Political Significance of Kant's Treatment of Religion" (unpublished ms.).

33. Reserving for the purposes of this chapter the question of the theoretical adequacy and coherency of these efforts, I shall cite only John Locke's *Letter Concerning Toleration* and its American progeny, like James Madison's "Memorial and Remonstrance."

34. Rorty, *Contingency*, xvi; see also "Priority," in *Objectivity*, 193.

35. See Rorty, *Contingency*, 74.

36. At the same time, however, "the only societies which give [ironists] the freedom to articulate [their] alienation are liberal ones" (Ibid., 89).

37. Ibid., 91.

38. See ibid., 184–185. Rorty takes a somewhat different tack in "Cosmopolitanism Without Emancipation," in *Objectivity*, 211–222. At this earlier point, he was not yet calling himself an ironist. In this essay, he was willing to say that "there is no *a priori* philosophical reason why this attempt [to create a cosmopolitan social democratic order] must fail," just as (*pace* Christianity, Kant, and Marx) there is no *a priori* reason why it must succeed and that "[t]hat failure to find a single grand commensurating discourse . . . does nothing to cast doubt on the possibility (as opposed to the difficulty) of peaceful social progress" (*Objectivity*, 217, 218).

39. Rorty, "The End of Leninism," 223.

40. Rorty, *Contingency*, 96.

41. See ibid., 97ff.

42. For a similar appreciation of the advantages of democracy for one whose goal is a certain sort of private fulfillment, see Plato, *Republic*, 557b–558c.

43. Rorty insists that Nietzsche and Heidegger—ironist theorists *par excellence*—were mistaken about the necessarily anti-liberal implications of their ironism. He seems to prefer Proust's rather unpolitical ironism. See ibid., 99.

44. Rorty, "The End of Leninism," 215.

45. See ibid.

46. Immanuel Kant, "On the Common Saying: 'This May Be True in Theory, But It Does Not Apply in Practice,' " in *Political Writings*, edited by Hans Reiss (Cambridge: Cambridge University Press, 1991), 89. I have altered the translation slightly.

47. For a contrary view, see William James Booth, *Interpreting the World* (Toronto: University of Toronto Press, 1986); for my response, see my "From Kant to Marx."

48. For my account of Kant's "statesmanlike" approach to the writing of history, see "The Politics of Kant's Philosophy."

49. See, for example, Thomas L. Pangle, *The Spirit of Modern Republicanism* (Chicago: University of Chicago Press, 1988); and Paul Rahe, "John Locke's Philosophical Partisanship," *Political Science Reviewer* 20 (1991): 1–43.

50. Consider Pangle's suggestion: postmodernism may produce a "deadening vacuum," "out of or into" which "may sweep . . . longings and irrationalisms of shattering and frightening proportions" (*Ennobling*, 55).

51. See Pangle's (*Ennobling*, 60) remark about a passage in Rorty, *Contingency*, 115.

52. On Rorty's "Rousseaueanism," see the observations of Lyotard, quoted by Pangle in *Ennobling*, 59.

53. For Rousseau, see, for example, *Second Discourse*, in *The First and Second Discourses* . . . , translated and edited by Victor Gourevitch (New York: Harper and Row, 1986), 161.

54. Rorty, *Contingency*, 191. I have explored Rousseau's view of the importance of patriotic narrowness in "Patriotism and Cosmopolitanism in Human Rights Education" (unpublished ms.).

55. Christopher Kelly has recently discussed Rousseau's turn to literature in "Novels Are Necessary for Corrupt Peoples: Fiction and Rousseau's Literary Project" (paper presented at the Annual Meeting of the American Political Science Association, San Francisco, 1996).

56. Jean-Jacques Rousseau, *Discourse on Political Economy*, in *On the Social Contract with*

Geneva Manuscript and Political Economy, translated by Judith R. Masters (New York: St. Martin's Press, 1978), 219.

57. See, for example, Rousseau, *Political Economy*, 222; and *The Government of Poland*, translated by Willmoore Kendall (Indianapolis: Bobbs-Merrill, 1972), 11, 19.

58. See Rorty, *Contingency*, 219: Moral progress consists in "the ability to see more and more traditional differences . . . as unimportant when compared to similarities with respect to pain and humiliation—the ability to think of people wildly different from ourselves as included in the range of 'us.' "

59. Rousseau, *Political Economy*, 222.

60. See Rousseau, *Second Discourse*, 175–176.

61. I have discussed this point at length in "Moving Beyond Fear: Rousseau and Kant on Cosmopolitan Education," *Journal of Politics* 51 (November 1989): 820–823. See also Rousseau, *Emile*, translated by Allan Bloom (New York: Basic Books, 1979), 222ff; and Bloom's commentary in *Love and Friendship* (New York: Simon and Schuster, 1993), 65–71.

62. Rorty, *Contingency*, 92.

63. In "Moral Universalism and Economic Triage," his contribution to the 1996 UNESCO Philosophy Forum, Rorty in fact does assert that "[m]oral universalism is an invention of the rich," that "[t]he assumption that our moral community should be identical with our biological species . . . could only have occurred to people who were lucky enough to have more material goods than they really needed." This "universalistic assumption" derives from Christianity and the Enlightenment, but it can stand alone as a pragmatic or postmodern project. See Rorty, "Moral Universalism," 4, 5, at http://www.unesco.org/phiweb/2rput/rort/rort.html

64. Rousseau, *On the Social Contract*, IV.8 (130, 131).

65. See Bloom's account of the "Profession of Faith," in *Love and Friendship*, 84–85.

66. Rorty, "Postmodernist Bourgeois Liberalism," 202. See also his essay on "Moral Universalism," cited in note 63.

67. See Huston Smith, "Postmodernism and the World's Religions," in Anderson, ed., *The Truth About the Truth*, especially 46–47.

68. See Pangle, *Ennobling*, 3.

69. Slavoj Zisek offers a similar criticism of the postmoderns in *Tarrying with the Negative: Kant, Hegel, and the Critique of Ideology* (Durham, NC: Duke University Press, 1993).

70. See Pangle, *Ennobling*, 55.

10

Bloom's Ineffectual Response to Rorty: Pragmatism, Existentialism, and American Political Thought Today

PETER AUGUSTINE LAWLER

Pragmatism is the dominant form of thought in America today, although it has significant opposition. America's leading professor of philosophy is the most clever, subtle, and witty pragmatist, Richard Rorty. Contemporary America's most formidable opponent of pragmatism may have been the author of the philosophic bestseller *The Closing of the American Mind*, Allan Bloom. Rorty teaches that human beings should view as true whatever they find useful in satisfying their desires, and that thus the experience of one's own mortality is neither useful nor true. He attempts to persuade us not to be moved by death. Bloom trumpets the existential truth that Rorty tries to hide about the limits to all pragmatic effort.

But Bloom may concede too much to Rorty to have his view of the truth prevail. He concedes too much to the Rousseauean view of nature Rorty assumes to be true, and so he is too open to the possibility that pragmatism has actually conquered death. The extent of Bloom's and Rorty's agreement on the condition of contemporary Americans should be troubling for those who hold or hope that history has not come to an end. After socialism's collapse, they may present the two fundamental alternatives in American thought today.

Pragmatism might be defined in large measure as the denial of death. Marx, Dewey, and Rorty never discuss the experience of one's awareness of one's own mortality. Marx does say that human misery is caused by the experience of individuality, but he explains that experience of nothingness as essentially economic. It can be transformed by a change in the economic system. Dewey, despite his many elegant accounts of human experience in terms of growth and decay, never discusses the experience of dying alone. He writes of the courageous denial of certainty, but only abstractly. He does not come to terms with the only certainty we have about personal change, the one from life to death. With amazing consistency, Dewey describes all of life in terms of what Heidegger called "average everydayness," a death- or self-avoiding immersion in life's ordinary details. Perhaps Dewey really does describe what a perfectly pragmatic life would be.[1]

My view is that the relationship between Rorty's and Bloom's thought may have been best expressed in advance by the great Hegelian Alexandre Kojève. The Hegelian wisdom possible at history's end combines the two dominant forms of contemporary thought, pragmatism and existentialism. Marx (Kojève's pragmatist) says that human beings gain their freedom and self-consciousness through historical struggle. But he vulgarly, or uncourageously, does not say what that self-consciousness is. The pragmatist cannot face without flinching what he really knows about his own existence, and so he writes to suppress it.[2]

Heidegger (Kojève's existentialist) says that human self-consciousness, what distinguishes human beings, is consciousness of one's own death. But Heidegger and Bloom do not make clear how human beings acquire that self-consciousness, not through passive contemplation of the human condition but through historical action. Bloom and Heidegger do not make clear that the identification of being with time could only have been made at or near history's end. Ironically, the final moment of the pragmatic struggle is coming to terms with the truth it was attempting to suppress, the natural limit of human existence and human satisfaction.

But the existentialist's victory over pragmatism lasts only for a moment. The perception of the truth about one's own mortality does nothing but make one miserable, and it reveals human distinctiveness to be nothing but a wholly contingent error. So that perception quickly disappears in the name of truth and contentment. What disappears is the truth of existentialism, the truth of the self-conscious mortal, what Bloom calls the philosophic experience. Then, in a way, pragmatism achieves complete success. Human beings finally can readily satisfy their desires through their own effort, because those desires have contracted to a subhuman level, that of Rousseau's brutish state of nature.

RORTY'S PRAGMATISM

Rorty follows Dewey most of all in feigning indifference to the existential questions. Rorty insists that some people think about death, others money, and still others sex. There is no object of thought that "is more philosophical by nature than any other."[3] Rorty's denial of the obvious seems too dense to be credible. We can say nothing about the human desires for money and power without speaking of the connection between the desire to acquire and fear and anxiety about one's contingency and mortality. Nor can we discuss human sexual desire without acknowledging what Allan Bloom calls the twinship between love and death.

Rorty writes essay after essay on Heidegger. But almost never does he discuss the existentialist's theme of anxiety in the face of death, and one's resolute or courageous response to it. In his hands, the founder of existentialism becomes remarkably unconcerned with death. When properly understood, Heidegger's concern with finitude is merely with the fact that we cannot acquire intellectual certainty or transhistorical truth. Rorty does say, on occasion, that human beings are mortal, and that there is no chance of surviving death. But he does not add that they are necessarily moved or even bothered by that fact. Rorty's Heidegger is really a pragmatist, as banal as Dewey.[4]

Rorty cheerfully admits that his Heidegger would have repulsed the historical Heidegger. For the latter, Dewey's or Rorty's pragmatism is "the most degraded form of nihilism in which metaphysics culminates."[5] Rorty's aim is "to stand Heidegger on his head, to cherish what he loathed."[6] What Heidegger loathed, perhaps most of all, is the specter of human beings unmoved by death and so the mystery of Being, the surrender of their authentic point of distinction.

Rorty agrees with Heidegger's proclamation of "the end of metaphysics." But he disagrees that that end "was a matter of despair or nihilism."[7] He mainly expresses his rejection of Heidegger's concern about the nihilism of our age through silence. But he does assert, outlandishly, that "the word 'Being' " was inessential to Heidegger's thought.[8] He creates the impression that Heidegger had a good insight and a bad mood. "Heidegger," Rorty reminds us rather seriously, "was not the first philosopher to have taken his own idiosyncratic spiritual situation for the essence of what it means to be a human being."[9] Heidegger's concern for Being and human being was really a quirk of his own psychological disorder, what caused him to view himself spiritually and take his political situation seriously. He was, at his best, an anti-essentialist, but at times he was part of the Platonic tradition of essentialist tyranny.

Rorty gives another argument against taking death seriously, in criticism of a poem about death and dying by Philip Larkin. Rorty says that " 'Death' and 'nothing' are equally resounding, equally empty terms." Fear is of something concrete, and so one cannot fear nothing or one's obliteration. For Rorty, the analytical philosopher Carnap's satire of Heidegger's desire to talk about nothing is decisive. After that criticism, Rorty suggests, nothing disappears as a philosophical category, even from Heidegger's writing. Rorty adds that "the word 'I' is as hollow as the word 'death.' " Because I do not really exist, neither does my death.[10]

Rorty goes on to deconstruct a noteworthy quote from Harold Bloom, one that resonates from the philosophical and poetic traditions: "every poet begins (however 'unconsciously') by rebelling more strongly against the fear of death than all other men and women do." Bloom appears to mean that all men fear death and rebel against it. But poets, or great creators, rebel with special intensity. Rorty gives a different view: "Such people [poets] are . . . to be thought of as rebelling against 'death'—that is, against the failure to have created—more strongly than most of us." They do not really rebel against the inevitable end of one's life or existence. "Death," for the great creator, really means "not having impressed one's mark on the language," not having distinguished oneself through

creative transformation. So the only "anxiety" felt by human beings and especially poets is that of not having any influence.[11]

Rene Arcilla explains that Rorty's goal in redescribing Larkin's and Bloom's
concerns is to cure human beings of their fear of death. Rorty, in an early book,
with uncharacteristic candor calls attention to the fact that people have that fear
as part of the "problem of personhood," originating in "pre-philosophical craving
for immortality." The philosophical and poetic approaches to that problem have
been ways of "expressing our claim to be more than the beasts that perish."[12]
The various poetic and metaphysical attempts to make that claim have been
failures. But Rorty, as Arcilla says, "puts his money" on his "redescriptive powers," which can eradicate the unique human need to make that futile claim about
uniqueness. Rorty can talk human beings out of that self-concern by describing
the self as a mortal out of existence. Arcilla interprets this redescription as a
victory of the self as mind over the self as body, but it is really a victory of the
poetic imagination over what the mind can really know about beings with bodies.
Rorty says that there is nothing really to be known, and so self-understanding or
the truth about oneself is simply a linguistic creation.[13] Because Rorty is trying
to describe away the desire to be person, as opposed to a beast, can we say that
his victory would be of the body over the mind or soul?

Rorty does at least obscure an obvious connection. Poets desire to create in
rebellion against death. Poetry is a characteristic of self-conscious mortals. Rorty
diverts us from the questions: Why are human beings alone among the animals
poetic? Would beings who come to be unmoved by death remain poetic?

The distinguished professor of philosophy Charles Hartshorne attempted to
get Rorty to consider a related question: Why do human beings alone among the
animals raise metaphysical questions? Metaphysical concern is not primarily epistemological, as Rorty would have us believe. It comes, Hartshorne says, from the
one great "certainty," that of "our own eventual death." Metaphysics is not so
much an inauthentic quest for certainty as a way of coming to terms with certainty. Generally, Hartshorne observes, Rorty "is overconcerned about problems
invented by philosophers and too little concerned about problems of human
beings, who are aware, unlike other animals, of their mortality." Pragmatists, by
denying with obvious untruth that anything is certain, avoids confrontation with
the really enduring philosophic issues. Pragmatism, despite its name, seems actually to be an escape from both theoretical and practical reflection on distinctively human life to a realm of empty abstraction.[14]

In response to Hartshorne, Rorty identifies the view that the concern with
one's own mortality is the source of the metaphysical impulse of human beings
with the early Heidegger. Rorty, usually silent on this core of Heidegger's
thought, does not comment on the correctness of the identification of death with
metaphysics. He just goes on to say that the later Heidegger concluded that poetry
was a better way than metaphysics for expressing that concern. Hartshorne errs
by wanting to back up the poet's, say, Wordsworth's, concern with mortality with
metaphysics. Rorty's view is that we should not ask whether any poetic descrip-

tion of reality is actually true, implying that he would criticize Wordsworth the way he did Larkin. Rorty ends up a long distance from Heidegger and Hartshorne: We cannot say that the poetic response to the inevitability of death is really a response to the truth. Again, we cannot say that "death" corresponds to death.

Rorty then quickly asserts the priority of a "poeticized culture," contending that all human awareness is a "linguistic affair." All of our experiences are a linguistic or poetic creation. We cannot say that they mirror any aspect of reality at all. So human beings can be moved through the linguistic manipulation of the imagination to say that "eternity" or "the silence of infinite spaces" do not matter, toward a world where religion, science, and metaphysics all seem like superfluous nonsense.[15]

Rorty's "philosophical therapy" is to assure us that the poets created and can cure us of our concern with death.[16] He reads the poet Shelley as saying "we should just forget about the relation between eternity and time."[17] Death need not seem essential or even important for human beings. It may seem, at first, inconceivable that we could lose such concern. But Rorty contends "we do not yet have any idea what is and what is not a conceivable experience." Language seems to have "no transcendental limits," and so Rorty conceives "of experience as potentially infinitely enrichable." There are no limits to how human beings might redescribe and so remake themselves. They should, of course, describe away the misery of self-conscious mortality. Rorty's approach to Hartshorne is condescending: He explains patiently that he solved in principle the problem that moved the philosophers to metaphysical reflection. Soon his solution will be implemented.[18]

Arcilla, one of Rorty's most sympathetic critics, complains that "Even as Rorty attacks positivism, his works seem prone to a positivistic impatience with existential mystery. It often summarily discounts any practical need we have to cope with the inelimability of such mystery, thereby reducing the scope of what can count as pragmatic thinking." Arcilla holds that a genuine pragmatism would help human beings live well with such experiences, to connect their morality with "the meaning of their mortality," and he reasonably aims to enlarge Rorty's pragmatism with that end in view.[19] But Arcilla knows that this enlargement of human concern makes him not a pragmatist, properly speaking. Rorty questions the goodness of those experiences Arcilla affirms, and the metaphysical dogma that they cannot be eliminated. Pragmatism uses language not to articulate but to correct human experience. Rorty actually works to make the impersonal science of the positivists as true as they believe it to be.

Rorty does, at one point, criticize the scientific or philosophic "desire for objectivity" as "a disguised form of the fear of death of our community," but not the fear of one's own death. The philosophical tradition as a whole, as Nietzsche said, has been "an attempt to avoid facing up to contingency, to escape from time and chance." But Rorty does not favor facing up to one's own death, but instead eradicating the experiences that caused one really to be moved by rebellion against time and personal mortality. The personal desire for objectivity—

or my desire to overcome time through thought—will disappear as impersonal or objective science finally becomes really true. There will no longer be beings in the world really defined by time and so death.[20]

By depriving human death of its weight, Rorty does the same for God and His death. The end of essentialism and logocentrism described by Heidegger are events of no great significance. They are merely parts of a gradual and salutary linguistic transformation of the world. They do not "entail . . . existentialist, Sartrean conclusions."[21] Rebellions against death, the abyss, meaninglessness, and so forth, as the personal examples of Heidegger and Sartre show, are theoretical misperceptions rooted in personal obsessions that produce tyrannical politics. In what might be his finest and intellectually unfashionable moment, Rorty says that Raymond Aron was right to call Marxism "the opium of the intellectuals," knowing that Aron was writing mainly against Sartre's Marxist existentialism.[22]

Rorty calls the project of secularizing the world the Enlightenment, which culminates politically in liberal democracy. He claims to be satisfied with liberal secularism. He has no personal experience that would cause him to rebel against it. He has no reason to sneer at the material satisfactions and personal freedoms that its success has brought ordinary people. Rorty also denies that the death of God, or the near disappearance of religious faith in the sophisticated, contemporary West, has been morally or socially corrosive. People simply stopped aiming at personal salvation and started working for their grandchildren. The desire for personal immortality was transformed into a genuinely pragmatic goal for the future.[23]

For Rorty, pragmatism is really a therapeutic doctrine designed to ensure the success of modern technology. He agrees with Dewey that poets and philosophers are really linguistic social or political engineers.[24] He says his task is to complete the Enlightenment project begun by Bacon and Descartes to remove metaphysical and theological discourse—the results of the capacity to be moved by self-conscious mortality—from respectable human conversation. Rorty observes that theology is already obsolete. All that remains is to do to the metaphysical assumptions still present in some intellectual discourse what Jefferson did to references to the supernatural in the Bible. Rorty takes Jefferson's avoidance of theology one step further. He aims to make all human thought merely useful or superficial, completing the secularization of thought and life.[25]

For Rorty, the truth of pragmatism is that human beings are completely self-created. All their experiences are shaped by and depend upon language. His true debt to Heidegger is the thought that "language speaks man," which he interprets to mean that what human beings view as good or bad or true or false depends entirely on linguistic manipulation, description and redescription.[26] There are no "truths independent of language."[27] If the words that articulate a particular experience disappear, then the experience will too. Pragmatism succeeds by describing the experience that produces existentialism out of existence. The truth of pragmatism is that language is more fundamental than experience.[28] So, for Rorty, the "heroes of humanity are people who dissolved the problems of their day by transcending the vocabulary in which these problems were posed."[29]

RORTY'S CHOICE

Rorty's pragmatic choice against the truth about death is a choice for the perfection of the modern or liberal utopia. He affirms the Enlightenment's goal of a more cosmopolitan, just, free, happy, secular, and well-ordered world. Rorty sometimes claims to be postmodern epistemologically, rejecting the foundationalism of the modern philosophers and affirming the radical contingency of all things human. But he also is perfectly aware that his moral and political choices are modern. Given the anti-foundational priority of politics or democracy to philosophy, Rorty knows he remains decisively modern or "bourgeois."[30] He may well be in every respect radically modern. He follows Machiavelli and Marx in aiming to make his view of the truth prevail in freedom from all illusions about the human dependence on nature and God. Like Machiavelli and Marx, he exaggerates how innovative his pragmatic anti-foundationalism is.

Rorty rejects the genuinely postmodern view expressed by Heidegger and Solzhenitsyn that if human beings were born only to be happy they would not be born to die. The beginning of postmodernism, in this view, is the recognition of death as the ineradicable limit to the modern project's success. For Rorty, human beings were not born to die or anything else, and so there are no ineradicable limits to their possibilities for happiness.

Rorty criticizes the postmodern moodiness of the cultural historian Christopher Lasch, who came to be "almost as dubious about the pursuit of happiness as Heidegger was." Lasch discovered the paradox that "the secret of happiness lies in renouncing the right to be happy." Rorty, suspicious of paradoxes if not of irony, holds that that discovery put Lasch in the camp of the religious fanatic Jonathan Edwards, away from the American democratic pursuers of happiness such as Jefferson, Emerson, and Whitman.

Lasch rejected the modern project's effort to conquer nature as an illusion, one that has culminated in a spiritual crisis, "a dark night of the soul." For Rorty, the only sound reason for renouncing the effort to transform the human condition in the pursuit of happiness is the possibility of "supernatural redemption," and nothing is more illusory than that. He sees no reason not to cheerfully "persist in believing that a merely material and secular goal suffices: mortal life as it might be lived in the sunlit uplands of global democracy and abundance." The Enlightenment goal is more reasonable than ever. We linguistic engineers know that our happiness or unconstrained material enjoyment need not be disturbed by the fact that we have not really conquered death.[31]

PRAGMATISM AND JUSTICE

Rorty, for the record, begins with the anti-foundationalist denial that there is "any neutral ground on which to stand and argue that either torture or kindness is preferable to the other."[32] But he quickly affirms the Enlightenment's choice of justice as "the first virtue," the foundation of human action.[33] Justice, Rorty explains, will be the result of the abolition of cruelty, the distinctively human aberration at the foundation of all injustice. Human beings unjustly inflict humiliation and suffering (Rorty even mentions killing[34]) upon one another. Sometimes Rorty denies the connection between cruelty and what is distinctively human by asserting that the pain inflicted by cruelty is prelinguistic, a merely animal feeling. But he adds that the other animals do not inflict cruelty on one another, and that cruelty includes verbal humiliation, the imposition of linguistic or "mental" or distinctively human pain.[35]

One source of cruelty, Rorty explains, is the "private pursuit of aesthetic bliss," personal obsessions (such as Heidegger's) which make one "incurious" about how such pursuit affects others. Rorty identifies this rare sort of cruelty with the "genius-monster." The liberal, Aronian Rorty diagnoses well the sort of "criminal," totalitarian cruelty Orwell and Solzhenitsyn described. The Communist theoreticians were genius-monsters.[36]

But the bourgeois Rorty also reports that most human beings are cruel because they are afraid. They strike out against pain and death by inflicting pain and death. If they no longer experienced such misery, they would no longer be cruel. They would become "nice," not "piggy," not selfishly insensitive to the suffering of others. They would never be angry. The philosopher, the novelist, and the journalist all contribute to the progress toward justice by using poetic narratives to manipulate the romantic or sentimental imagination to correct experience. We know no limits to the malleability of the human imagination, and so we reasonably hope that human beings can be induced to move from fearful, selfish calculation for themselves, their family, tribe, or country, to feeling compassionate sentimentality for all other human beings. Rorty suggests that the choice, which he tends to endorse, to limit the imagination's expansion to include all other human beings is arbitrary. There really is no morally important difference between our species and some of the others, or there will not be once we are freed from fear.[37]

Rorty does not address the concern that Tocqueville would raise about this sentimental education. Its cosmopolitan scope would undermine human love as it actually exists. Because our powers for knowing and loving are limited, we can really be moved only by a limited number of others. Rorty, rejecting the idea of fixed, natural limits (which brings death to mind), does not acknowledge the force of this objection. But he may accept it implicitly by usually seeing that his goal is universal niceness and not universal love. The reduction of the passionate intensity might be the price to be paid for secularizing Christianity and so dispensing with the omnipotent and omniscient God of love. Maybe it is a price well worth paying: Love in the strong sense is inconceivable without hatred and cruelty, and we are better off without it.

Rorty does not emphasize the extent to which he would truncate love by disconnecting it from death. What would be left, his positive message goes, would not be destructive of ourselves or others. Rorty does write of the "solidarity" that would include all others indiscriminately. He even calls Dewey's pragmatism "power in the service of love," but he means a vague "Whitmanesque" love of "democratic community." The pragmatic sentiment is a cosmopolitan love for humankind, not the love of particular self-conscious mortals or citizenship in some strong, positive sense.[38] But we can wonder whether the achievement of a risk-free existence would erode even the nice sentimentality of global community. It is my compassion, or revulsion against cruelty, that extends my imagination to others. If the liberal utopia abolishes cruel suffering, then surely it also abolishes compassion. "The ultimate synthesis of love and justice," Rorty writes, "may turn out to be an intricately-textured collage of private narcissism and public pragmatism."[39] The love of one human being for another and even solidarity disappear.

Part of Rorty's optimism about the prospects for sentimental education is the astounding progress it has already made in America, due to the fortunate combination of Enlightenment propaganda and economic prosperity. He reports that the American students' sentiments are now quite easy to manipulate. They are "already so nice that they are eager to define their identity in nonexclusionary terms." They are nice to everyone but those "they consider irrational—the religious fundamentalist, the smirking rapist, the swaggering skinhead."[40] Rorty, of course, helps them expand that category to include metaphysical philosophers, theologians, and so forth. The students make that connection with little prodding, having already divided the world into the nice and the not nice.

For Rorty, all that is required to complete the actualization of the Enlightenment utopia is to make the whole world as nice, secure, and well off as American students already are. Indignation against injustice as the foundation for social progress has almost become obsolete. As long as people are indignant, or not nice, they are still mistakenly rebelling against the fact of death. It is impossible to imagine a revolution, however progressive its results, that would not include a significant amount of gratuitous killing or cruelty.

Rorty finally tells students to abandon the distinctions between justice and injustice, good and evil, rational and irrational. Those who have been called bad, the cruel or not nice, are better called deprived. They are not deprived, as Platonists say, of truth or moral knowledge. What they lack is a "risk-free" life, one freed from fear. Only with such security can human beings "relax" enough to be affected by Rorty's "sentimental education." That sort of life is possible with modern technology's conquest of scarcity, but it requires more. Sentimental education and living a risk-free life are interdependent.[41]

Rorty's astute diagnosis is surely better expressed existentially. He never says it because he knows so well that human beings are distinguished from the other animals by their self-conscious mortality. The most potent effect of that consciousness is to make them miserable in a way other animals never are. Its existence seems an unfortunate, monstrous, cruel aberration from natural order. As Rousseau explained, it can hardly be understood to be good for one's own self-preservation or that of the species. As the pragmatist says, it is not useful.

We cannot, as the Christians do, understand self-consciousness as a gift from a benevolent God who made us in His image. If it came from God, we would have to blame Him for His cruelty. If we act in His image, we act cruelly. Human beings are cruel because their very existence is cruel. The worst form of misery is not what we do to each other, but what has been inexplicably done to each of us. Until that cruel experience is eradicated by some therapy, until human beings stop being moved by knowledge of our deaths, we will not stop being cruel to each other. If justice is the abolition of cruelty, then it is the abolition of self-conscious mortality. God promises us eternal life, but everyone who is not a "know nothing" knows that promise is an illusion. Modern technology will never actually conquer nature in the decisive sense: Death will remain inevitable for all beings with bodies. The pragmatist promises not to free us from death's in-evitability, but to free us from being bothered in any way by it.

PRAGMATISM, HISTORY, AND WISDOM

The relationship between Rorty's pragmatism and the truth about human existence turns out to be rather ambivalent. The core of pragmatism, at first glance, is anti-philosophic or anti-scientific. Its goal is to get human beings to view arguments about the truth about nature, God, and oneself with indifference.[42] "Metaphysicians think that human beings by nature desire to know," and they are wrong.[43] Rorty contends we have neither access to nor desire for the truth, and that there is nothing privileged about the philosopher's perspective. No one has any standpoint from which to criticize the morality that happens to guide one's society. This affirmation of the conservative side of anti-foundationalism makes Rorty the enemy of leftists, but only because they do not share Rorty's observation that the Left has already won.[44]

Rorty learned what the Hegelian Francis Fukuyama, Kojève's disciple, learned from the fall of communism. It is now impossible even for philosophers to imagine a plausible alternative for the future to liberal democracy, the just, universal, egalitarian political order. All that remains to be done is to attend to the details of its implementation. One argument Rorty gives for his views about language, selfhood, and so forth is that they "cohere better with the institutions of liberal democracy than available alternatives do."[45]

Rorty also says that he *knows* that to be human is to be finite or contingent or historical all the way down. What he refuses to say about one's own existence he says about all things human. There is one great certainty after all. Rorty actually suggests that our time is somehow privileged, because it has become unprecedently easy to perceive the truth.[46] In spite of himself, Rorty approaches the Hegelian view that wisdom is the complete articulation of the only truth we can know for certain: man is a completely historical or temporary and contingent being. So he also approaches the view that we are at history's end, because wisdom is becoming possible, even easy and common. He opposes Heidegger's "nostalgia" by saying that our century is a particularly good time for thinking about "the most elementary words of Being."[47] Conceding that he sometimes asserts that his defense of the principles of our time is merely groundless chauvinism, we notice that Rorty cannot help but oppose Heidegger with Hegel.

Rorty, the Hegelian in spite of himself, says that we should understand our recent past as the gradual implementation of the principles of the French Revolution. That progress has not been the work of reason, but the sentiments. He says he follows not Hegel the wise man, but Hegel the constructor of fantasies about the future. Hegel's true innovation was the substitution of "hope for knowledge." Today's pragmatist knows that progress comes from linguistic manipulation, not the pursuit of wisdom.[48] Rorty accepts in principle "Nietzsche's criticism of Hegel's attempt to escape finitude by losing himself in the drama of history," but he admits that some such escape is required if we are to know how to hope and act.[49]

Rorty says that descriptions of history, the past, present, and future, are never merely factual, but propaganda in pursuit of some purpose. He thinks he is following Hegel in telling a story of progress, one created in the service of promoting the characteristics of his time of which he approves. That progress, finally, is toward freedom from cruelty. In Hegelian fashion, Rorty claims that "Christianity did not know" what we can know, "that its purpose was the alleviation of cruelty." Christianity had to be secularized in the form of sentimental niceness to achieve its purpose. For the Hegelian, the secularization of Christianity is almost the final moment in the progress of thought.[50]

Rorty differentiates his story from that of the Hegelian "metanarrative" only as an afterthought. He says that the Deweyan or Hegelian pragmatist "urge[s] us to think of ourselves as part of historical progress which will gradually encompass all of the human race." In that light, he is "willing to argue that the vocabulary of twentieth-century Western social democrats is the best vocabulary the race has come up with so far." It is certainly the one that best uses "modern technology." The progress directed by the combination of that technology with social or liberal democratic vocabulary aims at a global society with equal freedom and prosperity for all human beings—the society Rorty calls cosmopolitan and egalitarian and Kojève calls universal and homogeneous.

Rorty adds, striving not to forget his ironic recognition of contingency, that today's vocabulary "will be superseded," as all vocabularies eventually are.[51] But its victory still seems definitive. Rorty himself contends that it is impossible and undesirable to go backward, to return to an enchanted, unjust, and deluded world. It is equally impossible, after the collapse of socialism, to imagine how we could radically go forward. Rorty is stuck with the Hegelian "hunch . . . that Western social and political thought may have had the last *conceptual* revolution it needs."[52]

Our ideas—the product of long cultural or historical development—are worthy of pride, Rorty asserts, because they are "the best hope of our species." They are the ones that have and deserved to have triumphed throughout the world.[53] Surely we cannot take pride in what is accidental or arbitrary. Rorty even asserts that we human animals have, in some Darwinian fashion, become "clever enough to take charge of our future evolution," to free ourselves from the experience of contingency.[54] Rorty may say his account of history is propaganda, but he cannot help but conclude that the real has become the rational. His Hegelian hyper-modernism triumphs over his attempts at postmodern ironism.

As a result of the controversy stirred up by Fukuyama's book, Rorty discovered Kojève and thought himself in disagreement with him. But this perception of disagreement is based on a misinterpretation. Rorty thinks Kojève's seeming ad-miration of the moral fervor that leads one to risk one's life to have one's freedom recognized is too serious. Rorty too quickly lumps Kojève with the anti-bourgeois thinkers, while siding himself with the bourgeois aversion to the gratuitous risk of life. For Rorty, bourgeois culture is distinguished by the anti-Socratic view that thought and action in response to one's self-conscious mortality is not im-portant at all.

Rorty does not see that Kojève himself finally affirms existence without thought or action, the end of history. But Rorty does recognize that the culture he affirms is the one Kojève finds at history's end, the "nihilistic wasteland" of Heidegger populated by Nietzsche's "last men."[55] This culture, in the eyes of such serious philosophers, is not a culture at all: "Nietzsche thought that the happy, prosperous masses who would inhabit Dewey's social-democratic utopia were . . . worthless creatures incapable of greatness."[56]

Rorty, like Kojève, knows what is lost with the emergence of bourgeois, liberal society: serious philosophy, artistic excellence, and noble deeds. He cheerfully acknowledges that "the typical character types of liberal democracies are bland, calculating, petty, and unheroic."[57] Their lives are disenchanted. Disenchant-ment is "the price we pay for intellectual and private spiritual liberation."[58] We are liberated, above all, from the need to respond passionately to our mortality. We are better off, and more just, because we are unmoved. Liberal culture "aim[s] at curing us of our 'deep metaphysical need.' "[59] Depriving people of that need, or, as Allan Bloom says, flattening their souls, is the way to stabilize or perpetuate liberal freedom.[60]

Rorty suggests strongly what Kojève concludes explicitly: Liberal society is the product of wisdom or genuine self-consciousness. It is full of people who can be understood to have surrendered that consciousness as a miserable error. Para-doxically, they surrendered wisdom in the name of wisdom, the truth about history. History, or human self-consciousness, is nothing but a misery-producing error, a unique, aberrant exception to the reasonable order of nature or the cosmos. Bourgeois thinkers can be understood to have experienced all that is implied in being a self-conscious mortal, as thinking at history's end. The thinker who defends bourgeois society against its reactionary critics is really defending its residents against their miserable perception of the truth, while defending their existence at history's end as a genuine manifestation of the truth.

CLEVER (POSTHISTORICAL) ANIMALS

Rorty is ambivalent about the distinctiveness of human beings in our time, and so about whether history has really come to an end. He seems to be saying that his self-contradictions are in the process of disappearing, and that human beings will soon be qualitatively no different from the other animals. He asserts at one point that, properly understood, bourgeois society is not held together by some conception of human rights rooted in shared human nature. We are coming to recognize ourselves as "clever animals" and nothing more.

Rorty has always said that human nature, properly speaking, is an oxymoron. But his usual argument is that human beings are not natural but historical, accepting the Hegelian distinction between human, language-based freedom and animal, determined nature. Human beings are those who somehow oppose spirit to matter (or nature) or, as Rorty says, engage in self-creation expressed in language. Rorty's massive and obvious contradiction is to say that human beings are both wholly historical and wholly natural.

But much of that contradiction dissolves as he goes on to explain that defining human beings as clever animals is not "philosophical and pessimistic," but "political and hopeful." The hope is that "if we can work together, we can make ourselves into whatever we are clever and courageous enough to imagine ourselves becoming."[61] But if we are clever animals in what sense are we political, or concerned with justice and injustice? Hopeful? Courageous? Imaginative? Those qualities surely depend upon self-conscious mortality, on some qualitative distinction between human and other beings. Does not the desire that animates self-transformation rest upon that distinction?

The pragmatist has clever answers for most of these questions. If we are merely clever animals, we would not rebel against our mortality. We would not imagine ourselves becoming anything we cannot be. The imagination would contract itself to producing goals toward which we can actually work. We would be "courageous enough," because there would no longer be any particular need to be courageous at all. For Rorty, "political" means fitting the requirements of our bourgeois society. The pragmatist accepts as his political project whatever is useful for his society's flourishing. That does not include thought and action in response to self-conscious mortality, or history in Hegel's sense. Self-consciousness may even get in the way of our potential for cleverness. The anxious dislocation, brooding fear, and dark melancholy it produces can inhibit the brain's calculative functioning. It can also block memory and put us in unproductive moods. We pragmatists can say that the experience of self-conscious mortality is untrue. Without it, we are clever animals and nothing more.

Clever animals, Kojève says, are what human beings are at the end of history. As a result of having become completely historical, they become completely natural. Because they have "definitively mastered" nature, they have "harmonized" their existence with it.[62] They no longer have any reason to oppose nature with history; they are content. Clever animal is the definition of our species that would have to be true for pragmatism to succeed completely.

Rorty calls the definition of human beings as clever animals Darwinian. Like the other animals, all they do is try their best "to cope with their environment" and "to enjoy more pleasure and less pain." "Words," in a Darwinian light, "are among those tools which those clever animals have developed," and nothing more. So Rorty "repudiates the question of whether human minds are in touch with reality. . . . No organism, human or nonhuman, is ever more or less in touch with reality than any other organism."[63] If human beings are really as unconscious as the other animals, they exist, in the decisive sense, in Rousseau's wholly brutish state of nature.[64]

Rorty agrees with Kojève that the common recognition that human beings are historical all the way down signals the coming of the world where they are not historical at all. Rorty's writing may be understood as propaganda for history's imminent end. It acknowledges implicitly by opposing radically the miserable truth about human or historical contingency. It aims to negate that truth in the name of the truth, the truth about the natural world in which clever animals are qualitatively no different from the other animals. Human beings will always be more than clever animals as long as Rorty writes. His incredible denials of the obvious, his contradictions, are evidence that he is troubled by his own self-conscious mortality. But he writes to eradicate that truthful perception of error, or history, on behalf of the prosperous, contented, and rational flourishing of our species, the true utopia of the Enlightenment.

LIBERAL IRONY

Rorty's irony is finally his recognition that his own human distinctiveness is without foundation, an error. His posthistorical wisdom contradicts his own existence as a philosopher. Rorty distinguishes between "liberal ironists" and most human beings even in his liberal utopia, the fully secularized society. In Jerry Weinberger's words, the liberal ironist "lives in the greatest possible awareness of the existential burden of irony."[65] The proper response to what he knows about his existence is irony or play. He is alienated even from his own social order, because he sees so radically how contingent and arbitrary all human creations are. Such radical irony is always an inherently private experience. Rorty admits he "cannot imagine a culture which socializes its youth in such a way as to make them continually dubious about their own process of socialization." Human beings cannot live well if they really recognize and reflect on their wholly historical existences.[66]

The ironist has the existential burden of recognizing how idiosyncratic, even ridiculous, his personal reflections are. He knows he should not find the death of God, the mediocrity of society without deep belief, or his own death to be sources of anger and anxiety. If he does have such feelings, he knows they are merely private fantasies. He experiences himself as more interesting and complex than others, but he knows he cannot credibly say why. All human beings have idiosyncratic fantasies, and there is no non-idiosyncratic way to rank their quality. That recognition is what makes the ironist liberal: All human beings should have an equal opportunity to fulfill their fantasies, as long as they are genuinely private or do not impinge on the fantasies of others. Contrary to Plato, Heidegger, and many philosophers in between, Rorty holds that healthy human life in no way depends on the efforts of great thinkers to create or pursue the truth. He ironically admits that he might find Nietzsche's and Foucault's fantasies to be particularly fascinating. But their intense personal obsessions are politically dangerous; they were not ironic or playful enough about the futility of attempts to make them more than idiosyncratic.[67]

The liberal ironist knows that it is pointlessly cruel for him to impose his obsessions on others politically. He may feel himself a genius, but he refuses to be a monster. He is both amused and repulsed by the cruel effects of political projects in response to theological, philosophical, existential, and other obsessions throughout history. He will leave other people alone or in peace. If he acts politically, it will be to expose the monstrous idiosyncrasy of the cruel impositions of others. His limited political goal is to free the world from the illiberal effects of anger and anxiety by discrediting the seriousness of thought and contributing to sentimental education.[68] That goal, of course, is really not so limited. It is nothing less than the completion of the actualization of the liberal or Enlightenment utopia. It is the creation of a world without cruelty and so without the experience of self-conscious mortality. It is, ironically, finally a world without liberal ironists.

Finally, the liberal ironist is ironic about his irony. He knows, as Rorty says, "there is no such thing as *inner* freedom," and there is no truth to "liberal individualism." He holds that "There is nothing to people except what has been socialized into them."[69] Irony, or any form of detached thought and feeling, is really impossible. The ironist cannot explain how and so must deny that his irony is possible. Clever animals are not ironic. Kojève became an ironist once he was certain history had ended, aware that there is no way really to articulate credibly or seriously the impossible superfluity of his personal dissatisfaction.[70]

IRONY AND PRAGMATISM'S TRUTH

Perhaps the ironist, most of all, cannot purge himself of his awareness of pragmatism's vulgarity. It seems actually to privilege the ordinary person's unironic, antiphilosophical, and uncourageous aversion to the truth. Rorty says quite cheerfully that his goal is to make people more banal or ordinary, and so to purge the world of both geniuses and monsters. The pragmatist replaces personal efforts to search for the truth in the depth of one's soul with the indiscriminate construction of private fantasies. Rorty encourages, even in the case of great creators or "strong poets," the democratic tendency to shrink away from the depths.

If self-realization is a radically private matter, then Rorty cannot avoid saying that it is the question of "what should I do with my aloneness?"[71] Part of Rorty's answer is not to dwell on the fact that one is alone. One begins with the denial that the "I" is really an I, that there really is such a thing as personal experience.

But Rorty cannot make that denial consistently, which is why he cannot sustain the definition of man as a clever animal. He sometimes acknowledges that "every human being" acts out "consciously or unconsciously . . . an idiosyncratic fantasy." Fantasizing or imagining is what distinguishes human animals from the others. We are more than clever; we are imaginatively self-deceptive, and it is impossible to speak of self-deception without acknowledging somehow the self. Rorty claims that his definition of human distinctiveness follows Freud, who democratized "genius" by reducing it to fantasy.[72]

Fantasies, Rousseau says, are imaginary reveries one employs to both fill and divert oneself from time.[73] What we call poetry and philosophy, Rorty explains, are idiosyncrasies that "just happen to catch on with other people," that they just happen to find useful.[74] But people cannot help finding certain fantasies useful for diverting themselves from what they really know. Part of Rorty's irony is that people "just happen" to find his poetry useful. Rorty's preference for the comfortable to the true is clear in his approval of Dewey's use of God and his appeal to the "religious attitude" in A Common Faith. Rorty praises Dewey's astute insight that "aggressive atheism" has "something in common with traditional supernaturalism." What they share is "the excessive preoccupation with man in isolation." Both the Christians and the existentialists dwell on the isolated individual's contingency and mortality, what Rorty would finally have to acknowledge to be the truth about the individual's existence. Dewey rightly corrects that preoccupation with the "religious attitude," which "connect[s] . . . man in the way of both dependence and support, with the world that the imagination feels is a universe." The human imagination opposes the truth, the miserable facts of contingency and isolation. Without such imaginary location, Dewey contends that man stands unprotected from the moods of "despair and defiance" that come with the perception of isolation.[75] Rorty acknowledges that we cannot live well in light of the truth and nothing but the truth, which is why to be human is to construct linguistic fantasies. The imagination's function is to protect us from the truth of existentialism and its destructive excesses of fatalistic despair and aggressive defiance.

Rorty's defense of solidarity is also acknowledged as a comfortable lie. He admits, uncharacteristically, that it may be impossible to eradicate "the hope of surviving our individual deaths through some satisfying transfiguration." Pragmatism may well not completely succeed, and human beings may well continue to long for immortality. So let them have some hopeful illusion about their community or species, but let that longing be as abstract or vague as possible. The key is that such "solidarity . . . be our *only* comfort, and to be seen not to require metaphysical support." Human hope should not require "a theory of the nature of man," reflection on to what extent individuals or the species are really immortal. The hope is a baseless lie that provides comfort for beings who have become incapable of strong longing or love.[76] The goal of education, Rorty explains, is "interesting conversations," but the purpose of those conversations is "not to seek the Truth but just to bind us together," presumably against the truth.[77] But the actual hope is that the need for solidarity itself will eventually wither away, in the name of the truth.

The pragmatist concludes that both the aggressive atheist and the traditional supernaturalist or metaphysician are far too serious about the truth. In this sense, pragmatism is "a philosophy of solidarity rather than despair."[78] Rorty has no objection, finally, to using God or the communal illusions as tools until the need for them completely withers away, until we have constructed a still better fantasy. That fantasy is that we are nothing but clever animals, because we are unmoved by the facts of contingency and mortality. But if that fantasy, which will be, Rorty must acknowledge, a sort of shared idiosyncrasy, is as successful as we have reason to hope, then it will actually become true. The need for fantasy will wither away, as Marx first said, even if Rorty explains better what that withering would actually entail.

Rorty cannot help but know that pragmatism is a lie. He really means to say that we do well to live by useful lies, including the lie that we should judge truth by the criterion of utility. Lies that spare us cruelty lose their effectiveness if we dwell on their untruth. We should say we have no transcendent or transhistorical truth, no certainty, by which to compare them. That way, anyone who has such metaphysical or theological opinions about the truth can be excluded from discussion in a liberal democracy. They can rightly be labeled mad. Whatever threatens our society's conception of freedom and justice—our common, idiosyncratic fantasy—we can call untrue. We can prove such opinions untrue by simply saying they do us no good. Rorty says our view of moral community is sufficient reason to drop metaphysical and theological questions "and the vocabulary in which such questions are posed." The disappearance of the vocabulary means the end of the questions.[79] Our deepest social and political hope is to make pragmatism true.

AMERICAN NICENESS AND FLATNESS

The irony of pragmatism is the human effort to make a lie true. Rorty says we are well on the way to making ourselves clever animals and nothing more, but he knows he is not really one. The possibility that such a project could succeed offends common sense. Nobody believed Fukuyama and almost no one believed Kojève when they said history had come to an end. We still know we are mortals; we still make history.

But there is some striking evidence that Rorty is right, the similarity between his and Allan Bloom's descriptions of the contemporary American students. We might suspect that is because Bloom is greatly indebted to the work of Kojève, even more than he acknowledged.[80] But Rorty did not read Kojève until his pragmatism was developed. Rorty did not learn much from Bloom, nor Bloom from Rorty. Nevertheless, they both describe American students as nice, and becoming more so.

Bloom describes the students he taught as having been formed by something very like Rorty's pragmatic, sentimental, officially relativistic pragmatism. Bloom sees clearly that such relativism is not really so relativistic, but a pragmatic, chauvinistic defense of bourgeois society. Relativism is a "moral postulate" that prevents students from being moved by critics of their society's egalitarian, pragmatic principles. It causes them to "worship . . . vulgar success," or vulgarly to regard antibourgeois criticism as not useful. Relativism supports "the only form of justice they know," and they "cannot even imagine" an alternative. They are taught not to extend their imagination to the past, when human beings were insanely cruel and unjust. As Rorty says, they have been deprived of antibourgeois words and so antibourgeois experiences.[81]

So today's students, according to Bloom, are unimaginative and unidealistic. They are nice, or pleasant, friendly, and inclusive, but "listless." Their niceness reflects their "lack of passion, of hope, of despair." They are untouched by "the sense of twinship between love and death." They are "competent specialists," or clever animals, and nothing more. Bloom himself finds their lack of passion "incomprehensible." The effort to understand and to come to terms with the twinship between love and death is what constitutes his distinctively human, but now quite idiosyncratic, life.[82]

Bloom reports that the eros of today's students is "lame" or one-dimensional, because it is free from all illusion and so from all distinctively human longing. Without such illusion, eros becomes simply sex, or mechanical rutting. The students' music is the rhythm of that rutting. "To strangers from another planet," Bloom explains, "what would be the most striking thing is that sexual passion no longer includes the illusion of eternity." *The* contemporary phenomenon is "the deeroticization of the world." The students have become just like the other animals, no longer beings with souls.[83] Bloom's "way of putting the educational question of our time" is "Are we lovers anymore?"[84] Because he tends to answer it in the negative, he, despite his recommendation of the Great Books antidote, tends to regards today's students as uneducable.

Today's students experience nothing as permanent, and so everything human as contingent. They "are the first historical or historicized generation, not only in theory but in practice."[85] As Rorty observes, it is becoming commonly known that human beings are historical all the way through, and that fact in a way informs their whole lives. But they are not moved by restless longing to thought or action. They are satisfied with their finitude without any effort. Bloom cannot believe they are really self-conscious at all. But he describes them as without illusion concerning their finitude. They recognize the truth about both history and eternity.

Like Rorty, Bloom understands this unprecedented flatness of soul as the culmination of the Enlightenment in America. He makes general statements about that development of thought and its effects on practice that do not depend upon his personal knowledge of his students. What Marx claimed was possible, Bloom insists the Americans have virtually achieved. They have freed human life from tension or contradiction. They have freed it from definition by necessity's constraints, especially the necessity of death.

Bloom finds three stages to the development of the Enlightenment in America. He instructively adds psychological detail to Rorty's rather abstract narrative, but he tells basically the same story and certainly reaches the same conclusion. First, the Americans "slowly executed" God. He lost out to "the sacred," a euphemism for scientific atheism. Next, "Love was put to death by psychologists," who replaced it with "sex and meaningful relationships." Polymorphous and largely insatiable longing has been reduced to readily comprehensible and achievable satisfaction. The American pragmatic expert explains that God and love really contribute nothing to useful and productive lives.

The perfection of the pragmatic science of sex produced another "new science, thanatology, or death with dignity." This science "is on the way to putting death to death." The only way wholly to separate death from indignity, as Rorty says, is not to be bothered by it. "Death," Bloom reports, "isn't what it used to be." It no longer terrifies. So philosophy, "Socrates' long and arduous education, learning how to die" is largely obsolete.[86] Socrates' education began with the pain that comes with questioning all that one holds most dear, and ends somehow with both intense pleasure and serene resignation. Today's student is incapable of feeling the pain that leads to that distinctively human pleasure. He has learned how to live comfortably with death, and with what is left of love.

Professors Bloom and Rorty recognize that the flat-souled or unserious niceness of their students is evidence of the Enlightenment's success. Death no longer defines human existence. Bloom says he is not certain what will replace it. He does report "a divination of Engels," a most scientific Marxist. What comes next is "the classless society," which "would last, if not forever, a very long time." The death of death means the Marxian-Hegelian end of history is now here. Justice, universally and homogeneously defined, has triumphed, because we are clever animals and nothing more. Human beings have definitively conquered nature; they have, Bloom reports, made themselves "perfectly at home on earth." Only their experiences of having to come to terms with God, love, and death prevented them from being so.[87]

BLOOM VERSUS RORTY

Bloom and Rorty agree on their descriptions of contemporary American students, and on the psychological analysis about what is required for the Enlightenment project really to succeed. "All one has to do is forget about eternity," Bloom concludes, and "the most intractable of man's problems have been solved."[88] The pragmatic method of problem-solving is forgetting through the manipulation or truncation of the imagination.

Bloom and Rorty do seem to differ radically on the level of evaluation. Rorty is all for effective problem solving. Bloom opposes the soul's flatness on behalf of "the deepest human experience," or "what is uniquely human, the very definition of man."[89] With the experience of the philosopher, Bloom claims to have a standpoint from which to criticize historical success. He asserts that "all the philosophers agreed that the fulfillment of humanity is the use of reason."[90] In the name of reason, Bloom shouts what he knows about the inevitability of his own and others' death, the truth Rorty unreasonably refuses to mention. Death, as Socrates said, is not a problem to be solved but a truth to be experienced. The experience of death, to be sure, is what makes much of our behavior unreasonable. But we have it, paradoxically, because we alone among the beings can reason, and it is unreasonable to deny that we have it.

The philosopher is the most complete human being because he is the least self-forgetful. "The essential difference," Bloom asserts, "between the philosopher and all other men is his facing of death or his relation to eternity." He neither flinches before or feigns unconcern with the fact of his mortality; his "facing of death" is "intransigent." The "reality of death" infuses "every thought and deed" of the philosopher. The philosopher seems, in Kojève's sense, actually to be wise: "No other way of life than the philosophic can digest the truth about death."[91] Bloom contends that "Philosophy is the rational," and presumably true, "account of the whole," and not just the quest for that account.[92]

With that truth, the philosopher sees the groundlessness of all human hopes. They are always hope for one's salvation. The philosopher can only "dissolve" human aspirations, and so most human beings find his "somber" insight "intolerable." The philosopher himself experiences an "intense pleasure" in compensation for the insightful misery of his self-conscious morality. Without that pleasure, which very few share, he too would find life in light of the truth intolerable.[93]

But, for non-philosophers, the truth is no clear guide for action. The social hopes for the future, for one's grandchildren, that Rorty encourages depend on forgetting that one will not likely be around to see them become reality. In any case, the achievement of such freedom and justice will not fundamentally transform one's existence. Hope for personal salvation is a more genuine, if illusory, response to the human longing. Bloom seems actually close to agreeing with Rorty that genuinely self-conscious mortality is useless. Most human beings cannot live well without it, and so would be better off without it. The radically different experience of the rare philosophers, Bloom's experience, seems too "idiosyncratic"[94] to oppose effectively this conclusion. But a complication is that Bloom says that today's students know the truth about death and certainly have no hope for salvation. They do not seem to find the truth intolerable or even somber. In what way are they less reasonable than the philosopher?

Rorty agrees with almost every particular statement Bloom makes about human finitude and contingency. He does not hope to be saved from death. He would acknowledge that he will die alone. He regards all metaphysical and theological statements about immortality to be untrue. Unfeeling acceptance of the transience and contingency of all things human, Rorty agrees with Bloom, is becoming more and more the common sense of our secular, postmetaphysical, nice, or unserious world.

Rorty joins the students against Bloom by denying that there is necessarily anything terrible about any of this. He never says he fears death or longs for immortality, and he adds that those who do have such fear and longing can be cured by sentimental education. We have reason to disbelieve Rorty's ironic self-denial, but the nice students he and Bloom describe really are that easygoing. They do not love anything at all. Bloom actually presents better evidence than Rorty that Rorty's pragmatism is true. Pragmatists may have very little left to do. Bloom is at least not certain that to be moved passionately by love and death is a permanent part of the condition of our species. It is the point of human distinction, but it may be on the way to disappearing. Surely Bloom has no reason to disagree with Kojève or Rorty that it would be perverse to work to restore death if it really has been overcome. Does Bloom affirm Rorty's priority of the pragmatist's linguistic manipulation to the existentialist's truth? They both agree that most human beings would be better off not knowing or being moved by the fact that they are going to die.

BLOOM, NATURE, AND HISTORY

Bloom's agreement with Rorty and Kojève on death seems to contradict what Bloom says about the way of life of the philosopher as a natural perfection. But considering all that he has written, the least we can say is that Bloom is not certain about the relationship between philosophy and nature. He reports, for example, that the philosophers regarded fear of death as natural. But he also notes that Rousseau, a philosopher, "flatly denies that man . . . naturally fears death."[95] Had he ever written on Rorty, Bloom certainly would have said that Rorty's position—and the Hegelian distinction between nature and history that it presupposes—was best expressed by Rousseau.

Rousseau and Rorty agree that awareness of death and so, in a way, death itself "is really a product of the imagination." By nature man enjoys an "idle and pleasure-loving life," one unconcerned with and so unresistant to death. So "men naturally know how die," because they do it unconsciously. They naturally are "Without the illusions about death that pervert life and require the Socratic effort." Death, and the corresponding human perversions, are historical, not natural, phenomena. The historical Socrates struggled to achieve imperfectly what natural man had easily and perfectly. Bloom shows that natural man, with Rousseau's help, is Socrates's best critic.[96]

Bloom reports that "the souls of young people [today] are in a condition like that of the first men in the state of nature." So it is not surprising that they are also Socrates's critics. They, like Rorty, use his method against him. Socrates's critical inquiries dispelled the illusions that gave weight to every way of life but his own. Why does the philosopher take death so seriously? What is his problem?

Today's young, Bloom goes on, "are exaggerated versions of Plato's [Socrates's?] description of the young in democracies."[97] He suggests that democracy's perfection is philosophy's end, because it is the end of death or being animated by the perception of invincible necessity. From Bloom's perspective, Socrates rightly thought democracy's perfection to be undesirable, but he wrongly thought it to be impossible.

What Rousseau says about death, he also says about love. It too is an imaginary illusion. It certainly does not point human beings in the direction of the truth. Instead, it aids in covering up their unnatural, perverted knowledge of death. So Rousseau tries to take love seriously for the perverted, social beings who must employ the imagination to live well. "The enigma of Rousseau's whole undertaking," Bloom observes, "is how can one believe in what one knows to be the product of the imagination?" That enigma plagues the fantasizing Rorty. But finally, Bloom shows, there is no enigma. The effectual truth of Rousseau's teaching on love, against his intention, has been to destroy it. It produced Rorty's belief that the imagination can be manipulated to allow human beings to live in abundance and without cruelty, as did natural man.

Rousseau criticizes the "modern philosophers," and the uncruel Rorty is surely one, for their "notably unerotic teachings." Rousseau, against their efforts, tried to restore the poetry of love to the world. But his criticism of the modern philosophers includes the acknowledgment that they "see nature as it is," unerotically or unpoetically. Rousseau and Rorty agree that there is no natural or true foundation for poetry and love. Rorty and Bloom describe a world in which Rousseau's modern view of the truth defeated his poetic creativity or illusion. The oxymoron flat soul is the true soul.[98]

Rousseau's teaching about nature is the foundation of the science or wisdom Bloom finds present among the students who have nothing to learn from him at history's end. Psychotherapy (or thanatology) of various sorts, including that practiced by Rorty, is restoring man, mentally diseased by history, to natural health. This cure is for the "wounds inflicted by society," gratuitous suffering or cruelty for which one has no responsibility.[99]

Bloom reminds us that Rousseau preceded Rorty in the abandonment of the moral language of virtue and vice. He replaced it with the medical language of health and disease. This reductionistic psychotherapy, Bloom claims, makes him the most modern of the moderns.[100] Kojève and Rorty do seem merely to follow his lead. The final goal of psychotherapy is euthanasia, the perfectly good death praised by the philosophers. The man who dies such a death is beyond the diseased realm of virtue or vice, or good and evil.

Bloom does say he has reason to disagree with Rousseau's diagnosis of the problem of human liberty and his proposal for a cure. Love and Friendship was written as "an attempt to recover the power, the danger, and the beauty of eros." The emphasis is not restoring the capability of human beings to be moved by death, but on the Socratic foundation for opposing Rousseau and his successors on man's natural solitude. "The difference between Nietzsche and Socrates,"

Bloom asserts, "comes down to the possibility of the most ultimate form of community, mutual understanding." This "logocentric" friendship is between philosophers who share the truth about "being," as well as a love of that truth.[101] Perhaps if that friendship did not exist, then love really is an illusion. All that would remain are idiosyncratic fantasies or solitary reveries.

But philosophic friendship, Bloom acknowledges, is extremely rare. The example he gives is the one between Montaigne and La Boetie, centuries ago. It seems mainly to have been the shared exhilaration of secret liberation from the religious illusions of their time. Could that exhilaration be experienced today, when the popularized religious indifference described by Bloom and Rorty has taken so much of the danger and the fun out of free thought? Is this philosophic friendship liberation from illusion for the truth about death? How can this truth, which would appear radically to isolate the individual, be the foundation of community?

Bloom may acknowledge that philosophic friendship is too rare and questionable really to be of human significance. He does say that friendship "in any sense intended by Montaigne" is virtually impossible in America today. Does he agree with Rorty that the possibility of philosophic friendship is too useless to be true? It seems to have no relevance to almost all human lives, especially lives today. Does Bloom really say or mean to say enough not to agree with Rorty that what Montaigne and La Boetie enjoyed was a private fantasy? In truth, were they so touched by each other that they were relatively untouched by death?[102]

CONCLUSION: RORTY AND BLOOM AT THE END OF HISTORY

Bloom, like Kojève, says philosophy is acknowledging all that is implied in without flinching about one's death. Does that include acknowledging that the very existence of human beings is historical or temporary? The end of history, of course, is the end of illusion, especially illusions about eternity that made human eros possible. Part of wisdom may be knowing that the human perception of it will pass away. Does Bloom acknowledge that philosophy has disappeared or is about to disappear? Does he share Rorty's or Kojève's ironic awareness of how idiosyncratic his personal experiences are?

Rorty thinks he disagrees with Bloom's portrayal of Americans as uneasy in the midst of a "deep spiritual malaise." The pragmatist denies that "our problem is . . . internal hollowness." It is only the apparent intractability of certain "external" or social problems, ones that really can be overcome through the linguistic manipulation of the imagination.[103] But Rorty misreads Bloom; the students he describes suffer from no such malaise. A flat soul is not a hollow one. One can fill up a hollow soul, but perhaps nothing can be done with a flat one. If Rorty had read Bloom more closely and sympathetically, he surely would have seen that Bloom may be more convinced than Rorty that Rorty is right about America's future.

AN AFTERWORD ABOUT A LEFTOVER

There is a very fundamental contradiction in Bloom's book about America, and it would be misleading to ignore it. He says that children of divorce are different from his other students. Their niceness is really rigidity. For them, the principles of egalitarian relativism are really "desperate platitudes" with which they try and fail to make sense out of "the chaos of their experience."

The children of the divorced have been subjected to "therapy," provided by psychological experts paid for by their parents. The therapy is linguistic. The psychologist speaks the platitudes about self-determination and the relationship between divorce and personal happiness. But the therapy usually fails because the "artificial language" about "artificial feelings" does not speak to the real longings within the soul of the child. The child may have nice manners and echo the expert's platitudes, but they are "a thin veneer over boundless seas of rage, doubt, and fear." Bloom says that the children of the divorced are "victims" who deserve our "pity." For them, "their disarray in the cosmos" is the appropriate "theme of reflection and study."[104] They are, as Walker Percy says, lost in the cosmos, and their lives are not those of clever, contented animals at history's end.

But Bloom does not actually present children of the divorced as exceptions to the rule. They are "symbols of the intellectual-political problems of our time." One of the consequences of the Enlightenment in America is the desocialization that comes with the de-eroticization of the world. All of life, including marriage, is redefined in terms of personal calculation. So the institution of marriage is failing, and no one knows what to do to save it. Divorce has become more pervasive, and even couples who stay together spend less time with and are less attached to their children. The children of the divorced "represent in extreme form the spiritual vortex set in motion by loss of contact with other human beings and the natural world."[105]

It makes sense to say that the extreme experience will become more common, and so students will more commonly experience themselves in cosmic and personal disarray. Does not the resulting fear, rage, and doubt show they have souls? The pragmatic project to de-eroticize the world is not really returning human beings to Rousseau's state of nature.

Does not this likely explosion of imperfectly repressed passion show that those who speak of the end of history only speak of a fragile and temporary surface of human reality? Why is the experience of "disarray in the cosmos" not closer to the truth than the self-avoidance of niceness? This line of inquiry could be Bloom's decisive refutation of Rorty, and we wonder why and are disappointed that he does not pursue it. It would lead, for example, to a new analysis of rock music, as full of anger and distorted human longing. Perhaps partisans of reason oppose the view that human beings are really lost in the cosmos, because they prefer not to say that human reality to some extent eludes reason.

NOTES

1. Harvey C. Mansfield, Jr., "Dewey: All-Out Democrat," *Times Literary Supplement* (January 24, 1992), 26.

2. Alexandre Kojève, "The Idea of Death in the Philosophy of Hegel," *Interpretation* 3 (1973). This article contains material that was left out of the English translation of Kojève's *Introduction to the Reading of Hegel*, translated by J. H. Nichols, edited by A. Bloom (Ithaca, NY: Cornell University Press, 1968).

3. Richard Rorty, "After Philosophy, Democracy," in *The American Philosopher*, edited by G. Borradori (Chicago: University of Chicago Press, 1994), 116.

4. Richard Rorty, *Contingency, Irony, and Solidarity* (Cambridge: Cambridge University Press, 1989), 150–158.

5. Ibid., 16.

6. Ibid., 113, note 15.

7. Ibid., 106.

8. Richard Rorty, *Objectivity, Relativism, and Truth* (Cambridge: Cambridge University Press, 1991), 71.

9. Rorty, *Contingency*, 110.

10. Ibid., 23, 71.

11. Ibid., 24, including the note.

12. Richard Rorty, *Philosophy and the Mirror of Nature* (Princeton, NJ: Princeton University Press, 1979), 70.

13. Rene Vincente Arcilla, *For the Love of Perfection: Richard Rorty and Liberal Education* (New York: Routledge, 1995), 98–99.

14. Charles Hartshorne, "Rorty's Pragmatism and Farewell to the Age of Faith and Enlightenment," in *Rorty and Pragmatism: The Philosopher Responds to His Critics*, edited by C. Saatkamp (Nashville, TN: Vanderbilt University Press, 1995), 21–22.

15. Rorty, "Response" [to Hartshorne], in Saatkamp, *Rory and Pragmatism*, 31–34.

16. Ibid., 34.

17. Rorty, "Expanding Our Culture," in *Debating the State of Philosophy*, edited by J. Nitzik and J. Sanders (Westport, CT: Praeger, 1996), 25.

18. Rorty, "Response," 35–36.

19. Arcilla, *For the Love of Perfection*, x. This book contains a useful comparison of Bloom and Rorty. But it is too abstract because Arcilla slights Bloom's connections among love, philosophy, and death, despite his intention to focus attention on the meaning of one's mortality.

20. Rorty, *Objectivity*, 32.

21. Rorty, *Essays on Heidegger and Others* (Cambridge: Cambridge University Press, 1991), 132.

22. Ibid., 137.

23. Rorty, *Contingency*, 85.

24. Rorty, *Essays*, 24–25.

25. Rorty, *Objectivity*, 175–196.

26. Rorty, *Contingency*, 113, text and note 13.

27. Ibid., 173.

28. Rorty, "[Untitled Comments]," in Nitzik and Sanders, eds., *Debating the State of Philosophy*, 114.

29. Richard Rorty, "Hermenutics, General Studies, and Teaching," *Synergos* 2 (Fall 1982): 9–10.

30. Rorty, *Objectivity*, 197–202. Rorty's title "postmodernist bourgeois liberalism" is clearly a joke—a lighthearted oxymoron.

31. Rorty, "Two Cheers for Elitism," *New Yorker* 70 (January 30, 1995): 88–89.

32. Rorty, *Contingency*, 173.

33. Rorty, *Objectivity*, 182.

34. See Rorty, *Contingency*, 40.

35. Ibid., 179.

36. Ibid., 146, 158, 161, 173, 182.

37. Rorty, "Human Rights, Rationality, and Sentimentality," *Yale Review* 81 (October 1993): 1–20.

38. Rorty, *Essays*, 48.

39. Rorty, *Objectivity*, 210.

40. Rorty, "Human Rights," 13–14.

41. Ibid., 13–20.

42. Rorty, *Objectivity*, 182.

43. Rorty, *Contingency*, 35.

44. Rorty, *Essays*, 25.

45. Rorty, *Contingency*, 197.

46. Ibid., 46.

47. Rorty, *Essays*, 47.

48. Rorty, "Human Rights," 6.

49. Rorty, *Essays*, 33.

50. Rorty, *Contingency*, 55, 73.

51. Ibid., 219.

52. Ibid., 63.

53. Rorty, *Objectivity*, 208, 216, 219.

54. Rorty, "Human Rights," 8.

55. Richard Rorty, "The End of Leninism and History as a Comic Frame," in *History and the Idea of Progress*, edited by A. Melzer, J. Weinberger, and R. Zinman (Ithaca, NY: Cornell University Press, 1995), 223.

56. Rorty, "Relativism—Finding and Making," in Nitzik and Sanders, eds., *Debating the State of Philosophy*, 43.

57. Rorty, *Objectivity*, 190.

58. Ibid., 194.

59. Rorty, *Contingency*, 46.

60. Rorty, *Objectivity*, 192.

61. Rorty, "Human Rights," 9.

62. Kojève, *Introduction*, 158–159, note 6.

63. Rorty, "Relativism," 38.

64. The intellectual Rorty, of course, cannot adhere to this position consistently: "But we of course go on to add that being an irrationalist . . . is not to be incapable of argument. We irrationalists do not . . . behave like animals" ("Relativism," 34).

65. Jerry Weinberger, "Technology and the Problem of Liberal Democracy," in *Technology and the Western Political Tradition*, edited by A. Melzer, J. Weinberger, and R. Zinman (Ithaca, NY: Cornell University Press, 1993), 264.

66. Rorty, *Contingency*, 87–89.

67. Rorty, *Objectivity*, 192; *Contingency*, 89, 53.

68. See Weinberger, "Technology and the Problem of Liberal Democracy," 262–265.

69. Rorty, *Contingency*, 177.

70. Hugh Gillis, "Anthropology, Dialectic and Atheism in Kojève's Thought," *Graduate Faculty Philosophy Journal* 18 (1995): 103.

71. Rorty, *Objectivity*, 13.

72. Rorty, *Contingency*, 36–37, 26.

73. Jean-Jacques Rousseau, *The Reveries of the Solitary Walker*, Walk 5.

74. Rorty, *Contingency*, 37.

75. Rorty, *Objectivity*, 69–70.

76. Ibid., 32. Rorty's new book, *Achieving Our Country* (Cambridge, MA: Harvard University Press, 1998), appeared too late to be considered here. But it is clearly an example of his easygoing atheism: Nationalism and the religious impulse are to be used today to achieve their obsolescence tomorrow. For more, see my "Rorty's America," *Perspectives on Political Science* (Fall 1998).

77. Rorty, "Hermeneutics," 10–11.

78. Rorty, *Objectivity*, 33.

79. Ibid., 183, 186–187, 190.

80. See Allan Bloom, *Giants and Dwarfs* (New York: Simon and Schuster, 1990), 256–267.

81. Allan Bloom, *The Closing of the American Mind* (New York: Simon and Schuster, 1987), 25–26, 90.

82. Ibid., 134, 123.

83. Ibid., 68–81, 123, 132–133; Allan Bloom, *Love and Friendship* (New York: Simon and Schuster, 1992), 15.

84. Bloom, *Closing*, 133.

85. Ibid., 106–108.

86. Ibid., 230.

87. Ibid.

88. Ibid.

89. Ibid., 273.

90. Ibid., 292.

91. Ibid., 277–285.

92. Ibid., 264.

93. Ibid., 277.

94. Ibid., 312.

95. Bloom, *Giants*, 185.

96. Ibid., 185–186.

97. Bloom, *Closing*, 87.

98. Bloom, *Giants*, 200.

99. Bloom, *Love and Friendship*, 44.

100. Ibid.

101. Ibid., 12, 542–543.

102. Ibid., 410–428.

103. Rorty, "Straussianism, Democracy, and Allan Bloom—I: That Old Time Philosophy," in *Essays on the Closing of the American Mind*, edited by R. Stone (Chicago: Chicago Review Press, 1989), 103.

104. Bloom, *Closing*, 121.

105. Ibid., 118–121.

11

Romanticism, Cultural Literacy, and the Great Books: The Goals of Education

MARY P. NICHOLS

For years we have been hearing numerous criticisms of American education and proposals for reform that include improved teacher training, stricter standards of accountability, and higher financial incentives for teachers. Several influential critics trace educational decline to the very ideas that we hold about education. The work of two of these, E. D. Hirsch and Allan Bloom, has received widespread attention. Hirsch, in *Cultural Literacy* and Bloom, in *The Closing of the American Mind*, claim that American education has failed American democracy.[1] Hirsch contends that our students lack a common body of information about their own culture. Without that shared cultural literacy, communication becomes impossible.[2] Bloom, similarly, complains that today's students are rootless, with no sense of continuity with the past, no connection to the great ideas and individuals of Western civilization, and no understanding of the philosophic foundations of their society. While Hirsch recommends teaching the basic facts of "cultural literacy" in the early years of schooling, Bloom suggests reading the Great Books in order to remedy the defects of our colleges and universities and to provide students with a liberal education. Both trace our current problems at least in part to the influence in America of Jean-Jacques Rousseau. In this essay, I shall examine the "romanticism" deriving from Rousseau that has influenced American education, and which Hirsch and Bloom regard as pernicious, as well as the alternative understandings of education that they propose. Do their analyses of the current crisis help us to understand the problems in education that confront us, and what we should do about them? While Hirsch and Bloom, I shall argue, correctly identify problems with Rousseau's romantic ideal, their alternatives are only partially successful. Indeed they suffer from some of the very aspects of romanticism that they criticize.

It is paradoxical to argue that Rousseau's influence on education undermines democracy, for Rousseau is known as one of the great democratic theorists. Not only his political philosophy but also his educational prescriptions were meant to "save" democracy, and to give freedom, self-government, and democratic community firmer foundations—and more elevated meanings—than they had previously. Underlying both his political and educational philosophy is his analysis of society and its effect on human beings. Rousseau argues that society itself deprives individuals of their freedom, enslaving them to its opinions and prejudices. Social man, for example, concerned with acquiring the good opinion of others, becomes what pleases them. He is "other-directed," as we would say today, a slave to those from whom he derives his direction.[3] Rousseau describes the pitiful state of the child made to perform for others, who recites verses he does not understand, displays a "learning" that has taught him nothing except to obtain the praises of the adults on whom he depends (E, 110–112; see also 109).[4] According to Rousseau, he has lost himself; he is only what others expect of him, a slave without an identity of his own.

Allan Bloom refers to a striking example of the kind of individual Rousseau criticizes, Woody Allen's Zelig (CAM, 144–146). Zelig is the classic other-directed man. He imitates those around him; he is a Republican among the rich and a Democrat among the kitchen help. Zelig wants to be liked and to fit in with others so much that his physical features and accent change so that he comes to look and act like those around him. He becomes black among blacks and Oriental among Orientals. He is all roles, and cannot find himself. When with the help of his psychiatrist he determines to be himself, he merely does the opposite of what is expected of him. Whenever anyone says anything, Zelig denies it. His psychiatrist admits that she has gone too far in teaching him to be himself. But such "assertiveness" is not being oneself, nor is it being free. A person who becomes a Democrat among the rich, or a Republican among the poor, is still determined by others. He is still reacting to his surroundings, even if he is reacting against them rather than imitating them. Rousseau's educational scheme is meant to save us from being Zeligs.

Society does not merely enslave us by inculcating its opinions and prejudices, and, in general, its ways of being, Rousseau argues. It also inflames our imagination, introducing us to new pleasures and arousing our desire for them. Satisfying these new desires becomes essential to our happiness and we become all the more dependent on society (E, 80–81). Social man, for example, desires to acquire property and to increase his possessions. But by acquiring possessions, Rousseau tells Emile, he will become dependent on those who can destroy those possessions; and his use of them, whether in commerce, finance, or public office, will force him to adjust his morals and behavior "to the example and prejudices of others" (E, 456). He may suppose that his pursuit of happiness is "as he sees fit," but in fact he is determined by desires, needs, and opinions that become the very fabric of his being as he grows up in society. Rousseau thought that it might be possible to rescue the individual from the tyranny of materialism and public opinion in a liberal society by means of the proper education. In his *Emile*, he proposes principles of education intended to keep his student free from the conventions of time and place. Preserved from desires for unnecessary things that individuals acquire in society, the student will be content with what he can attain solely through his own efforts. He will not depend on others to satisfy his desires, or on society to determine their objects. Only this free being, according to Rousseau, is happy (*E*, 98; see also 61, 107, and 117).

It is not the case, however, that Emile's tutor is a stern master, teaching the child to control his desires lest he become a slave to them. According to Rousseau, a child does not by nature have desires that he needs to master. Individuals naturally desire only what is necessary. The desires that enslave them are ones learned from society (*E*, 87). For example, Rousseau traces an infant's desire to dominate to the missteps of his caretakers, who teach him the pleasure of ruling others by spoiling him. The spoiled brat, dependent on those he tries to command, is no longer moved by nature, but by society. As Rousseau writes, "there is no original perversity in the human heart. There is not an original vice to be found in it of which it cannot be said how and whence it entered" (*E*, 92).

It is this idea of the goodness of natural man that lies at the heart of romantic philosophies of education. Because man is good by nature, education should not be an acquisition of anything, neither the cultural information that Hirsch thinks necessary or the enlightening and ennobling ideas that Bloom finds in the Great Books. Rather, education should be an attempt to preserve the child from outside influences so that nature can emerge. Romanticism, Hirsch writes, holds not only that "human nature is innately good, and should therefore be encouraged to take its natural course, unspoiled by the artificial impositions of social prejudice and convention," but also that "the child is a special being in its own right with unique, trustworthy—and indeed holy—impulses that should be allowed to develop and run their course." Such theories have dominated education "ever since Rousseau's *Emile*."[5]

Emile's education does not include cultural information, for Rousseau does not want him to possess a particular tradition, to be a Frenchman, or an Englishman. Rather, he wants to create an "abstract man," free of time and place (*E*, 42).[6] The acquisition of a literate culture in Hirsch's sense resembles the socialization from which Rousseau wants to preserve Emile. Nor is Rousseau interested in introducing Emile to the Great Books, to the liberal education that Bloom advocates. What are the Great Books, he would ask, but the chronicles of the many errors human beings have made or the images of the many vices to which they have yielded (*E*, 236–237)? Of the works of philosophy, which are especially prized by Bloom, Rousseau declares, "It is not philosophers who know men best. They see them only through the prejudices of philosophy, and I know of no station where one has so many" (*E*, 243).[7] As for the works of history, Rousseau finds no greatness for Emile to admire, no models for him to imitate, no alter-

native ways of being and thinking that help him to transcend his own ways. Far
from it. The history that Emile learns is a history of human weakness and the
suffering it has produced. Its effect is to make him even more content with himself
and his education which has preserved him from the artificial lives, the corrupt
passions, and the hurt and pain that result, from what has been up to that time
the human lot (E, 236–244, especially 244). If Emile "just once prefers to be
someone other than himself [when he reads the stories of history]," Rousseau
proclaims, "were this other Socrates, were it Cato—everything has failed" (E,
243).

For better or worse, Rousseau has been a dominant force in American edu-
cation in the twentieth century, primarily through the influence of John Dewey.
As Hirsch observes in *Cultural Literacy*, "The theories that have dominated
American education for the past fifty years stem ultimately from Jean-Jacques
Rousseau" (CL, xiv). As the originator of romantic education, Hirsch writes,
"John Dewey is usually given too much credit (or blame), and Jean Rousseau too
little" (CL, 119). One can see Rousseau's influence in the attempt to allow the
child to develop naturally, with a minimum of external direction. Proposals for
child-centered education, the view of the teacher as a guide who should help the
pupil to achieve his own purposes, the praise of "open classrooms," the move
toward greater participation of students in the development of the curriculum,
are indebted to Rousseau. So is the notion of a "content-neutral" skills-oriented
education. Only such an education, it is said, is truly free, for its product, the
free individual, has the tools to learn whatever he desires. Only he has not been
smothered by the choices of others, filled with their values and ideas, and thus
made subject to external authority, whether of his teachers, of his society, or of
civilization itself.[8]

Hirsch presents a powerful argument against romantic education. He contends
that the "openness" of current education, its attempt, for example, to teach skills
without content in the name of freedom, actually deprives students of freedom.
Specifically, it does not give them the basic information they need to thrive in
the modern world. Without widely shared information, he says, individuals are
not able "to communicate effectively with one another in our national community" (CL, xvii). They lack the "background information" necessary to make
sense of the spoken and written word. Any communication, Hirsch explains,
assumes that its addressees have basic information that is part of the culture in
which they live—knowledge of literary references, for example, or historical facts,
or the meaning of scientific terms. Such background information is necessary for
any effective communication, from receiving directions to reading a newspaper.
Such "cultural literacy" is necessary for individuals to relate "what they read to
the unstated context which alone gives meaning to what they read" (CL, 2). We
have previously taken for granted this context for communication, Hirsch argues,
but it is now slowly eroding among us due to the influence of romantic education
in our schools. No longer taught an "adult culture," our children are growing up
"culturally illiterate."

This cultural illiteracy, according to Hirsch, constitutes a crisis for our national life. "Only by piling up specific, communally-shared information," Hirsch claims, "can children learn to participate in complex cooperative activities with other members of their community." Cultural literacy is thus "the only sure avenue of opportunity to disadvantaged children" who will otherwise remain "poor and illiterate" (CL, 1). Moreover, without cultural literacy, we cannot exercise democratic citizenship: "Illiterate and semiliterate Americans are condemned not only to poverty, but to the powerlessness of incomprehension," Hirsch writes. They do not understand issues, they are prey to oversimplification; unable to "deliberate and communicate with one another," they cannot be "active participants in our republic" (CL, 12). Far from independent or self-sufficient, culturally illiterate Americans are dependent on others, economically and politically. The romantic education that was supposed to embody the democratic principles of freedom and equality has backfired: it fosters only dependence and inequality. Only if education provides "content," teaching children "what literate Americans know" (CL, 146), will these democratic values be truly served.

While Hirsch may be successful in arguing against a contentless education, is his understanding of the content of education adequate? Just as the Romantic educator refuses to impose his own values on his students, so too is Hirsch careful not to judge the value of a specific literate culture, or of any of its particular elements. Indeed, he maintains that one literate culture is no better than another. We must acquire knowledge of our own literate culture simply because it is ours; only by knowing what others know can we communicate with them. To think that our own culture has any "inherent merit" is "cultural chauvinism and provincialism": "no single national vocabulary is inherently superior or privileged above all others" (CL, 107; see also xvi). Similarly, when Hirsch compiles a list of items that the schools should teach in order to promote cultural literacy, that list is intended to be merely descriptive rather than prescriptive (CL, xiv and 137).[9] He is attempting to describe what literate Americans know, not what they should know. As he says, "the specific contents [of a national vocabulary] are far less important than the fact they are shared" (CL, 106). Although he recommends "content" for education, and censures those educators who abdicate their responsibility "to make decisions about curricular content" (CL, 144; see also 21), the content for which he takes responsibility is value free.[10] Hirsch—and the teachers he is trying to persuade—would not impose their values on anyone. Like skills-oriented education, Hirsch's cultural literacy provides only the conditions for individuals to pursue their own values. Cultural literacy, as Hirsch presents it, is only another skill.[11] In spite of his proposal to give education content, the justification he finally gives for that content is surprisingly abstract—the communication it makes possible rather than what is communicated, the participation that it permits rather than the kind of community in which individuals participate.

Allan Bloom's criticism of American education in The Closing of the American Mind also suggests the inadequacy of Hirsch's approach. Like Hirsch, Bloom blames education for abdicating its responsibility and refusing to provide a "content" for education (CAM, 329 and 341). He also notes that students are cut off from tradition, that they share no common body of knowledge or beliefs (CAM, 51 and 109). And he too blames progressive education and its philosophic originators and disseminators such as Rousseau and Dewey for the "openness" of American education that is really "a great closing" (CAM, 35). However, this is where Bloom's similarity to Hirsch ends. The openness that for Bloom is so harmful is nothing other than the cultural relativism that characterizes Hirsch's position.[12]

While the culturally literate individual may have superficial knowledge of the facts of Western culture, his belief in the relativity of all cultures would make him indifferent to his heritage; he has been taught in effect that nothing is worth loving.[13] While his education gives him information about a variety of subjects so that he becomes adept in his dealings with others who share such information, nothing of what he has learned need have any meaning for his life.[14] A proper reform of American education for Bloom demands not merely a commitment to teaching facts in Hirsch's sense, but a profound overhauling of the ideas that currently hold sway in America. Specifically, students must be taught to read books as if books might teach them how to live, how to satisfy their deepest longings. Such an exposure to the Great Books, according to Bloom, forms a student's character, and even changes him profoundly, for it makes him free. Rather than becoming free to engage in politics and business, as would one who possesses a literate culture, he becomes free of the prejudices of his own time and place. He becomes free to think.

Bloom's emphasis on freedom, however, makes his view of the value of tradition ambiguous. While he laments that education no longer presents the Great Books and ideas of the Western tradition, those books and ideas, he believes, will free one from tradition itself.[15] Bloom upholds Western civilization not because it is ours but because it is *the* civilization, modeled as it is on Socrates' way of life, that questions itself and all civilizations. "Only in the Western nations, i.e., those influenced by Greek philosophy," Bloom writes, "is there some willingness to doubt the identification of the good with one's own way" (CAM, 36). Moreover, "one has to have the experience of really believing before one can have the thrill of liberation" (CAM, 43). The community that Bloom thinks that education makes possible is less of people who share a tradition than of those who have been liberated from one (see CAM, 252). It is the community of philosophers, of "potential knowers," "the true friends" who "think together" (CAM, 381).

Bloom's emphasis on freedom has been missed by those who accuse him of a "Platonic appeal to immutable standards." Richard Rorty makes this claim in his attack on Bloom in *The New Republic*.[16] Rorty points out that Socrates's life is one of "openness and curiosity," a life more consistent with American democracy, Rorty suggests, than the ideal proposed by Bloom.[17] But Bloom praises Socrates not for any truth that he found but for his pursuit of the truth. It is not that Socrates finds answers to his questions; rather, "Socrates lives with the essential conflicts and illustrates them" (CAM, 266). Similarly, the university's task, Bloom says, is in the first place "always to maintain the permanent questions front and center. . . . [W]ithout having the answers, the university knows what openness is and knows the questions" (CAM, 252–253; see also 249).[18] Bloom speaks of a tiny band of men who "participate fully in the [philosophic] way of life" and who "are the soul of the university." They are united by their common experience, their way of life devoted to reason, rather than by any common teaching (CAM, 271). It is not their view of the good, but their disagreement about the good, that makes them "absolutely one soul as they [look] at the problem" (CAM, 381).

If Bloom eludes Rorty's criticism, however, does he not reinstate openness as the highest good? Bloom distinguishes "the openness of indifference" which he associates with our current education, from "the openness that invites us to the quest for knowledge and certitude" (CAM, 41). But there is no certainty that certitude is possible. Indeed, Bloom gives no reason to think even that it is likely. That is one reason why philosophy is for only the few, in Bloom's opinion. Only a few can live the life of openness that the university at its best represents: the university, Bloom writes, is "for the sake of preserving the freedom of the mind . . . for some individuals within it" (CAM, 252).[19]

Could Bloom, then, like Hirsch, be in his own way guilty of what he criticizes current education for doing—emphasizing form over content? Bloom might respond that the permanent questions, to which philosophy is devoted, provide the content of education. But Bloom's treatment of these questions is curiously abstract. "Concreteness, not abstractness, is the hallmark of philosophy," he proclaims (CAM, 255), but then gives little attention to political philosophy or political science, which might offer concrete subjects for reflection (CAM, 275–276; 283).[20] After all, as he says, "all societies look pretty much the same from the heights" (CAM, 292–293).[21] Bloom's statement that all societies look pretty much the same from the heights resembles Hirsch's observation that no culture is better than another (CL, xvi). But while Hirsch thinks that in spite of this fact it is natural and good that individuals live within a particular culture (CL, xiv), Bloom thinks that philosophers at least can live outside of one. Indeed, this is finally why some societies do look better to Bloom than others—for just as Western philosophy is preferable because of the self-questioning at its core, so societies are preferable that permit philosophers to rise more easily to the heights to which they aspire. While Hirsch ultimately prefers liberal democracy because of the opportunities it permits the many if they are given the proper educational opportunities, Bloom prefers liberal society because of the opportunities it allows the few.[22] While Hirsch speaks against the elitism of a Great Books program (CL, xiv),[23] Bloom speaks eloquently of "the heights" occupied by philosophers.

From these heights the philosopher "applies what he sees in nature to his own life," Bloom says. " 'As are the generations of leaves, so are the generations of men'—a somber lesson that is only compensated for by the intense pleasure accompanying insight" (CAM, 277). They "live more truly and fully" when they "are forgetting their accidental lives" (CAM, 380). Is not Bloom's philosopher much like Rousseau's Emile, "abstract man," a member of no class, a citizen of no country, connected to no particular time or place, and curiously void of human attachment?[24] The philosophic ascent that Bloom thinks reading the Great Books makes possible sounds strangely like the deplorable state of today's youth, influenced by German philosophy, that Bloom describes: it is a time when "country, religion, family, ideas of civilization, all the sentimental and historical forces" lose their power over human minds—so that nothing stands "between cosmic infinity and the individual" (CAM, 85; see 277). Although Bloom is correct to remind us that critical distance from one's own is a mark of humanity, he leaves out of his account the moving forces of philosophy, the particular human beings—friends, family, teachers, and fellow citizens—whom we desire to understand and who help us in our search.

Bloom, as we have seen, refers to Woody Allen's Zelig as an example of an other-directed man. According to Bloom, the movie's criticism of other-directedness has nothing positive to offer about how human beings *should* live. Zelig is "a haunted comedy," Bloom writes, "that has nothing to tell us about the inner-directedness" which to Allen is "simply empty or non-existent" (CAM, 144–146). Consistently, Bloom leaves out the positive end of the movie, in which Zelig is rescued from his fear of being himself by the woman psychiatrist who is treating him—not simply because she is a good therapist but also because she loves him. Indeed, her love makes her a good therapist, for her love for Zelig is possible only if he is someone rather than a variety of contradictory roles; her love proves that he does not have to change himself in order to get the acceptance he is seeking. The answer is not "inner-directedness," which separates a person from others just as surely as other-directedness assimilates him to them. The answer is understanding that one is connected to others—in the love that a man and a woman have for each other, for example. The movie therefore does have something positive to teach, even though it does not lift us to the heights from which all societies—to say nothing of human beings—"look pretty much the same."

At the end of the movie, the happily married Zelig is reading Moby-Dick, a book that he once pretended to have read in order to impress people. In his early life, we could say, he tried to be a culturally literate man, knowing enough about Moby-Dick to take part in "intellectual" discussions. In the end, however, he is reading a Great Book, in order to "see how it came out."[25] But Bloom sees only "a mixture of petulance and facile, self-conscious smugness" in the "health" Zelig attains (CAM, 145). Nor does Bloom mention any significance in Woody Allen's choice of Moby-Dick. In that novel a man who isolates himself from human society in a lone quest for the infinite destroys himself and others in the process, while a man who befriends others is saved. Ishmael, not Ahab, is a model for the reformed Zelig, and Moby-Dick illustrates that at least not all of the Great Books must be read as Bloom would read them. Woody Allen's positive teaching warns us not merely against the other-directedness of the unredeemed Zelig, but also against the inner-directedness of Ahab. *Moby-Dick* demonstrates that there is something that stands between the individual and cosmic infinity, for Ishmael lives to tell Ahab's tale to us. In a way, Bloom leaves himself out of his account of philosophy, his own skills as a teacher, and the seductive eloquence of his writing. But he surely knows of the power of love and friendship. He is, in the end, a surprisingly modest man.

Bloom's proposal for a Great Books education does provide a needed complement to Hirsch's concept of cultural literacy. Bloom teaches us that education should lead us to a deeper understanding of our lives, giving us something to love, something to live for, rather than merely conveying cultural facts. But Bloom's interpretation of the Great Books, and of the philosophy they foster, tends to isolate human beings from one another. Cultural literacy itself, I believe, can in turn correct this tendency. If Bloom's tiny band of men seem to be as "liberated from all conventional attachments to religion, country, and family" as the college students he finds so lifeless (CAM, 109; see also 85 and 119), this is not true of those who possess a literate culture. Such individuals share particular or concrete objects of knowledge that connect them to their own country and tradition. Cultural literacy is not at odds with reflection, or even criticism, while reflection itself need not lead to rejection rather than deeper appreciation. Can we not therefore learn something from cultural literacy about the possibility of the bonds between human beings, bonds that some believe that education should sever? Indeed, by exploring the community implied in cultural literacy, I believe that we can satisfy our desire for something higher from education, even our desire for freedom, to which both romantic education and Great Books programs appeal. And I believe that we can do so without denying our own communities or traditions.

Consider, for example, Hirsch's discussion of what items of basic information should be taught in our schools. Educators, he says, must choose "between degrees of worthiness" (CL, 25), but the test of worthiness is whether something is generally known by other members of one's culture. He gives the example of Virginians having to choose between learning about Abraham Lincoln or Jeb Stuart. "The concept of cultural literacy," he writes, helps us to decide in favor of Lincoln "because it places a higher value on national than on local information." Knowledge of Lincoln is more useful for communication with Americans throughout the nation: "the priority [of learning about Lincoln] has nothing to do with inherent merit, only with accidents of culture" (CL, 26). But is it simply accidental that Lincoln is remembered and not others? Many items of cultural literacy like Lincoln are part of our national culture precisely because of their merit. It is because Lincoln's statesmanship added an important dimension to American culture that he is remembered. He is remembered because he is worth remembering. When Hirsch lists "what literate Americans know" he includes Lincoln—as well as the Emancipation Proclamation, the Gettysburg Address, and John Wilkes Booth—and not Millard Fillmore, for example, and many other

United States presidents. This is not due to chance. We can understand more about our country and about human life from studying Lincoln than from studying Fillmore. What literate Americans know is to some extent what they should know. The trivial does not endure.

Consider also the story Hirsch tells of a memo that his father sent to associates in the commodity business, a story intended to illustrate how background information functions in communication. His father wrote only "There is a tide," counting on his associates to recognize Brutus' words from *Julius Caesar*, and thereby understand that time is ripe for action. But does this story illustrate the role merely of facts in communication, as Hirsch suggests (CL, 9)? Why does Hirsch's father quote Brutus rather than directly urge his associates to act? Brutus' words indicate—and the play illustrates—that there are times when individual action makes a difference for one's life and for the lives of others, but that those times pass. They remind us—more or less depending on our familiarity with Shakespeare's play—of human freedom and its limits, along with a concomitant responsibility to act when action is called for. Hirsch's argument why we should learn "familiar quotes" indicates nothing of this larger sense of humanity's freedom and responsibility. His father's use of Brutus's words conveyed this sense of the importance of one's actions. Although he applies this quotation from *Julius Caesar* to dealings in the business world, he evokes its context—risk for the sake of something important—and thereby finds in otherwise mundane dealings a broader concept of humanity. There is more to cultural literacy, we might say to Hirsch, "than is dreamt of in your philosophy." Indeed, there may be something in it that resembles a Great Books education, if that education is understood to teach a person his connection with the great individuals and ideas of his tradition. And however more deeply some may understand *Julius Caesar* than others, there is not the radical disproportion between them that Bloom finds between the philosophers and the rest of mankind (CAM, 291), between those who devote their lives to learning and teaching and those who, for example, are involved in the commodity business.

Culturally literate Americans should understand not only who Abraham Lincoln was, but *why* he is important to their literate culture. They should not merely remember certain lines in Shakespeare's plays that others also remember, but they should understand why those lines are remembered. That is, they should understand what they mean for human life. Cultural literacy cannot be value free. To teach it as if it were is to fail to provide what is necessary for communication. For in the background of communication and necessary for it to occur successfully are not merely bits and pieces of cultural information but understandings of what is better and worse, noble and base. The facts that Hirsch wants educators to convey cannot be divorced from the values that give them meaning.

Cultural literacy suggests not merely a group of people who can communicate because they have the same background information, but a moral and intellectual community. As a community based on shared understandings of what is admirable and base in human life, it might provide a firmer foundation than a list of facts for the deliberation and choice that are essential to democratic self-government (*CL*, 12). When our children are taught their literate culture, they become part of larger wholes, traditions formed by Western civilization and by the life of the American nation. Although cultural literacy might very well make possible economic and political advancement, it is therefore not merely a means to private goals. Rather, it constitutes a basis for individual and community identity. Culturally literate Americans are not "abstract" humanity or free-floating philosophers; they are twentieth-century Americans, with ties to their nation and their civilization.

Cultural literacy so understood is analogous to a Great Books education, if that education also fosters an understanding of our tradition. Learning about one's culture can do for younger students what Great Books can do for older ones, and, indeed, should help to prepare them for that later education. To foster aspects of a Great Books education in the early acquisition of cultural literacy makes cultural literacy more than a skill; it would be important in the formation of character and mind. To encourage reading Great Books in the spirit of cultural literacy so understood would help students become more reflective members of their community, not expatriates who look down upon it with indifference. Only together can Hirsch's and Bloom's educational proposals offer an antidote to the educational malaise these men so eloquently describe. There need be no radical difference between the education of the working class Americans with whose prospects Hirsch is concerned and that of the privileged youth in the universities on whom Bloom focuses.

The educator who teaches cultural literacy in this way or who introduces students to the Great Books does not curtail freedom, imposing his own values on students as he leads them to understandings that go beyond mere information. Rather, he makes freedom possible, for he encourages the reflection that frees an individual from, in Hirsch's words, "the powerlessness of incomprehension" (*CL*, 12). That powerlessness, however, is not merely the one with which Hirsch is concerned, one stemming from an inability to communicate with others. It is a more subtle powerlessness, perhaps unknown to its possessor, that comes from lack of reflection on the meaning of the culture in which he lives and from which to some extent he derives his identity. There is much truth, in other words, in Rousseau's contention that we are slaves to the society that forms us and in Bloom's view that education should release us from the prejudices that society gives us. Regardless of whether critical reflection can lead some to a philosophical transcendence of time and place, however, it is the necessary support for democratic self-governance. Such an education might well change a person profoundly, as Bloom says education should do, but it could make him more, not less, a citizen of democracy.

Although an individual's belonging to a particular literate culture may be a historical accident, how he understands his culture, how he responds to it, how he assimilates it is not necessarily due to chance. We have seen Hirsch emphasize the extent to which the elements of a literate culture are accidents of history.

But he also speaks of "the culture makers . . . in the early days of a nation," who while they "are limited . . . by the range of materials that history has made available to them" make "choices . . . from those possibilities [that] are not always inevitable" (CL, 84). These culture makers, of whom Hirsch appears to approve, did not transmit mere descriptions; they chose what they thought was worth remembering, having reasons for their choices. And although there are "persistent, stable elements . . . at the educational core [of a literate culture]," as Hirsch says, the content of a literate culture changes in part even from generation to generation (CL, 28–29). "Cultural revision," Hirsch writes, "is one of our best traditions" (CL, 101).

Literate culture is not static, and whether it is determined primarily by the accidents of history or the choices of human beings depends on whether they make those choices. Hirsch's insistence on merely describing what literate Americans know leaves change to chance. By so doing, he surrenders the freedom implied in education—the "not always inevitable choices" of *what* students learn. The freedom of the culture makers is shared by teachers and students in the classroom: just as culture makers embody what they think worth remembering in literate culture, teachers lead students to see the significance of the elements of their literate culture. Their understanding allows them to choose, in the words of the nineteenth-century authors of *Everyday Classics* quoted by Hirsch, "the best things in [our] moral and intellectual heritage" (CL, 132).[26] Teachers who merely transmit bits and pieces of information because they are elements of a literate culture and students who merely receive such information are only passive instruments. This is true as well of those who compile lists of information that only reflect what exists in the minds of others, and leave change to the accidents of history.

Since the culturally literate individual, whether culture maker, teacher, or student, does make choices, he is not bound by the given. But because his choices are informed by his reflection about the elements of his culture and their meaning, his freedom presupposes a dependence of human beings on civil society. As a member of a particular culture, a culturally literate person is neither isolated within himself nor stationed on heights above humanity. He does not possess the radical independence of the abstract romantic or the transcendent philosopher, nor would he want to, for, as Hirsch shows, such a life leads only to poverty and dependence, and alienation from the community in which he lives. More importantly, the possession of a particular culture is natural to man, as Hirsch maintains (CL, xv–xvii). The concept of cultural literacy as I have developed it would lead us back to Aristotle's understanding that human beings are political by nature—and to the freedom and community implied in that understanding. It therefore provides a firmer foundation for democratic self-government than either romantic education or an Ahab-like pursuit of freedom.

Moreover, my interpretation of cultural literacy is consistent with the American political tradition and the principles embodied in its Founding documents, the Declaration of Independence and the Constitution. American independence was declared by a free people who chose to establish a better government for itself when its rulers became oppressive and who justified its actions before humanity. So too do culturally literate individuals evaluate their culture, offer different emphases and revisions, and give reasons for their choices. The concepts of freedom and responsibility embodied in the Declaration of Independence are thus preserved in cultural literacy. But like a people who accept the limits of law, the authority of a Constitution, and a presumption in favor of precedent, culturally literate individuals recognize the place of tradition in forming individuals and giving them an identity. The concepts of continuity and permanence indispensable to constitutional government are thus preserved in cultural literacy. Indeed, the Declaration and the Constitution, and the political history of the nation that developed under their guidance, occupy the core of the education of culturally literate Americans. Highlighting such a core constitutes the kind of choice that Hirsch hesitates to make. Such choices are essential to democratic self-government. Only with such an understanding of cultural literacy can we approach, as Hirsch wishes us to do, "the fundamental goals of the Founders at the birth of the republic" (CL, 145).

NOTES

1. E. D. Hirsch, Jr., *Cultural Literacy* (Boston: Houghton Mifflin Company, 1987), and Allan Bloom, *The Closing of the American Mind* (New York: Simon and Schuster, 1987). I will cite these works in parentheses in this chapter as CL and CAM, respectively, followed by page numbers to these editions. For Hirsch's argument that American education has failed democracy, see, for example, *Cultural Literacy*, pp. xiii–xiv. Bloom's book is subtitled "How Higher Education Has Failed Democracy and Impoverished Today's Students."

2. Hirsch does not find the concerns he expressed in *Cultural Literacy* any less relevant today. In his 1996 *The Schools We Need* (Garden City, NY: Doubleday, 1996), for example, Hirsch expresses many of the same concerns. This later book, he writes, "takes the earlier one [*Cultural Literacy*] as its foundation. . . . In recent years, further empirical evidence has supported the basic correctness of the book's inferences" (12). Hirsch thus offers not a "qualification of [his earlier] argument, but an *extension* of it" (14).

3. See, for example, Jean-Jacques Rousseau, *Discourse on the Sciences and Arts*, in *The First and Second Discourses*, edited by Roger D. Masters, translated by Roger D. Masters and Judith R. Masters (New York: St. Martin's Press, 1964), 179.

4. *Emile or On Education*, translated by Allan Bloom (New York: Basic Books, 1979), will be cited in parentheses as E, followed by page numbers to this edition.

5. Hirsch, *The Schools We Need*, 74. This book takes as its central theme, Hirsch claims, what was "only adumbrated in *Cultural Literacy*—the disastrous consequences of educational naturalism," 15.

6. Rousseau's comprehensive view on education, of course, is more complex than this quotation suggests. Consider not only *The Government of Poland*, translated by Wilmore Kendall (Indianapolis: Bobbs-Merrill Library of Liberal Arts, 1972), but also his prescrip-

tions for the education of Sophie in the *Emile* itself. Unfortunately, the simplified formula tends to be more influential than its more complicated qualifications.

7. It is also true that from time to time Rousseau praises particular philosophers (see, for example, *Discourse on the Sciences and Arts*, 43–45 and 63), but his praises always remain ambiguous.

8. See John Dewey, *John Dewey on Education: Selected Writings*, edited and with an introduction by Reginald D. Archambault (New York: Random House, 1964), and Archambault's description of Dewey's view of the teacher, xxiv; see also xxvi. Carl R. Rogers argues against teaching in favor of "facilitation of learning," which must "permit individuals to go charging off in new directions dictated by their own interests." See "The Interpersonal Relationship in the Facilitation of Learning," in *Humanizing Education: The Persons in the Process*, edited by Robert R. Leeper (Washington, DC, 1967), reprinted in *Innovations in Education*, edited by John Martin Rich, 3rd ed. (Boston: Allyn and Bacon, 1981), 41.

9. Hirsch does make an exception for science, of which the literate American, he thinks, lacks "the essential basic knowledge" (148).

10. One change that Hirsch made between the publication of *Cultural Literacy* and *The Schools We Need* is the name of what he recommends—from "cultural literacy" to "core knowledge." He did so, he reports, when "teachers pointed out that the term 'Cultural' raised too many extraneous questions, whereas the term 'Core Knowledge' better described the chief aim of the reform" (*The Schools We Need*, 13). The change indicates even more clearly Hirsch's attempt to avoid the appearance of imposing any cultural values on others through educational reform.

11. On the other hand, there are those who argue in criticism of Hirsch that any list necessarily reflects its compiler's values. In spite of his intention, they say, Hirsch prescribes rather than describes. Critics of Hirsch also object to his notion that there is a single national culture that all Americans share. Paul B. Armstrong, for example, claims that "pluralistic literacy" is more appropriate to the heterogeneous world in which we live than cultural literacy. He argues that "neither 'culture' nor 'literacy' . . . is as monistic or as codifiable as Hirsch assumes." He criticizes Hirsch for thinking that he knows what cultural literacy is and can tell us. "Pluralistic Literacy," *Profession 88* (Publication of the Modern Language Association, 1988), 29. Such criticisms of Hirsch indicate how pervasive Rousseau's influence is.

12. Some who note the differences between Hirsch and Bloom praise Hirsch for the very "openness" that they think Bloom lacks. See, for example, Jeff Smith, "Cultural Literacy and the Academic 'Left,' " *Profession 88*, 25.

13. See also Helene Moglen's suggestion that Hirsch's program for conveying cultural information discourages thought. "Allan Bloom and E. D. Hirsch: Educational Reform as Tragedy and Farce," *Profession 88*, 59. Moglen is not, however, supportive of Bloom's proposals, either.

14. To be sure, Hirsch does not think that the vague information that constitutes cultural literacy is the only important element in education. He distinguishes "the extensive curriculum" that should be common to all culturally literate Americans from "the intensive curriculum," which provides "a fully developed understanding of a subject, making one's knowledge of it integrated and coherent" (CL, 128). But the content of "the intensive curriculum," according to Hirsch, should vary from school to school, and even from individual to individual. He offers no criteria for choosing the content of one's intensive curriculum. Indeed, it seems to be a matter of personal taste. "The intensive

curriculum is the more pluralistic element of my proposal," Hirsch writes, "because it ensures that individual students, teachers, and schools can work intensively with materials that are appropriate for their diverse temperaments and aims." It is in this context that Hirsch cites Dewey with approval (CL, 128).

15. Harry V. Jaffa has observed that Bloom writes "in the tradition of the great expatriates." "Humanizing Certitudes and Impoverishing Doubts," *Interpretation* 16 (Fall, 1988): 118. According to Jaffa, Bloom shows neither knowledge of nor interest in the American books "that form and represent American character," 118. The same is true of the American Founding and the great issues of American history, 119–131, especially 126.

16. Richard Rorty, "That Old-Time Philosophy," *The New Republic* (April 4, 1988): 28–33.

17. Ibid., 31.

18. Rorty's 1988 criticism of Bloom is not dead. Lawrence W. Levine in his 1996 *The Opening of the American Mind* restates Bloom's position: "He characterized the contemporary university as 'open to all kinds of men, all kinds of lifestyles, all ideologies,' and thus 'closed' to the absolute truths of the classical writings and great books that alone constitute true education." *The Opening of the American Mind* (Boston: Beacon Press, 1996), 18–19. I can find no mention of "absolute truths" in any of the pages of *The Closing of the American Mind* that Levine cites. According to Levine, Bloom finds dangerous those perspectives that "open students to the possibility that *their* culture is not necessarily superior and potentially weakens the conviction that Western culture and 'Civilization' are synonymous," 19. He thus misses Bloom's argument that *the* advantage of Western thought is its willingness to question the identification between one's own and the good, as I quote in the text of this chapter.

19. It is not surprising that Bloom has been criticized as antidemocratic and elitist. See, for example, Rorty, "That Old-Time Philosophy"; Martha C. Nussbaum, "Undemocratic Vistas," *The New York Review of Books* (November 15, 1987): 20–26, and Benjamin Barber, "The Philosopher's Despot: Allan Bloom's Elitist Agenda," *Harper's Magazine*, Vol. 276, No. 1652 (January 1988): 61–65. Harvey C. Mansfield, Jr., defends Bloom against this charge: it is a virtue of liberal democracy, he argues, that it "makes room for outstanding people—for a 'natural aristocracy,' in Jefferson's phrase. . . . Elitism is a necessary feature of pluralism." "Democracy and the Great Books," *The New Republic* (April 4, 1988): 34. There is nevertheless in Bloom's view an incommensurability between the philosopher and the rest of mankind. Bloom says that "the gulf [that separates philosophers from all other men] is unbridgeable." "The philosophers in their closets or their academies have entirely different ends than the rest of mankind" (CAM, 290–291). While elitism may be a feature of democratic pluralism (as Mansfield argues), philosophic incommensurability goes beyond democratic elitism. See also Eva Brann, "Allan Bloom's *The Closing of the American Mind*," *The St. John's Review* 38 (1988): 73.

20. Although Bloom proclaims the importance of political philosophy or political science, its importance lies less in what it might teach the philosopher about politics and the nature of man than in its protecting philosophy from the political community (CAM, 275–276). But since the political community's fear of the philosopher—who questions its most authoritative opinions—is well founded, the philosopher must practice deception. "Presumably he would prefer not to practice deception," Bloom says, "but if it is a condition of his survival, he has no objection to it." Political philosophy thus becomes "a gentle art of deception" (CAM, 279).

21. Bloom makes this statement in the context of criticizing intellectuals who complain

about the vulgarity of modern society. This is something, Bloom, claims, that "philoso-phers [are] willing to live with," inasmuch as "all societies look pretty much the same from the heights" (CAM, 293).

22. As Bloom writes, "a peaceful, wealthy society where the people look up to science to support it is worth more than splendid imperia where there are slaves and no philos-ophy" (CAM, 293).

23. Hirsch notes that William Bennett's endorsement of the ideas in *Cultural Literacy* has led people to incorrectly identify cultural literacy with the reading of Great Books. Hirsch distinguishes cultural literacy from such an approach. According to him, literate Americans require only vague knowledge of the cultural facts that other Americans know. They should know what *Das Kapital* is, for example, but need not have actually read it. The goal that Hirsch advocates is "literacy for *all* our citizens" (emphasis Hirsch's) (CL, xiv).

24. Nussbaum also claims that Bloom's notion of philosophy "seems remarkably empty of content," but berates Bloom for an insufficient interest not in political philosophy but in "the traditional subjects of 'the contemplative life' such as metaphysics, cosmology, and mathematics" ("Undemocratic Vistas," 25). She nevertheless argues that Bloom's ideal philosophic education is insufficiently practical, active, and broadly distributed. She then criticizes Bloom for neglecting analytic philosophers—"serious writers" in philosophy of science and language and in ethics (20, 24). Can analytic philosophy, we wonder, be the broadly distributed philosophy that Nussbaum prefers to one restricted to a small elite?

25. Woody Allen, *Three Films of Woody Allen* (New York: Random House, 1987), 129.

26. These authors, A. H. Thorndike and F. T. Baker, define a classic as "what, in brief, *every child in the land ought to know*, because it is good, *and because other people know it*" (emphasis in Hirsch). While Thorndike and Baker give two reasons, Hirsch italicizes the latter reason and ignores the former (CL, 131).

12

The Illiberal Leo Strauss

ROBB A. McDANIEL

The liberalism of Leo Strauss has always been questionable. While Strauss and his students have been strong supporters of the American regime against its rivals, Strauss's thought appears foreign and forbidding, and his defense of the Constitution strikes much of academic liberalism as decidedly "antiliberal."[1] Most disturbing to liberals, Strauss issues a rousing call to arms against modern egalitarian ideals. That Strauss left behind a faithful school of followers ready to defend classical aristocracy only adds to his perceived threat.

Strauss announces his elitism in an apocalyptic rhetoric, one that focuses on the "crisis of the West" and highlights his divergences from modern liberalism. Resurrecting the classical Greeks, Strauss describes a hierarchical "natural" order in which "philosophers" and "gentlemen" rule over the "vulgar" democratic masses. Inequality is not only natural, it is radical: the differences between human types are not ones of degree but ones of kind. For Strauss, some human beings are simply more noble than others. The great gap between these human types produces essential conflicts, requiring that philosophers conceal their true beliefs. Of course, Strauss also musters a defense of liberal democracy, albeit on grounds far removed from the ideals of liberty and equality. While this alternative legitimation should raise questions, it more typically draws battle lines. Strauss's critics object to the implicit immorality of Strauss's disseminating "philosophers" and the arrogance of those Straussians who see themselves as belonging to that exclusive club.[2] Strauss's rediscovery of "esoteric teaching" renders suspect his own political rhetoric. Naturally, Strauss's defenders protest that he is innocent and misunderstood.[3]

Generally missing from this debate is a systematic analysis of Strauss's anti-egalitarianism. There are some genuine ambiguities at the heart of Strauss's account of natural inequality, most notably in his articulation of the "philosopher." Given the centrality of the philosopher to Strauss's work, any examination of equality must take a critical look at these ambiguities. The gap in Strauss between the wise and the vulgar is more nuanced and graduated than is often recognized. "Wisdom" and even "philosophy" are continually put into question in his work. When these ambiguities are taken into account, Strauss's defense of liberal democracy takes on added complexity—it is, paradoxically, staunchly antiliberal while also genuinely accommodating of liberalism. In this essay, I suggest that an examination of this ambiguity may prove useful for those who would think through liberalism, not for its outright destruction, but for its eventual ennobling.

Strauss's disavowal of democratic equality is one of the most conspicuous themes of his writing, even if he often presents this as a friendly critique.[4] Although Strauss finds liberal democracy far superior to its immediate challengers, communism and fascism, this does not mean that he is a liberal democrat. It certainly does not mean that he endorses liberalism as it is commonly understood: "the safeguarding of . . . rights."[5] Being an "ally" of liberal democracy is not the same thing as actually "being" a liberal democrat. At the same time, Strauss adapts his antiliberalism to surprisingly modern idioms.

Strauss devotes much of his work to an attack on the natural rights doctrines that underlie modern democracy, a critique made in the name of "classical natural right." This "classical" conception is based in a hierarchical ordering of human souls, one anchored not in "freedom" but in "virtue."[6] Freedom is an empty goal. The liberal argument that government must provide only a negative freedom *from* restraint ignores the fact that the individual concerned with living the best possible life must necessarily ask, "Freedom *for* what?" Philosophical liberalism thus refuses to address what for Strauss is the ultimate question—what sort of human beings are capable of maintaining the "good life"? While liberals hold that those who are protected in their freedom will gladly help protect others in theirs, Strauss is not so sure. From a political standpoint, Strauss argues that modern liberalism increasingly lacks both the intellectual resources and the courage of conviction to defend itself against outside attacks.[7] What is needed is a return to virtue, both political and philosophical. The American regime is praiseworthy only insofar as it vaguely resembles the classical "mixed regime" (i.e., our institutions are not simply "democratic") and allows for liberal education, "the necessary endeavor to found an aristocracy within democratic mass society."[8]

Strauss thus appears to share parts of the "communitarian" critique of liberalism and modernity.[9] But Strauss takes what seems a more radically anachronistic turn. He argues that the paragon of virtue is the "philosopher," whose pursuit of universal truth makes him an imitation of God. Nature is hierarchically ordered, and the soul mirrors this natural order. Reason, which "distinguishes man from the brutes," is the soul's highest faculty.[10] Those who perfect reason are the highest human type. Taking his point to its extreme, Strauss makes the philosophic "way of life" the central theme of his writing, often describing this life in ways that cause his critics great concern. Specifically, he argues that "philosophers form a class by themselves."[11] This class has its own "selfish interest" which necessarily conflicts with that of society as a whole.[12] Strauss refers approvingly to those classical writers who recognized "that the gulf separating 'the wise' and 'the vulgar' was a basic fact of human nature" and that "philosophy . . . was essentially a privilege of 'the few.' " These writers saw that philosophy "was suspect to, and hated by, the majority of men."[13] Since the city rests on popular beliefs, and since the questions of a skeptical philosopher undermine this foundation, conflict is inevitable. It derives from the variety of human ends: materialism, honor, and truth. Although these drives can coexist, one end will generally predominate. If humans are determined by the principles that guide them, and these principles differ essentially, the city is grounded in a strong sense of human plurality.

Despite their classical pretensions, Strauss's ruminations on the philosophic "class" and its "selfish interests" are the formulations of a modern "sociology."[14] His argument that, starting with Socrates, philosophers realized that they had to learn to live peacefully with their essentially incompatible neighbors is a model for post-modern liberal accommodation—political peace without the sacrifice of group identity. The fact of persecution, a realization that the conflict of principles is often violent, makes the question a pressing one, one that Strauss often ties to the problems of modern Judaism.[15] Much like the communitarians, then, Strauss accommodates his "classical" critique to the language of modern liberalism and post-modern pluralism. Liberals are unlikely to be reassured. Strauss does not relegate inequality to the private sphere in good liberal fashion. Instead, he argues that some ends are inadequately accounted for by liberalism. The quest for honor is necessarily political and cannot be quietly pushed to the private sphere. As long as there are internal conflicts and external borders there will need to be guardians who can be trusted to serve the common good.

In opposition to modern egalitarianism, Strauss draws from the Greeks a hierarchical legitimation of government—one that accounts for each human end and which, at the top, seems to feature "the secret kingship of the philosopher."[16] Nature indicates that the "best regime is that in which the best men habitually rule, or aristocracy." Since it "would be absurd to hamper the free flow of wisdom by any regulations . . . rule of the wise must be absolute rule."[17] A philosopher's tyranny, however, is "impracticable" if not "impossible."[18] The only thing more unlikely than the masses asking philosophers to rule is the philosophers trying to convince the masses. Strauss argues that the practically best regime is that in which rule of law substitutes for the rule of wisdom and where "gentlemen"— "the political reflection, or imitation, of the wise man"—administer the laws "equitably."[19] This is the "mixed regime" in which elements of kingship, aristocracy, and democracy are judiciously combined. The best balance places emphasis in the middle, on the aristocratic senate occupied by the "urban patriciate." The "landed gentry" are "well-bred and public-spirited, obeying the laws and completing them, ruling and being ruled in turn."[20] Our present system falls short of this model. In the name of equality, we have substituted materialistic businessmen and lawyers for the naturally political and patriotic patricians.[21] Strauss suggests that our current arrangement may not be able to protect a society from serious threats. Leaders driven by concern for their own bottom line are unlikely to make ultimate sacrifices for others.

While the "gentleman" is central to Strauss's political theory, his critics tend to be more concerned by the notion that philosophers, hiding behind a veil of secrecy, manipulate gentlemen for their own subversive purposes. Strauss indicates that the philosophic life, in questioning social beliefs, undermines morality. More seditiously, he hints that the philosophers do not even respect morality: "justice and moral virtue in general can be fully legitimated only by the fact that they are required for the . . . sake of the philosophic life. From this point of view the man who is merely just or moral without being a philosopher appears as a mutilated human being."[22] The philosopher should still obey the law, but Strauss clearly implies that obedience can only be in letter and not in spirit. Once again, however, this picture is noticeably "liberal": contractualist, morally minimalist, and demanding only self-interested consent to the law, not pious devotion to it. Strauss indicates that Socrates submitted to Athenian authority because of a "tacit contract."[23] If the philosopher wants to enter politics by giving leaders advice, nothing stands in his way except for the fact that no one may want to listen. Strauss fully recognizes that a deaf ear is a likely possibility.[24]

Strauss's elitism could be construed as an attempt to convince those who would think of themselves as "wise men" that it is in their interest to support liberal constitutionalism. If the reasons for this support appear at first glance to derive from the premises of "wisdom," the motives are presented in a liberal language of "interests." Given the crisis of German intellectuals under the Nazis—epitomized by Martin Heidegger and Carl Schmitt—such persuasion could be understandable. But the broader status of Strauss's politics remains unclear. While he adopts a language that is more modern and liberal than is often realized, he raises serious objections to the liberal framework. Liberalism tends to exclude political claims of radical difference, especially when articulated in terms in inequality. The liberal Strauss is not, therefore, the last word.

To understand Strauss's critique of liberal egalitarianism more fully, we must turn to "the philosopher" in Strauss's most important work on these subjects, *Natural Right and History*, tracing his elitism to its philosophic roots. *Natural Right* is not a standard philosophical treatise, however, but is "historically dialectical."[25] Strauss puts ethical theories into dialogue with one another. He presents Greek thinkers answering modern questions, responding to a modern dialogue in a way the "real" Greeks could not have. More specifically, Strauss's Greeks appear in the text as a rebuttal to the twin terrors of modern ethical thought—Weberian positivism and Heideggerian existentialism. In *Natural Right*, Strauss seeks a remedy for the failure of these two thinkers to derive a natural right (or human Ought) from human nature. We should be careful, however, before placing Strauss with simplicity on the side of the ancients. Strauss holds elsewhere that a return to the Greeks can be at best "tentative or experimental."[26] Strauss's classicism is always a move *through* the moderns.

Strauss grounds both inequality and natural right in an account of nature and "the ideas." He uses "idea" in a dual sense.[27] First, the ideas are "natural kinds": those things about which we can ask common-sensically, "What is . . . ?" And second, the ideas are "fundamental problems," since to ask what something "is" will generate any number of conflicting opinions. Some ideas, such as "justice" or "man" or "the good" would seem more important and contestable than others such as "tree"—the former are "fundamental" problems.[28] How then do the ideas relate to "nature"?

Eidos means primarily the "look" or the "surface" of the thing—the ideas are those things which, at first glance, look like they belong to a common "kind" or "class." These ideas are what is "first for us," as we would ordinarily experience them. Any inquiry must begin here, "from what comes to sight first, from the phenomena."[29] These classes are not unproblematic. Instead, they are formed by "opinions" about the classes. It is in "what is said about the things" that we actually first come to see "the things." To take a simple example, a whale might be said to be a fish. They appear to belong to the same kind—they swim in the ocean, have small eyes and large tails. Another examination reveals that a whale is not a fish but a mammal. While we may alter our opinion as to which class a whale belongs, we still recognize it as belonging to a class. To clarify the matter we must ask what a whale actually "is." Philosophy thus begins as the quest to understand the things as they are "in themselves," or according to their "principles."[30] Accordingly, Socrates begins with the "opinions about the natures of things" and attempts to ascertain the genuine class character of a thing. Contradicting opinions about the nature of a given thing draw attention to its problematic class character, especially when the thing queried is something as complex as "the good." In an even stronger sense, however, to ask about the character of a "thing," such as a whale, points inevitably back to the character of the thing that forms the opinion, or to the "human" thing—the "idea of man."

The dual sense of the ideas reveals a dual sense of "nature" or "the whole." First, nature is the "natural horizon," or the totality of that which first appears to us by opinion. To borrow a term from modern phenomenology, nature is the immediate "lifeworld," that which, from the outset, we are "given" to understand.[31] This horizon appears to us as a contextual "whole" within which the "parts" of the whole are seen in their referential totality—that is, they must be understood in light of their "being parts" of a greater whole, one that constitutes and makes clear their meaning *as* parts. According to Strauss, "All knowledge, however limited or 'scientific,' presupposes a horizon, a comprehensive view within which knowledge is possible."[32] The parts, understood in their character as distinct parts, are the "ideas," the natural "classes" of things. But as noted, the classes (or the parts) reveal themselves to us, in opinion, as problematic. Our opinions differ as to the genuine character of each of the parts. We must then go to the things as they are "in themselves" or in their first principles. But if we must do this for the parts, we must also do this for "the whole" which makes possible the parts as parts. Here is "nature" in Strauss's second sense. Philosophy is the quest for nature, or the whole as it "is" in itself, in its character *as the whole*.[33]

The great difficulty is that, "the whole cannot 'be' in the same sense in which everything that is 'something' 'is'; the whole must be 'beyond being.' "[34] In other words, we typically understand a part by comparing it to other parts: the whale is understood by comparing it to fish or mammals or humans or the ocean. The whole, on the other hand, cannot be seen by reference to other wholes—there are none. At the moment in which we get outside what we think is a whole (our lifeworld) in order to see its character as a whole, we become aware that it is itself merely a part of some even larger whole. The whole-as-whole can only be understood in contradistinction to the parts which it makes possible. But the whole and the parts are not of the same order. To speak in Heideggerian terms, there is an "ontological difference" between the two. An awareness of nature as a whole is not available to us in the same way that knowledge of the parts is. Nature is a ground that hides itself from sight, behind the ideas, even as it mysteriously makes possible our vision of the ideas. With Strauss's Socrates, we might call this a "knowledge of ignorance," that is, "knowledge of the elusive character of the truth, of the whole."[35]

At the same time, however, "the whole is the totality of the parts."[36] In its hiddenness, nature as the whole makes available to us a certain reflected sight of the ideas—the nature of "things" in their class character. As Strauss goes on to say: "The whole has a natural articulation."[37] If we are ignorant about the whole, our ignorance helps to alert us to a certain understanding of the parts. A difficulty emerges here. It was noted earlier that our understanding of the parts is developed in the realm of opinion and that the conflict of opinions produces the realization that, in order to understand, one must ask of that part the question "What is it?": for example, What is a whale? Is it fish or mammal? But the unavoidable reference to opinion makes it clear that our access to that "thing" is always mediated. "We" get in the way. We think the whale is a fish. For this reason, to understand the nature of a thing one must also ask about the nature of man, or "the idea of man." The "Socratic turn" toward the "human things" is therefore a *necessary* one, not one made for purely "political" purposes.[38] Philosophy, to be what philosophy genuinely "is," as a "quest for knowledge of the whole," must always already be political philosophy.[39] The phenomenon of "man" should be seen as it is revealed socially, hence in terms of law and politics.[40]

What then is man? Strauss, following Socrates, makes two approaches to this question: "by appeal to the 'facts' " and also "from the 'speeches.' "[41] The first approach is an examination of man as a thing, the second, of man as an opinion. First the facts. Strauss argues that conventionalist arguments, which equate "the good" with "the pleasant," fail to account for the human constitution that grounds our wants, which in turn determines what we find pleasant. Man, as a natural class, is distinguished from animals in terms of its wants by "speech or reason or understanding."[42] The life of the mind is the defining part of man's constitution.

But why is human essence drawn from its distinction (or its height) rather than from its common animality? Strauss argues from the phenomenon of "admiration": the experience of excellence in others that contains "no reference to one's selfish interests."[43] Admiration transcends concern with one's "own." It is freely given regard for the superiority of another. This phenomenon points in turn to man's natural "sociality": the fact that "Man refers himself to others, or rather he is referred to others, in every human act."[44] Man is "constituted" socially as the animal who compares. Love, affection, friendship, and pity are all based in man's natural social constitution and not in a utilitarian calculation. This is important for two reasons. First, man can be said to be that being which desires "to be" what it admires—hence, what it "is" not. Man has a *telos*. Second, admiration and sociality point together toward man's high regard for justice, the notion that society should give people what they deserve. If man has a *telos* and man is social, man writ large (or society) also has a *telos*.[45] It is here that Strauss begins his discussion of the city, culminating in his analysis of the best regime. Aristocracy is that regime which, by uniting sociality and admiration, achieves justice. It is where the "best men," those "who embody the admired habits or attitudes" are seen as authoritative "in broad daylight."[46] From an elaboration of the phenomenological facts, Strauss contends that the human being "is" in such a way, both individually and socially, that it pursues an authoritative Ought.

The question now becomes one of what sort of being man should admire or "should be." Strauss now turns away from the facts to the "speeches." The philosophic turn to the "human things" is itself precipitated by the observation that our view of "the things" is conditioned by our opinions about the things. This seems especially true of the "experience" of admiration. While the facts show human "actuality," the speeches show human "potentiality." Since man "is" that being who strives to be what he is potentially, human nature requires a turn to speech. An analysis of the facts of human nature can only establish *that* man admires and aspires, but not *to what* he admires and aspires. So far then, Strauss has only managed to arrive at the Weberian "categorical imperative": "Thou shalt have ideals!"[47] Strauss notes that this is a purely formal imperative lacking in content. To understand man fully, one must understand man's best opinion of man, or man as an "ideal." In accord with the principle of admiration, one should turn to the most admired or authoritative opinions. For Strauss, if not for the world at large, this means the opinions of the great philosophers. He presents three possible variations of "natural right": the Socratic-Platonic, the Aristotelian, and the Thomist.[48] Given Strauss's consistent celebration of Socrates, we may provisionally assume that Socrates is his authority. But Socrates is not simply the most profound thinker to have walked the earth. Rather, Socrates, paralleling Plato's "just city," is that philosopher who exists "in speech." As Strauss says elsewhere: "The Platonic dialogues 'idealize' Socrates."[49] Plato's Socrates is man as he is potentially.

What does possibility mean for Strauss? Discussing the possibility of the best regime, Strauss notes that it "was perhaps never actual" and may never become so. In fact, "It is of its essence to exist in speech as distinguished from deed."[50] The same may be said of the best man: "In order to reach his highest stature, man must live in the best kind of society."[51] The highest human possibility then exists essentially only in speech. As Strauss goes on to say, "Human nature 'is' in a different manner than its perfection or virtue. Virtue exists in most cases, if not in all cases, as an object of aspiration and not as fulfillment. Therefore, it exists in speech rather than in deed."[52] If Socrates is man as he potentially is, he is also man who "is" only potentially. He is the utopian man. Why should we accept the authority of Socrates? An answer to this question depends upon the logic of speech, or the relation of opinion and truth.

Strauss describes philosophy as an "ascent from opinions to knowledge or to the truth, in an ascent that may be said to be guided by opinions."[53] As such, philosophy is dialectical or conversational. This "ascent" is necessary because of the contradictory nature of mere opinions. Strauss continues:

Recognizing the contradiction, one is forced to go beyond the opinions toward the consistent view of the nature of the thing concerned. That consistent view makes visible the relative truth of the contradictory opinions; the consistent view proves to be the comprehensive or total view. The opinions are thus seen to be fragments of the truth, soiled fragments of the pure truth. In other words, the opinions prove to be solicited by the self-subsisting truth, and the ascent to the truth proves to be guided by the self-subsistent truth which all men always divine.[54]

Here is the movement between the two kinds of nature, nature as "the whole" and nature as original "lifeworld." By getting outside an immediate horizon, one comes to see its contradictions, hence its limited character, but one also comes to a broader view. As long as this broader view remains consistent it will be comprehensive, if also provisional. The "quest for an adequate articulation of the whole" has an "unfinishable character."[55] For this reason, philosophy is not a matter of arguing from evident premises. The ideal is never attained. Truth reveals itself only negatively, through our ability to reject contradictory views and rise to higher consistency. For Strauss, "the ascent to the truth proves to be guided by the self-subsistent truth." Truth draws human understanding forward even as our backs are turned.

This explains why Strauss's Greek return passes through the moderns. To determine the truth about human nature, Strauss must arrive at a consistent view, one that reconciles the most comprehensive opinions. In their concern with the facts, however, the great moderns give short shrift to man in his possibility as it appears in speech. The source of the modern failure to secure an Ought can be found in Machiavelli's and Hobbes's efforts to turn possibility into actuality— possibility becomes "power."[56] In the process, man's aspiration toward the good life (what he ideally "may be") becomes limited to what he is capable of (what he actually "can do"). Strauss's turn to the classics thus depends upon there being a "possibility" which, while consistent with human nature, cannot be fully converted to actuality. There must be an "ideal," or object of admiration, that exists only in speech. Plato's Socrates is the ideal because he is, on a provisional basis, the most consistent expression of human possibility that is also irreducible to actuality. He is the ordered soul, self-sufficient and lacking in contradiction.

What does it mean to be an "ordered" soul? The psychology of Socrates can be understood in relation to the different types of men. In *Natural Right*, Strauss deals primarily with three types: the philosophers, the gentlemen, and the vulgar. If there is but one idea of man (Socrates), what is the basis for Strauss's claim that there are essential differences between the human types? The human being is that creature which, by virtue of its social constitution, admires and reasons. But there are many possible objects for reason and admiration. Not everyone wants to be Socrates. The objects of admiration can be understood in terms of nature and the whole. Nature as "the whole" has a "natural articulation" in terms of "the parts." A particular part is a "thing." But not all parts are created equal. One thing is privileged—the human thing or things.[57] This is because the "human thing" is the only part which is aware of its "being" a part. Man is that part of the whole that has some awareness of the whole. For Strauss, "the human soul is . . . therefore more akin to the whole than anything else is."[58]

We can categorize three distinct levels within nature:

1. nature proper: "the whole" in its character as the whole;

2. the human: that "part" which is aware of, and reflects, the whole; and

3. the things: those "parts" which are unaware of the whole-as-whole.

Man is both nature and thing, that part which "is" insofar as it is "toward" the whole. Since nature is complex, there are different patterns of relatedness to the whole. The distinct types of human correspond to these three levels of nature. First, the "philosopher" is the one who strives for knowledge of the whole through a reflected understanding of the ideas, or the discrete parts taken as wholes. The philosopher views man in his possibility of being toward nature as a whole. In being open to the human in its highest possibility, the philosopher is open to the whole. The second human type is the "gentleman," who Strauss calls "the political reflection, or imitation, of the wise man."[59] The gentleman is the "political man" whose concern is local justice. Where the philosopher rejects human particularity for the "ideas," the gentleman "cannot accept this radical deprecation of man. . . . He must 'care' for man as such."[60] Like the philosopher, the gentleman is open to man as man, hence in his possibility. But the gentleman is "attached" to the human and does not necessarily admire the philosopher. Gentlemen are open to human possibility only in man's class-character (hence in the capacity for communal justice), not in the quest for the first or natural things. For this reason, the gentleman appears to the philosopher as a "mutilated human being."[61] Finally, the "vulgar" are those who are not at all open to the human in its possibility. The vulgar only regard others in terms of their usefulness, or as "things." On this level, even love is merely a concern with one's "own."[62]

Here is the source of radical inequality. Understanding humans as they are requires an understanding of them as they would be. Human "ends" are complex and heterogeneous, rooted in the three-fold relation of man to nature, other men, and things. This schema also grounds the Socratic psychology. Each human relation represents a part of the human soul or the human whole: reason, spiritedness, and desire.[63] Socrates is that individual man whose openness to the whole through his investigation of the idea of man orders his three constitutive relations. At its highest level, the human is attuned to the whole. Knowledge, as *theoria*, orders the soul in accord with nature by existentially subordinating spiritedness (i.e., anger or moral indignation) and desire to reason. According to Strauss, this philosophic openness tends to produce a benevolent detachment from the egoistic relations that obtain between "actual" human particulars.[64] Lower down, the soul's full relations to its world are concealed from it, preventing it from being aware of what it could become in possibility.

For Strauss, the complex structure of nature reveals a corresponding pattern of natural right or the human Ought. The fact of admiration, or what could also be called the "experience of inequality," shows how humans pursue different ends (wisdom, honor, and gain) at each level of the relation to nature. Accordingly, Strauss's ethics depend upon a delineation of three economies of admiration—one for intellect, a second for politics, and a third for material gratification. Radical inequality is grounded in the ideal distinction between these three economies.

The idealism of Strauss's ethics should not be taken in isolation from his politics however. The theory of natural right is only half of "Natural Right and History." If ethics requires a turn from the real to the ideal, politics requires a movement from possibility back to actuality, or to the empirical realm of history. What then is the politics of radical inequality?

On the concrete plane of history, revelation becomes the key obstacle to Strauss's ethics. Revealed religion alters and obscures the possibility of philosophy. Because philosophy is essentially the pursuit of a possibility—that of the Socratic ordered soul—philosophy ceases in some sense "to be" when its possibility is forgotten. As noted, Strauss views the history of philosophy in terms of the flight from possibility conceived starkly *as* "possibility," a flight into power and "actuality." He traces this decline to the intrusion of early Christianity into philosophy.[65] The modern philosophers then merge the traditions of Greek philosophy and Biblical morality. Starting with Machiavelli, who imitates Jesus, and ending with Heidegger, who wants to create a space for a "world religion," the modern "philosophers" are a succession of secular messiahs trying to create a city of Man.[66] History is the story of how the "possibility of philosophy" slips into a revolutionary "pseudo-philosophy" defending "superstition" by means of "propaganda."[67]

As a practical question, we might wonder what Strauss actually wants to *do* about this "crisis of the West." In *On Tyranny*, Strauss debates Alexandre Kojève on the fate of philosophy in the current age. They agree that philosophic "actuality" is sought in modern thought by the dispersion of knowledge. But Strauss plays Nietzsche to Kojève's Hegel, asserting that one contradiction has not and *cannot* be politically reconciled. Against Kojève's "world-state" at the "end of history," Strauss contends that the "last men" cannot be universally satisfied:

But perhaps it is not war nor work that constitutes the humanity of man. Perhaps it is not recognition (which for many men may lose in its power to satisfy what it gains in universality) but wisdom that is the end of man. . . . But if the final state is to satisfy the deepest longing of the human soul, every human being must be capable of becoming wise. The most relevant difference among human beings must have practically disappeared. . . . The actual satisfaction of all human beings, which allegedly is the goal of History, is impossible.[68]

Strauss speaks about the philosopher "class" in a sense reminiscent of Marx's proletariat.[69] He even hints that he is waging a class war: "The philosophers in their turn will be forced to defend themselves or the cause of philosophy. They will be obliged, therefore, to try to act on the [Final] Tyrant."[70] The sometimes apocalyptic tone of Strauss's rhetoric derives precisely from his acceptance of the historicist's version of history.

What would a philosopher's revolution look like? Strauss could not accept a reconciliation of the contradiction. There would need to be a permanent revolution. To avoid the ideological capture of philosophic "possibility," the philosopher and the state must be brought to see the ineradicable nature of their conflict. Instead of convincing the city that the philosophers are harmless, Strauss would need to antagonize the city and sow dissent among the philosophers. This would explain Strauss's rhetorical advocacy of esotericism and the necessity of maintaining a radical "gap" between the wise and unwise. Yet Strauss can only act in the liberal West, since communism and fascism both destroy philosophy as a possibility. At the same time, philosophers would need to remain politically limited to avoid the subversion of "possibility" in modern ethics. This is a difficult tightrope to walk, both intellectually and rhetorically. Strauss puts himself in the position of demanding a revolution to end philosophy-driven revolutions.

Of course, it is by no means obvious that a "revolution" is possible. There is something comical about philosophers waging a class war. There are structural barriers as well. Strauss is concerned about the combination of technology and empire that modern thought has encouraged.[71] These occurrences, combined with the obscuring of philosophy in its original possibility, make him suspicious of modern democracy in a way that his Plato need not have been. Granting the dispersion of knowledge and the increase of power that these developments imply, it seems unlikely that the genie of "enlightenment" can be put back in the bottle. Strauss really has nowhere to re-turn as a *political* radical.

Moreover, who would fight such a revolution? The philosophers are an elusive bunch. Strauss's ethic requires that there have never really been any philosophers in the strictest (Socratic) sense. In somewhat broader terms, one could say that the actual "philosophers" are those who live, to the highest practical degree, in pursuit of the Socratic ideal. Strauss opens this possibility in his discussion of Weber: the Weberian imperative "might seem to create a universal brotherhood of all noble souls; of all men who are not enslaved by their appetites, their passions, and their selfish interests; of all 'idealists.' " But Weber's relativism cannot support such an "invisible church."[72] Strauss, on the other hand, returns to this possibility in his analysis of how Socratic natural right answers the call for a "world-state":

what is divined in speaking of the "world-state" as an all-comprehensive human society subject to one human government is in truth the cosmos ruled by God, which is then the only true city, or the city that is simply according to nature because it is the only city which is simply just. Men are citizens of this city, or freemen in it, only if they are wise.[73]

As Strauss indicates, this ethical ideal "obviously transcends the limits of the political life" and implies that actual political justice "can only be imperfect."[74] Strauss offers us philosophy as an elite Greek Calvinism: the visible church strives hopelessly to be Socrates. Philosophy has entered the age of religious revelation and an era of historical resignation.

While Strauss's ethics points to an invisible church, his history implies that there are no more "philosophers" even in this broader sense. If being a philosopher depends upon having a certain reflected wisdom—one that helps approximate a well-ordered soul—and this wisdom has been lost, then there are no more ordered souls. Rousseau and Heidegger certainly were not well-ordered individuals. At some point, Strauss's "moderns" all sacrifice intellectual motives to political ones. Strauss is quick to comment that the genuine philosopher is truly "rare" and may not even be alive in our lifetime. He also says that "We cannot be philosophers, but we can love philosophy."[75] Following the principle of admiration, we should become the lovers of the lovers of wisdom. If even Rousseau was not fully "philosophic," it would be strange for Strauss's students to think that they somehow were. It also would not have been very Socratic of Strauss to go around showing people how wise they really were. On the other hand, openly admitting that philosophy is merely a regulative "possibility" undermines the rhetorical effort to free "wisdom" from its subservience to politics.

One might also ask if the historical trend Strauss describes really starts with Christianity. Strauss hints that Aristotle actually begins the mass education of political leaders that lays the groundwork for Machiavellian propaganda.[76] Even Plato, in his own "conservative way," begins to influence politics in a way that Socrates had not.[77] And, of course, much of Strauss's later work shows that even Socrates was not really "Socrates." The utopian "citizen-philosopher" Socrates who exists in speech could not have been attacked so justifiably by Aristophanes.

Philosophy may *never* have been more than an object of aspiration. This seems logical given the difficulty of loving an "object," such as wisdom, that can never actually "be" an object because of its ultimate unavailability.[78] Philosophy only becomes a theme in Plato's *Republic* by abstracting from the bodily desires.[79] While Strauss makes this claim in order to argue that the "just city" can never exist in actuality, it is reasonable to ask the same question of "the philosopher." Is it ever possible, "in deed," to abstract from the body? In Plato's *Laws*, where the bodily *eros* is not abstracted, "philosophy" never becomes an explicit theme and is only barely mentioned. In the *Sophist* and the *Statesman*, the "philosopher" comes to light only negatively, in terms of what he "is not." If the essence of philosophy lies in its pursuit of an unattainable possibility, we might wonder if it is ever possible, even in the broader sense of an invisible church, to call someone a philosopher.

Given the elusiveness of wisdom, the notion that there is a "radical" gap between the wise and the unwise is questionable, at least if understood in terms of a privileged class of philosophers existing "in deed." Strauss can still hold that some people are oriented toward understanding and that others are not. It may even be true that, at its best, the quest for knowledge can produce the sort of virtuous individuals that Strauss celebrates. But this last conclusion should be taken with a grain of salt. Strauss recognizes that the cultivation of reason guarantees nothing in itself and that political usurpation in the name of wisdom is always suspect on its face.[80] Placed in its proper ethical context, radical inequality is primarily rhetorical—it is a call for heightened responsibility, moderation, and respect for human limits. The philosopher ideal is more a reflection of ethically ordered thinking than a commentary on the brilliance of that thinking. Esotericism is a cautionary warning about the limitations of wisdom.

On the other hand, the questionable status of the philosopher does not invalidate Strauss's insights into human inequality. Once one accepts the premise that learning is possible, even in some limited sense, inequality follows as a natural fact. Strauss's phenomenological observation that human "difference" is initially experienced in terms of inequality is a sound one. The parent-child and teacher-student relationships are only the most obvious examples of how concrete human relations are inscribed with qualitative evaluations of worth. Even horizontal relationships, such as friendship and marriage, begin in a perception of inequality. To some extent, interpersonal *eros* is fueled by a sense that the desired other is better than oneself. This does not imply a relationship of submission and dominance. Two friends may each regard the other as a superior in some respect. Lasting relationships often consist in mutual admiration. A relationship of equal regard is often an interwoven pattern of alternating inequalities. Furthermore, "superiority" is itself ambiguous. A parent's love is heightened by the possibility that the child represents. Equality, unlike the simple perceptions of inequality, is always a complex achievement.

The political question is not then one of a simple choice between equality and inequality. Rather, we should ask when and where inequality is appropriate.

Relations of inequality can be legitimate if they are dynamic and grounded in an appreciation of human possibility.[81] It is here that Strauss's ethic of the philosopher offers grounds for fresh debate. In his concrete politics of the philosopher, Strauss distinguishes between "philosophic politics" and the "politics of the best regime."[82] The former concerns the education of the potential philosophers, the latter is a matter of producing the "just city" where sociality and admiration come together "in broad daylight."[83] Philosophic politics attempts to secure constructive private inequalities; the politics of the best regime provides for constructive public ones. While there are difficulties in Strauss's practical elaboration of these two politics, neither demands a complete rejection of democratic liberalism.

According to Strauss, Socrates goes to the marketplace primarily "to fish there for potential philosophers," and the philosopher writes esoterically to instruct "the puppies of his race."[84] Strauss's concern for liberal education is a logical outgrowth of his desire to render philosophical thought responsible. There is no open conflict with liberalism here. The private inequalities of a philosophic education are generally compatible with the political equality of democratic liberalism. At the same time, philosophy can become power in a way that creates a radical gap between wise and unwise. Machiavelli may have played a small part in Italian politics, but he has been a force in Western history. If modern thought from Machiavelli to Heidegger has defined itself in terms of power, Strauss's ethics may address a liberal blind spot. The radical possibility of philosophy means that private inequalities can become dangerous public ones. Despite his elitism, Strauss's doctrine of natural right is actually an attempt to rein in this power politically without destroying it. At the same time, his reflections on history show that this is almost assuredly an exercise in futility.

While "philosophic politics" can exist alongside liberalism, the "politics of the best regime" appears genuinely antiliberal. Democratic liberalism has no room for an aristocracy ruled by gentlemen of the landed gentry. Once again, however, Strauss's ideal types are not always what they seem once they are moved from ethical theory to political practice. The gentleman is a suspect figure in Strauss, a "mutilated human being." The problem is not only that the gentleman is "merely" moral, but also that his morality is profoundly ambiguous. Preoccupied with honor, he follows the spirited part of his soul, the source of anger and moral indignation. As long as the rewards of honor are guided by a good legal code, the gentleman will be an admirable completer of that code, capable of interpreting and enforcing it. But righteous indignation can become vindictive and honor can be derailed to serve tyrannical ends.[85] Aristocracy is always in danger of drifting into oligarchy or tyranny, making its defense of inequality openly hypocritical.[86] Nevertheless, Strauss maintains its superiority to democracy. If the gentleman is a requirement of the political *ethos*, that is, a regulative morality defending the "common good" and illuminating the limits of "political man," I do not think Strauss runs into much difficulty. The gentleman satisfies the natural demand that laws treat citizens equitably.

Strauss often takes this position further, however, making the aristocratic gentleman an *economic* ideal. While Strauss recognizes that the "superiority" of the gentleman is questionable—"partly a matter . . . of the accident of birth"—he justifies the position with an argument from economic necessity.[87] Scarcity means that not everyone can afford a proper education. The poor need their children to work. Strauss contends that the rural gentleman is likely to be virtuous because he is concerned only with maintaining his estates and not with increasing them. Monetary necessity is thus unlikely to become an obsessive concern. Strauss understands that this is not a foolproof principle.[88] But even granting its logic provisionally (in a moment of charity), the problem of scarcity is transformed by modern technology, expanding capital, and the diffusion of wealth. There is no reason that the merely preliminary requirement of liberal education cannot be broadly met in an advanced and urbanized constitutional democracy. Although it is legitimate for Strauss to raise the sociological question of how best to maintain an ethical elite, his turn toward the aristocracy seems nostalgic and little more. His celebration of the "patriciate" is inadequate as an approach to the problems of wealth and technology in modern economies.

Here is both the problem and the promise of Strauss's politics. Ultimately, Strauss is unable to provide a concrete or fully satisfying alternative to liberalism. Unlike virulent antiliberals like Schmitt or Nietzsche, Strauss rests content at the margin of liberalism. Importantly, however, he suggests a cautionary comportment between philosophy and politics, one that rests upon respect for the rule of law. For Strauss, liberalism is less an enemy than an unsympathetic host, one that requires tempering in its moments of excess. In this analysis, Strauss shares some ground with "communitarian" thought, an association which becomes closer once the nuances of his account of nature and inequality are taken into account. If Strauss's aristocratic rhetoric, both tragic and comic, is hard to accept as a full-fledged politics, it nonetheless accents his critical distance from liberalism without forcing him to reject its obvious strengths. Through his philosophic *ethos*, Strauss begins to think against modernity, not for its outright rejection, but for its pragmatic amelioration. Read critically and undogmatically, Strauss should be welcomed in the contemporary search for an ethical legitimation of liberal practices and institutions.

NOTES

1. Stephen Holmes, *The Anatomy of Antiliberalism* (Cambridge, MA: Harvard University Press, 1993).

2. See, for example, J.G.A. Pocock, "Prophet and Inquisitor," *Political Theory* 3 (1975): 385–401; M. F. Burnyeat, "Sphinx Without a Secret," *New York Review of Books* 32 (May 30, 1985): 30–37; Shadia Drury, *The Political Ideas of Leo Strauss* (New York: St. Martin's Press, 1988); Richard Rorty, "That Old-Time Philosophy," *The New Republic* 198 (April 4, 1988): 28–33; Holmes, *The Anatomy of Antiliberalism*.

3. See, for example, Werner Dannhauser, "Leo Strauss: Becoming Naive Again," *The*

American Scholar 44 (1974–1975): 636–642; Harvey C. Mansfield Jr., "Reply to Pocock," *Political Theory* 3 (1975): 402–405; Harvey C. Mansfield Jr., "Democracy and the Great Books," *The New Republic* 198 (April 4, 1988): 33–37; Thomas L. Pangle, "Editor's Introduction," in Leo Strauss, *The Rebirth of Classical Political Rationalism* (Chicago: University of Chicago Press, 1989), vii–xxxviii; Hadley Arkes, "Strauss and the Religion of Reason," *National Review* 47 (June 26, 1995): 60–63.

4. Leo Strauss, *Liberalism Ancient and Modern* (Chicago: University of Chicago Press, 1968), 24; Strauss, *The Rebirth of Classical Political Rationalism*, 6.

5. Leo Strauss, *Natural Right and History* (Chicago: University of Chicago Press, 1953), 181–182.

6. Leo Strauss, *What Is Political Philosophy? and Other Essays* (Chicago: University of Chicago Press, 1959), 36.

7. Strauss, *Natural Right and History*, 1–6; Leo Strauss, *The City and Man* (Chicago: Rand McNally, 1964), 1–3.

8. Strauss, *Liberalism Ancient and Modern*, 5.

9. To take only the most prominent examples from the communitarians, compare Alasdair MacIntyre, *After Virtue: A Study in Moral Theory* (Notre Dame, IN: University of Notre Dame Press, 1984); and Michael J. Sandel, *Liberalism and the Limits of Justice* (New York: Cambridge University Press, 1982).

10. Strauss, *Natural Right and History*, 127.

11. Leo Strauss, *Persecution and the Art of Writing* (Chicago: University of Chicago Press, 1980), 8.

12. Strauss, *Natural Right and History*, 143.

13. Strauss, *Persecution and the Art of Writing*, 34.

14. Ibid., 7 ff.

15. Ibid., 32 ff.; Strauss, *Liberalism Ancient and Modern*, 230 ff.

16. Strauss, *Persecution and the Art of Writing*, 17.

17. Strauss, *Natural Right and History*, 140.

18. Ibid., 140; Strauss, *Liberalism Ancient and Modern*, 14.

19. Strauss, *Natural Right and History*, 142; Leo Strauss, *On Tyranny, Including the Strauss-Kojève Correspondence*, edited by Victor Gourevitch and Michael S. Roth (New York: Free Press, 1991), 193.

20. Strauss, *Natural Right and History*, 142.

21. Strauss, *Liberalism Ancient and Modern*, 15–17.

22. Strauss, *Natural Right and History*, 151.

23. Ibid., 119.

24. See Strauss, *The City and Man*, 125; Strauss, *Liberalism Ancient and Modern*, 14; Strauss, *On Tyranny*, 186 ff.

25. Thomas L. Pangle, "Platonic Political Science in Strauss and Voegelin," in Leo Strauss, *Faith and Political Philosophy: The Correspondence Between Leo Strauss and Eric Voegelin, 1934–1964*, translated by Peter Emberley and Barry Cooper (University Park, PA: Pennsylvania State University Press, 1993), 342.

26. Strauss, *The City and Man*, 11.

27. See Stanley Rosen, *Hermeneutics as Politics* (New York: Oxford University Press, 1987), 127–131; Thomas L. Pangle, "Introduction," in Leo Strauss, *Studies in Platonic Political Philosophy* (Chicago: University of Chicago Press, 1983), 2–8.

28. Strauss, *Natural Right and History*, 32–35, 125–126; Strauss, *What Is Political Philosophy? and Other Essays*, 38–39.

29. Strauss, *Natural Right and History*, 123–124.

30. Ibid., 82.

31. Strauss often speaks as if there is a genuinely natural horizon that is "pre-theoretical," or determined completely by the "common sense" articulations of political phenomena (*Natural Right and History*, 77–82). The natural horizon is Strauss's social substitute for the asocial "state of nature"—it is a post-theoretical attempt to grasp the pre-theoretical situation that makes it possible. This can only be achieved by an abstraction from what is taken to be subsequent; that is, it cannot be simply historical but is also ideal. For Strauss, as for Rousseau, it becomes politically important to recapture the pre-theoretical "nature" post-theoretically.

32. Strauss, *Natural Right and History*, 125.

33. Ibid., 82, 124–126.

34. Ibid., 22.

35. Strauss, *What Is Political Philosophy? and Other Essays*, 38–39.

36. Strauss, *Natural Right and History*, 122.

37. Ibid., 123.

38. Ibid., 121.

39. Strauss, *What Is Political Philosophy? and Other Essays*, 11.

40. Strauss, *The City and Man*, 20; Strauss, *The Rebirth of Classical Political Rationalism*, 133.

41. Strauss, *Natural Right and History*, 126.

42. Ibid., 127.

43. Ibid., 128.

44. Ibid., 129.

45. Ibid., 134.

46. Ibid., 137.

47. Ibid., 44.

48. Ibid., 146.

49. Leo Strauss, *Socrates and Aristophanes* (New York: Basic Books, 1966), 3–4.

50. Strauss, *Natural Right and History*, 139.

51. Ibid., 135.

52. Ibid., 146.

53. Ibid., 124.

54. Ibid.

55. Ibid., 125.

56. Ibid., 194 ff.

57. Ibid., 121–122.

58. Strauss, *What Is Political Philosophy? and Other Essays*, 39; see Strauss, *The Rebirth of Classical Political Rationalism*, 164.

59. Strauss, *Natural Right and History*, 142.

60. Strauss, *On Tyranny*, 198.

61. Strauss, *Natural Right and History*, 151.

62. Strauss, *What Is Political Philosophy? and Other Essays*, 35; Strauss, *On Tyranny*, 89.

63. Strauss, *The Rebirth of Classical Political Rationalism*, 165–168.

64. Strauss, *On Tyranny*, 199 ff.

65. Strauss, *Natural Right and History*, 144; Strauss, *Persecution and the Art of Writing*, 168.

66. Strauss, *What Is Political Philosophy? and Other Essays*, 45; Strauss, *The Rebirth of Classical Political Rationalism*, 42; see Strauss, *Natural Right and History*, 172–191.

67. Strauss, *Persecution and the Art of Writing*, 155 ff.; Strauss, *What Is Political Philosophy? and Other Essays*, 45.

68. Strauss, *On Tyranny*, 209–210.

69. Strauss, *Natural Right and History*, 143.

70. Strauss, *On Tyranny*, 211.

71. Ibid., 23–27, 194; Strauss, *What Is Political Philosophy? and Other Essays*, 37.

72. Strauss, *Natural Right and History*, 45.

73. Ibid., 149–150.

74. Ibid., 151.

75. Strauss, *Liberalism Ancient and Modern*, 3–7.

76. Strauss, *The City and Man*, 21; see Strauss, *Natural Right and History*, 162.

77. Strauss, *Persecution and the Art of Writing*, 17.

78. Strictly speaking, there cannot be an "idea of nature." If an "idea" is a discrete "part" that is taken as "a whole" unto itself, it becomes a category mistake to speak of an idea of *the* Whole. This is why "nature" must be taken in the dual sense discussed above— the natural lifeworld and the Whole. The former provides an *analogia* for the latter. Since the lifeworld ceases to be natural at the very moment it is revealed as partial, that is, at the moment when "nature" itself becomes an issue, nature always eludes—it is the "fundamental problem."

79. Strauss, *The City and Man*, 62, 111, 138; Strauss, *The Rebirth of Classical Political Rationalism*, 165.

80. Strauss, *Natural Right and History*, 6, 141; Strauss, *On Tyranny*, 193.

81. Questions of distributive justice would thus be of the utmost importance for political philosophy; see Michael Walzer, *Spheres of Justice: A Defense of Pluralism and Equality* (New York: Basic Books, 1983), for an analysis of this problem that shares some commonalities with my reading of Strauss.

82. Strauss, *On Tyranny*, 205.

83. Strauss, *Natural Right and History*, 137.

84. Strauss, *On Tyranny*, 205; Strauss, *Persecution and the Art of Writing*, 36.

85. Strauss, *The Rebirth of Classical Political Rationalism*, 168.

86. Strauss, *Liberalism Ancient and Modern*, 21; Strauss, *On Tyranny*, 182.

87. Strauss, *Liberalism Ancient and Modern*, 193; see Strauss, *What Is Political Philosophy? and Other Essays*, 37; Strauss, *The Rebirth of Classical Political Rationalism*, 146.

88. Strauss, *Liberalism Ancient and Modern*, 21.

13

The Experience of Totalitarianism and the Recovery of Nature: Reflections on Philosophy and Community in the Thought of Solzhenitsyn, Havel, and Strauss

DANIEL J. MAHONEY

Totalitarianism, the central political phenomenon of the twentieth century, began in 1914 with the guns of August and ended definitively with the collapse of Soviet authority between 1987 and 1991. However, the mainstream of American social science has stubbornly resisted the legitimacy of the category of totalitarianism. They dismiss it as an unscientific term of cold-war opprobrium or, quite rightly, note that in practice no "so-called" totalitarian regime, not even during the worst period of Stalinist or Nazi terror, ever succeeded in establishing total control over society or the recesses of the human mind.

But these objections miss the essential point. The concept of totalitarianism long predated the Cold War, and the best analysts of totalitarian rule have understood that the aspirations toward total domination of the individual and civil society were a *consequence* of a more fundamental ideological determination to create a different "logic" of social life.[1] Raymond Aron, Aleksandr Solzhenitsyn, Václav Havel, Alain Besançon, and Leszek Kolakowski have all located the wellspring of totalitarianism in the phenomenon of ideology.

The totalitarian regimes were above all *ideocracies*, despotisms characterized by the project for the ideological reconstitution of man and the world. These analysts have all freely made a judgment that the social sciences with their aspirations to value-neutrality and their commitment to methodological asceticism (that is, to silence about human nature or human ends) are unable to make: they have judged ideology to be mistaken in its object because, in the decisive respects, it is anti-natural. They have judged ideology in its aspirations and consequences to be a lie. This lie is not to be confused with ordinary or "Machiavellian" lies coextensive with political life itself. It is rather a radical or ontological falsehood that leads to the effort to overcome the natural order itself.[2]

Kolakowski, Havel, Besançon and Solzhenitsyn challenge the "agnostic" sensibilities of a social science which rejects the category of human nature. They argue that totalitarianism is defined not by the achievement of "total" control over human beings, which in principle is impossible, but by the creation of a "surreal" world of ideological discourse and practice. This "surreality" aims to fill and to obfuscate the gap between a mundane or real or natural world resistant to the caprice of the revolutionary will and the requirements of historical necessity, and the "revolutionary" aspiration of ideology itself. According to these thinkers, ideology itself is a powerful testament to the reality of a "natural world," one which can be distorted and deformed by the social engineering of ideologies but one which inevitably "comes back" (Horace). Human nature stubbornly resists the pretenses of revolutionaries to create a "New Man."

In this chapter, I would like to highlight the contribution that Aleksandr Solzhenitsyn has made to our understanding of the phenomena of ideology and natural right. I will also make some references to the remarkably complementary analyses of ideology and "conscience" by the Czech writer and statesman Václav Havel. (I will refer only to the pre-1989 "dissident" writings of Havel.) In the final section of the chapter, I will turn to the work of the political philosopher Leo Strauss who has done as much as any thinker of our time to defend the idea of natural order against the purported authority of History.

THE LIMITS OF THE PHILOSOPHY OF HOBBES

Let us begin with Solzhenitsyn and Havel. The analyses of these two thinkers challenge the superficial self-confidence of a cheerful "nihilist" such as Richard Rorty. Rorty announces that totalitarianism reveals above all the dangerous implications of taking ideas too seriously. He insists that good ("anti-foundational") liberals learn from reading anti-totalitarian writers such as Orwell and Solzhenitsyn a prejudice that "cruelty is the worst thing to do," although he insists that this insight in no way entails the knowledge of a "moral fact."[3] Rorty surely knows that this is not the lesson that Solzhenitsyn or even Orwell wishes us to draw from their work. It is in fact the insight less of a nihilist than of a less than self-conscious Hobbist who dogmatically clings to certain foundational supports after all. According to Rorty, a belief in truth causes men to fight, and from this insight he draws the conclusion that the bodily preservation of the individual is therefore the defining mark of a liberal regime with its accompanying categorical imperative to reject cruelty.

But Solzhenitsyn and Havel point out the limits of Hobbism as a moral and societal principle. Men and women who believe that physical suffering is the greatest evil may, even must, do whatever is necessary to stay alive. But neither Solzhenitsyn nor Václav Havel nor other "dissidents" who stood up to ideological falsehood and risked their liberties and lives are Rortyean liberals. They are partisans of the natural world, and of the legacy of a European morality rooted in natural conscience and Christianity. Solzhenitsyn writes of their indebtedness to the "small change in copper that was left from the golden coins our great-grandfathers had expended, at a time when morality was not considered relative and when the distinction between good and evil was very simply perceived by the heart."[4]

Jan Patočka and Havel in their turn speak about the "solidarity of the shaken"[5] but this is not to be understood as an easygoing plea for the superiority of mere life, or an endorsement of compassion as *the* modern virtue. It is rather a call to affirm our humanity despite the ravages inflicted by ideology's assaults on the bodies and souls of men. It is their answer to those who dogmatically and pathetically assert "the death of God" as the truth about our late modern predicament or situation.

We must reflect philosophically about the meaning of ideology and totalitarianism. This is surely as worthy of study as the Jacobin episode, which, narrowly understood, lasted only two or three years but which paradoxically has enriched political and philosophic reflection for the last two hundred years. Surely, the far more extensive, radical, and humanly destructive experience of totalitarianism in the twentieth century ought to be the subject of an analogous reflection by political theory. And there is reason to suggest that such a reflection needs the experiential framework and resources of moral imagination that writers such as Solzhenitsyn and Havel can provide. As Alain Besançon and Martin Malia have suggested, our best guides through the radical evil of totalitarianism often have been writers who are freed from the methodological constraints of the "human sciences." They are able to grasp the lie imaginatively and to vividly pose the human alternatives present in a world constituted by the lie.

The greatest effort by political theory to conceptualize the "essence of totalitarianism," was a failure, although worthy of serious consideration and highly instructive.[6] Hannah Arendt certainly understood the contingency and originality of the ideological project. Yet she did not sufficiently appreciate its roots in the most radical and radically evil denial of natural right ever known. She, of course, was correct to locate National Socialist totalitarianism within the family of biologically reductionist or "vitalist" ideologies. But she failed to appreciate that its naturalist roots in vulgarized Darwinian or scientific thought were far less fundamental than its revolutionary and post-naturalist exaltation of the human will. She believed that there was something essentially despotic—hierarchic or inegalitarian—about all "essentialist" notions of human nature. She therefore located nature and history as the twin, co-equal grounds of revolutionary totalitarianism and terror. She failed to see that only a non-reductionist account of nature and human nature provides any reasonable foundation for rejecting the amoral impositions of human willfulness or Historical Necessity. A generation ago, Raymond Aron and Eric Voegelin rightly located her error in her not always obvious acceptance of the categories of "German metaphysics," particularly in her pathetic insistence in *The Origins of Totalitarianism* that through totalitarianism "human nature as such is at stake."[7]

THE WORST OF EVILS: THE PARTICIPATION IN THE "LIE"

Solzhenitsyn and Havel follow a different and, I think, ultimately more truthful and fruitful road. They agree that in some decisive moral sense totalitarianism threatens the integrity if not the reality of human nature. They certainly recognized that human *liberties* are at stake. But the question is not whether ideology can close the gap between reality and surreality. That is not an open question, because given the nature of things, the lie will remain a lie. The question rather is whether human beings can maintain their "point of view,"[8] as Solzhenitsyn calls it, or their links to the world of conscience which provide access to the prereflective givens of good and evil, truth and falsehood, responsibility, restraint and awe before the mystery of being and the order of nature, as Havel puts it.[9] The worst evil for the dissidents is not cruelty per se (although cruelty is a malevolent symptom of the systemic anti-naturalism or "constructivism" or "rationalism" of the totalitarian project) but the severing of the individual from his "point of view" or "natural conscience." The worst evil is forced or voluntary participation in the lie. For both Solzhenitsyn and Havel, the ideological lie is the most radical, self-conscious, intensive, and consistent version of a lie at the heart of the modern rationalist and technological project: the subordination of the ends or goals of human nature, of the human soul to a "technology of power" (Havel) that knows nothing about either the natural world of prereflective human experience or the final ends or aims of human life. Havel speaks about the "impersonality of power" as such[10]; Solzhenitsyn locates the modern lie in an anthropocentric humanism that replaced a despotism of the soul in need of correction with a despotism of the body and which measured human things by the impersonal standard of "success" or "progress."[11]

To repeat, the "dissidents" pose a radical challenge not only to Rorty's dogmatic and deceptive anti-foundationalism but also to modern and liberal agnosticism about the good. Ideological despotism has revealed emblematically the moral vacuity and philosophical falsehood of the *entire* modern rejection of the accessibility and knowability of the human soul as a rational and moral entity rooted in a natural order of things.

The Anglo-American intellectuals whose house organ is the *New York Review of Books* despise the "reactionary" and Russian Solzhenitsyn. They rightly sense that he has contempt for "subservience to progressive little notions,"[12] as he put it, echoing Dostoevsky, in his "Nobel Lecture," and most certainly does not believe in the doctrine of Progress in any of its forms. These same intellectuals fawn over the more easygoing and culturally attuned Havel with his sympathies for the energy and youthfulness of popular culture. (They only understand Havel as engaged writer and politician rather than as witness to the truth.) Yet Havel repeatedly makes clear his indebtedness to and admiration for Solzhenitsyn. In *Power of the Powerless*, he endorses the fundamental insight of Solzhenitsyn's Harvard address of 1978, the recognition of the "illusory nature of freedoms not based on personal responsibility and the chronic inability of the traditional democracies, as a result, to oppose violence and totalitarianism."[13] He concludes his most philosophical statement, *Politics and Conscience*, by applauding Solzhenitsyn as a witness to the truth that "it is possible to oppose personal experience and the natural world to the 'innocent' power and to unmask its guile, as the author of *The Gulag Archipelago* has done."[14] Solzhenitsyn and Havel are allies not necessarily in their programmatic statements or intentions but rather in their common dissection of the "modern" and "ideological" lie. They both recognize ideology's link to a more restrained version of the lie at the heart of "modern" theory and practice. Solzhenitsyn and Havel, in somewhat different idioms and with different cultural bearings, call for the reconstitution of the regime of modern liberty on new, postmodernist *foundations*. These foundations must be found in the natural world of "good and evil" that provides a bridge between scientific objectivity and the objectivity of human subjectivity and which must draw also upon the Christian heritage of the West with its "great reserves of mercy and sacrifice," as Solzhenitsyn puts it in his Harvard address.[15] Solzhenitsyn and Havel are partisans of a postmodernist, post-totalitarian foundationalism or naturalism.

Let us turn to a fuller discussion of Solzhenitsyn's penetrating if unsystematic discussion of ideology and natural right in *The Gulag Archipelago*. Finally, we will look at the ways in which the "dissident" call for a postmodernist naturalism supplements but also corrects and challenges the classical rationalism articulated and defended most seriously in our time by Leo Strauss.

SOLZHENITSYN AND THE UNMASKING OF THE LIE

As Martin Malia has observed, *The Gulag Archipelago* is too often read as an epic monument of "man's inhumanity to man," as a book directed against brutality and authoritarianism in its most inhuman forms. It is therefore received as a work of noble but repetitive and mind-numbing overkill. Read in this spirit, after a hundred or two hundred pages the reader puts the book away with a feeling of slightly apologetic relief. There is some truth to this common evaluation of Solzhenitsyn's epic witness to the reality of Soviet oppression and tribute to the memory of the world of the Zeks. Solzhenitsyn's work is long and sometimes repetitive. But it is not finally depressing or devoid of hope. If Orwell's *1984* shows the final defeat of the "last man" in Europe, Winston Smith, at the hands of the Machiavellian inquisitor and ideologue O'Brien, Solzhenitsyn's work reveals the impossibility of ideology transforming or conquering human nature. Human nature cannot be overcome but rather in the course of confronting its sometimes deadly efforts some are led to rediscover the meaning of human existence. They are led to rediscover their "souls" and the possibility of its "ascent."[16] The ontological structure of the world, characterized by permanent natural limits and by ineradicable evil in the hearts of men, cannot be eliminated. The effort to do so, hubristic and corrupting, unleashes unheard-of individual and social evils. The stories, digressions, historical reconstructions, and authorial musings and reflections which characterize *The Gulag Archipelago* are united by a sustained reflection on and rejection of ideology and all its works.

Raymond Aron has aptly and accurately captured the central and animating focus of Solzhenitsyn's works:

Solzhenitsyn's message can be summarized, it seems to me, in two fundamental sentences: There is something worse than poverty and repression and that something is the Lie; the lesson this century teaches us is to recognize the deadly snare of ideology, the illusion that men and social organizations can be transformed at a stroke.[17]

The Gulag Archipelago is then fundamentally a work directed against the ideological lie. It is only secondarily an assault on repression, dictatorship, or even cruelty per se. Solzhenitsyn's corpus, from *Cancer Ward* to *The First Circle*, from *The Gulag Archipelago* until his 1974 appeal to the Soviet peoples, "Live Not by Lies," has been characterized by an analysis of "the lie as a form of existence."[18] A multitude of lies about the past, present, and future, about the reality of Soviet life, about the nature of things, came to characterize the matrix of life under "really existing socialism." Language became dominated by "newspeak," by a wooden, ideological language totally divorced from the elementary facts of social and political life, the evidence of science, and especially the ordinary insights of common sense and the human conscience. The cultured despisers of Solzhenitsyn, largely ignorant of the nature of the lie, were confused by Solzhenitsyn's claim in *From Under the Rubble* (1974) that "the absolutely essential task is not political liberation, but the liberation of our souls from participation in the lie forced upon us."[19] Solzhenitsyn's critics dismiss this as an illiberal and "mystical" affirmation of a "Slavophile Russian." But let us repeat Solzhenitsyn's words, "the absolutely essential task." There are other, less than absolutely essential tasks, among them the maintenance and recovery of political liberty.

The lie as a form of existence is a product of the fundamental ontological denial or negation present at the core of the ideological project: the belief that men and societies can be transformed at a stroke. Behind this illusion lay the mistaken belief that "revolution" or the "historical process" can eliminate the human condition as a world characterized by permanent contradictions and sometimes tragic choices and by the permanent and "mixed" existence of good and evil in each human being. Solzhenitsyn reaffirms something resembling the Christian doctrine of original sin but does so, at least in *Gulag*, on "naturalist" or "experiential" grounds. He discovers the "truth of all the religions of the world"[20] based upon his rational reflections on his experience in the Gulag. Solzhenitsyn writes in the chapter of Volume 2 of *The Gulag* entitled "The Ascent": "They struggle with the *evil inside a human being* (inside every human being). It is impossible to expel evil from the world in its entirety, but it is possible to constrict it within each person."[21]

Solzhenitsyn continues by locating the essential falsehood of ideological revolution in its denial or obfuscation of the following fundamental truth that he discovered during his years in captivity: "They destroy only *those carriers* of evil contemporary with them (and also fail, out of haste, to discriminate the carriers of good as well). And they then take to themselves as their heritage the actual evil itself, magnified still more."[22]

Solzhenitsyn's speech at Lucs-sur-Bologne in the Vendée in the fall of 1993 shows that he believes that this understanding of the possibility of political action, of the exercise of "human sovereignty" which would eradicate evil from the world, first displayed itself during the French Revolution.[23] The Soviet revolution more completely, because essentially ideological, and without its Thermidor, revealed the falsehood of this claim in an unambiguous way. Solzhenitsyn repeatedly calls this falsehood, tied to the historicism of Marxist-Leninist ideology, "the Progressive Doctrine."

Solzhenitsyn summarizes his understanding of the mixed character of human beings in two famous passages from Volumes 1 and 2 of *Gulag*. The first occurs in the chapter entitled "The Bluecaps" where Solzhenitsyn reflects on the unselfconscious refusal of young men like himself to become members of the "organs" or secret police. Some inner intuition held them back, a revulsion against the moral corruption inherent in carrying out the criminal misdeeds of the regime while really advancing one's lust for power and insatiable material desires. Solzhenitsyn is led to a deeper "Socratic" reflection guided by the imperative to "know thyself!" But the self or rather soul that one knows, experientially, noetically, is light years from the man of the Progressive doctrine, totally devoid as he is of all interiority or self-consciousness. Solzhenitsyn writes:

If only it were all so simple! If only there were evil people somewhere insidiously committing evil deeds, and it were necessary only to separate them from the rest of us and destroy them. But the line dividing good and evil cuts through the heart of every human being. And who is willing to destroy a piece of his own heart?

During the life of any heart this line keeps changing place; sometimes it is squeezed one way by exuberant evil and sometimes it shifts to allow enough space for good to flourish. One and the same human being is, at various ages, under various circumstances, a totally different human being. At times he is close to being a devil, at times to sainthood. But his name doesn't change, and to that name we ascribe the whole lot, good and evil.

Socrates taught us: *Know thyself!*[24]

Solzhenitsyn insists that his book is not a "political exposé." It is rather an act of moral recovery and catharsis. It is a repudiation of the lie promoted by almost every current of modern thought. This "lie" asserts that historical and technological progress have displaced, either inevitably, through a science of historical necessity, or freely, through the exercise of the human will, the knowledge or improvement of the soul as the primary purpose of human existence. Most radically, the lie denies any transcendent meaning to human existence. The experience of totalitarianism becomes an opportunity to rediscover the reality of the soul and the moral "drama" of human existence. Solzhenitsyn writes in "The Ascent" in an autobiographical passage which is arguably the most famous in his corpus:

Gradually it was disclosed to me that the line separating good and evil passes not through states, nor between classes, nor between political parties either—but right through every human heart—and through all human hearts. The line shifts. Inside us, it oscillates with the years. And even within hearts overwhelmed by evil, one small bridgehead of good is retained. And even in the best of all hearts, there remains . . . an unuprooted small corner of evil.[25]

Ideology locates evil in the accidental or ephemeral. Revolution can dispose all too easily of recalcitrant classes, reactionary political parties, authoritarian states. But ideology is not aware of what every decent and self-reflective human being knows. It does not know the "mixed" character of the moral nature of man. It therefore does not recognize the reality of the conscience, of natural and sacred awe before the limits of the human condition. It is for providing an opportunity for discovery of self-knowledge that Solzhenitsyn can acclaim in a thoroughly non-masochist sense, "Bless you prison for having been in my life!"

Most fundamentally, Solzhenitsyn discovered that ideology itself is a kind of tribute that falsehood pays to truth. It is a confirmation of the moral nature of man. He writes: "To do evil a human being must first of all believe that what he's doing is good, or else, that it's a well-considered act in conformity with natural law. Fortunately, it is in the nature of the human being to seek a *justification* for his actions."[26]

The phenomenon of ideology shows that human beings respect moral and natural limits even in the very process of violating them. And yet the respect that the ideological negation pays to the natural order of things also allows for and demands the radical intensification of violence and oppression.

Solzhenitsyn explains this process of intensification by comparison with the limited and "natural" character of the crimes of Shakespeare's evildoers: "Macbeth's self-justifications were feeble and his conscience devoured him. Yes, even Iago was a little lamb too. The imagination and the spiritual strength of Shakespeare's evildoers stopped short at a dozen corpses. Because they had no ideology."[27]

It must be noted that this Christian and anti-Communist does not locate the evil of our time in communism per se but in communism as the most "perfect" of ideological justifications for individual and collective evildoing. Christianity itself can be distorted for ideological purposes, and Jacobinism, and especially

Nazism, provide anticipations (in the case of Jacobinism) and rivals (in the case of Nazism) to communism as social theories of ideological justification. Solzhenitsyn writes:

Ideology is what gives evildoing its long-sought justification and gives the evildoer the necessary steadfastness and determination. That is the social theory which helps to make his acts seem good instead of bad in his own and others' eyes, so that he won't hear reproaches and curses but will receive praise and honors. That was how the agents of the Inquisition fortified their wills: by invoking Christianity; the conquerors of foreign lands, by extolling the grandeur of their Motherland; the colonizers, by civilization; the Nazis, by race; and the Jacobins (early and late), by equality, brotherhood, and the happiness of future generations.

Thanks to *ideology*, the twentieth century was fated to experience evildoing on a scale calculated in the millions. This cannot be denied, nor passed over, nor suppressed.[28]

Solzhenitsyn insists that ideology allows ideologues and revolutionaries to pass a precise line of moral demarcation which cuts them off from their own humanity. Ideology invites moral corruption and evildoing on a previously unimaginable scale. When one crosses that line by participating in the repression of real or imagined class enemies, by suspending ordinary moral judgment, by participating in fantastic and unjustifiable falsehood, an individual paradoxically is no longer able truly to justify himself to "the living or to posterity, or to his friends, or to his children."[29] He can only live in the lie of ideological self-justification. In the worst cases, one crosses a "threshold magnitude,"[30] to use a term that Solzhenitsyn borrows from physics, and risks losing one's capacity for repentance once and for all. Ideology cannot "change human nature" but it can magnify the evil inherent in the human heart. To use theological language, it becomes an agent of damnation, where the higher dimensions of the soul risk becoming permanently enslaved to the basest instincts of human nature, without any possibility of *metanoia* or moral recovery.

Solzhenitsyn knows that the temptation of ideology is not irresistible. The lie can be resisted, as his own case powerfully testifies. Solzhenitsyn presents numerous cases of resistance to ideology. In the final chapter of Volume 2 of *Gulag* he tells the story of Anna Petrovina Skripnikova who repeatedly stood up to Bolshevik deceits, despite half a dozen arrests and numerous firings from jobs. She continued to live as a free soul and free citizen, in the midst of a totalitarian regime. She eventually succeeded in working successfully for the release and rehabilitation of prisoners during the Khrushchev period. Anna Skripnikova refused to "participate in the lie," and her refusal was simultaneously spiritual and civic. "And if everyone were even one quarter as implacable as Anna Skripnikova the history of Russia would be different."[31]

Anna Skripnikova had a "point of view." That point of view could not be abolished by the imprisonment or torture or even killing of her body. She was one of the strong souls who knew that her soul was precisely the one possession or treasure which could not be taken from her. The human spirit and conscience are irreducible and remain in principle intractable to the engineering implicit in ideology. Felix Dzerzhinsky himself could not shake the philosopher-theologian Berdyayev during interrogation in Cheka prisons in 1922. Berdyayev maintained his dignity and his principled defense of liberty, and thereby showed that "a human being has a point of view."[32] Unable to risk a public trial, the Cheka released him and sent him into exile. And some prisoners perished rather than lose their souls by abandoning friends or families or their elementary sense of right and wrong. They were unwilling to do anything base or ignoble in order to stay alive.

The communists who were the victims of the purge trials of 1936 often broke down, not merely because of excruciatingly cruel and severe torture, but because they lacked a principled "point of view."[33] They had disarmed their own humanity. They who lived in the lie had no weapons of resistance and no resources of integrity available.

So far, I have avoided a detailed discussion of Solzhenitsyn's Christianity and its relation to his affirmation of a *natural* moral order. Solzhenitsyn is quite clearly a theist who has publicly communicated his belief in the "living God." He is a convert to and practicing member of the Orthodox Church. He is assuredly a serious and orthodox Christian. But his moral vision as presented in his novels and especially in *The Gulag Archipelago* is decidedly phenomenological, experiential, and naturalistic. His distinctly sectarian and even theological affirmations and references are rather muted. Solzhenitsyn affirms the natural world where good and evil find their home in the soul of man. Solzhenitsyn insists in all of his works on the necessity of "repentance and self-limitation" for individuals and peoples. He does so not only because he is a Christian but because repentance and self-limitation are among the highest qualities or manifestations of the well-ordered human soul.

Solzhenitsyn also speaks as a Russian patriot who recognizes what few of his compatriots appreciate: the failure to repent for evil and to punish evildoers, the agents of totalitarianism in the party-state and secret police, the failure of Russian citizens to repent for their role in the perpetuation of the lie, implant evil in the next generation by reinforcing the amoral and anti-civic belief that vice is not only unpunished but is in fact rewarded. This is why Solzhenitsyn applauds the post-World War II process of de-Nazification in Germany; this is why he insists that repentance is the *sine qua non* of the moral recovery of a free Russia.[34] Solzhenitsyn knows what the entire tradition taught: the natural conscience needs the support of habit and education. If there is no comprehensive act of national repentance, if there are no judicial trials for tyrants and murderers, the lie will not be expunged and will continue insidiously to corrupt the life of the nation. Solzhenitsyn proclaims what many of his compatriots do not want to hear. "It is going to be uncomfortable, horrible, to live in such a country!"[35]

THE POLITICAL IMPLICATIONS OF SOLZHENITSYN'S MORAL VISION

Let me conclude my remarks on Solzhenitsyn by briefly discussing the political implications of his moral vision. Solzhenitsyn is not the political reactionary, or Czarist, or theocrat, of media and academic superstition. These are grotesque distortions that ought to be put to rest by Edward Ericson's excellent recent work *Solzhenitsyn and the Modern World*.[36] As the quickest perusal of *Rebuilding Russia* or of Solzhenitsyn's numerous public statements since his return to Russia reveals, Solzhenitsyn even has some kind words to say about democracy, particularly local self-government as a training ground for civic virtue and responsibility. This Russian has read his Aristotle, Montesquieu, and Tocqueville and has clearly established his credentials as a partisan of political liberty.[37] (Did the author of *Gulag* need to establish them in the first place?) He is a liberal conservative of a distinctly conservative cast of mind, part of a long and respectable current of European and Russian political reflection.

Yet there is a limited truth in the criticism of Solzhenitsyn's political stance. He is, of course, no simple reactionary. He rejects a return to monarchy, he criticizes the Middle Ages for an unbalanced despotism of the soul over the body. Yet he seems to imagine a *solution* to the theological-political problem in which the concerns of the body and those of the soul would be perfectly balanced.[38] The moral development of man would become a central, perhaps the central concern of social life. There is perhaps an element of "spiritualism" or "angelism" in Solzhenitsyn's political reflection. The same utopian spiritualizing can be found, in a more modernist idiom, in Havel's expectation that the "apolitical politics" of the dissident experience can define the functioning political life of a modern commercial republic. Solzhenitsyn's and Havel's powerful witnesses to "living in truth" risk becoming a form of conservative "literary politics" if they expect their recovery of the natural world to become the direct and self-conscious basis of modern politics.

Modern politics certainly does not demand a thoroughly "naked public square." But modern liberty is based on a clear separation of power and opinion, a demarcated separation of statecraft and soulcraft. This demarcation may be moderated in numerous ways, but it will not be essentially eliminated or overcome. To reject this separation against the wills of modern peoples, against modern men decisively formed by that separation, would be a revolutionary and perhaps an ideological act. The public vocation of advocates of a reinvigorated naturalism must be more indirect and educative. We must concentrate our resources on the education of opinion within civil society and on the cultivation of those habits and mores which provide support for the maintenance of constitutional government. We must articulate the experience of the natural world which in principle is available to human beings as human beings.

After raising this caveat about a nascent utopianism in Solzhenitsyn's thought,

I would like to draw your attention to a beautiful passage from the third volume of *The Gulag Archipelago* where Solzhenitsyn articulates the limits and possibilities of politics in light of the experience of totalitarianism. He distances himself from the spiritualists who expect nothing from politics (except hindrances, compromises, and repression) and the modern exaltation of social and political action for the sake of the transformation of the world. Chiding Tolstoy's apolitical spiritualism, and seemingly anticipating my objections, Solzhenitsyn writes:

Such were the circumstances in which Tolstoy came to believe that only moral self-improvement was necessary, not political freedom.

Of course, no one is in need of freedom if he already has it. We can agree with him that political freedom is not what matters in the end. The goal of human evolution is not freedom for the sake of freedom. Nor is it the building of an ideal polity. What matters, of course, are the moral foundations of society. But that is in the long run; what about the beginning? What about the first step? Yasnaya Polyana in those days was an open club for thinkers. But if it had been blockaded as Akhmatova's apartment was when every visitor was asked for his passport, if Tolstoy had been pressed as hard as we all were in Stalin's time, when three men feared to come together under one roof, even he would have demanded political freedom.[39]

Earlier in this chapter I characterized Solzhenitsyn's position as soliciting a fuller articulation of a post-modern foundationalism or naturalism. I suggested that some of the politico-philosophical essays of Václav Havel point in the same direction and expressly indicated their indebtedness to the analysis and witness of Solzhenitsyn. An adequate discussion of Havel's distinctive but related presentation of the dissident recovery of the possibility of "living in truth," and the relationship of that insight to his larger critique of modernity's efforts to "systematize" both thought and the world, must be the subject of another essay. Instead, I would like to conclude with a few reflections on the relationship between Solzhenitsyn's recovery and rearticulation of a natural moral order and the classical rationalism most intelligently defended in our time by Leo Strauss.

LEO STRAUSS AND THE RECOVERY OF NATURE

My suggestion is that Strauss's rationalism, in its completed expression, entails a profoundly important but partial and one-sided recovery of the natural world. Strauss's work reveals the disastrous theoretical and practical consequences of modern thought's "decapitation" of human beings. Modern thought severs human life from ends or purposes knowable by human reason. Strauss's presentation of classical natural right, on the other hand, includes the phenomenology of the natural world and the human soul. According to Strauss, these have been distorted or denied by centuries of sedimented theoretical speculation and by dogmatic historicism and reductionism.

Like Arendt, Voegelin, and the Eastern dissidents, Strauss wished to make sense of the political evil of the century: he wished to come to terms with the specifically modern form of tyranny, totalitarianism. He did not believe that totalitarianism was reducible to or identifiable with classical tyranny, but he did claim that totalitarianism was fully intelligible to classical thought. Its two principle "modern" presuppositions, "the conquest of nature" and the "popularization of philosophy or science," were known but rejected by the classics as " 'unnatural,' i.e., as destructive of humanity."[40] Strauss feared the semi-permanent establishment of a "universal and homogenous state," as his debate with Kojève in *On Tyranny* evidences. He feared this possibility, though, primarily as a partisan of philosophy: "the coming of the universal and homogenous state will be the end of philosophy on earth."[41]

But he also opposed ideological despotism in the name of humanity, in the name of human liberty and excellence. A universal and homogenous state, a universal communist despotism, would entail the victory of Nietzsche's "last man." It would establish an unholy alliance between thought and an unprecedented, modernized version of "Asiatic despotism." Strauss, in his "Restatement of Xenophon's *Hiero*" strikingly called for an alliance of warriors, workers, statesmen, and philosophers to defend the possibility of genuinely human thought and action. "Warriors and workers of all countries, unite, while there is still time, to prevent the coming of 'the realm of freedom.' Defend with might and main, if it needs to be defended, 'the realm of necessity.' "[42] This alliance required partisanship for liberal or constitutional democracy. Liberal democracy, although by no means the best regime available to human beings, includes real respect for political limits, allows a place for a moderating rule of law and prevents "the absolute rule of unwise men." Most importantly, it allows space for philosophy and some possibility for the sustenance of human excellence. Constitutional democracy, in Strauss's view, is a modern descendent and reformulation of the mixed regime, one which has accepted the technological mastery of nature and the emancipation of popular appetites and leaves room for popular participation in political life. But like all comparatively decent or moderate regimes, it is a more or less tolerable compromise between "wisdom" and "consent."[43]

I have already spoken of the phenomenological dimensions of Strauss's rearticulation of the problem of natural right. On the one hand, Strauss seems to speak as a partisan of the "humanity" of man. He articulates the classical understanding of the order of the soul against all forms of modern reductionism and historicism. He presents the natural constitution of man as it comes to sight to "common sense," to a human being whose understanding is not distorted by low or base appetites or instincts. The order of the soul is characterized by hierarchical and political governance by the soul of the body. Strauss in his role as phenomenologist of the soul does not speak for philosophy in contradiction to poetry or statesmanship or even to piety. He speaks as a witness to the elementary self-understanding of decent and civilized men: "the proper work of man consists in living thoughtfully, in understanding, and in thoughtful action."[44]

In Chapter 4 of *Natural Right and History* entitled "Classical Natural Right,"

Strauss convincingly articulates "the phenomenon of admiration of human excellence," an admiration which "cannot be explained on hedonist or utilitarian
grounds."[45] One suspects that Strauss had in mind his own admiration for Winston Churchill whom (in his correspondence with Karl Löwith) he freely identified with the magnanimous man described by Aristotle in his *Ethics*. In the same
chapter of *Natural Right and History* Strauss anticipates the argument of Solzhenitsyn about the respect for nature implicit in the very act of ideological justification. Strauss writes:

There is no relation of man to man in which man is absolutely free to act as he pleases
or as it suits him. And all men are somehow aware of this fact. Every ideology is an
attempt to justify before one's self or others such courses of action as are somehow felt to
be in need of justification, i.e., as are not obviously right.[46]

These remarks show in a concrete way the support that "theory" can give to
sound practice against ideological and theoretical assaults on the foundations of
common life. Yet in the same chapter of *Natural Right and History* Strauss proceeds
to explain the "contradictions" inherent in the moral and political perspective.
This is a wholly legitimate enterprise and only a fanatic would deny that the
commonsensical, decent moral consciousness, no matter how natural, needs the
guidance and direction provided by rational reflection. But Strauss moves in
another, and I fear less salutary and reductionistic direction. His rich developments of the Socratic, Platonic, Aristotelian, and Thomistic accounts of the
problem of natural right can only be alluded to here.[47] But his conclusion, a
conclusion that he identifies with the philosophic core of Plato's and Aristotle's
teaching, is in tension with the rich account of the order of the soul and of the
natural world that introduces his chapter. In the course of presenting the variety
of classic natural right teachings, Strauss becomes the partisan of philosophy—
dare I say, against the constituent elements of the natural world. Reasonable
action is reduced to the status of a kind of human deformation and mutilation
finding its partial and derivative dignity as an instrument of the philosophic life.
And the superiority of the noble Churchill to the "erotic" tyrant itself becomes
a genuine question from Strauss's newly formulated "philosophic" perspective.
Strauss writes with uncharacteristic boldness:

If striving for knowledge of the eternal truth is the ultimate end of man, justice and moral
virtue in general can be fully legitimated only by the fact that they are required for the
sake of that ultimate end or that they are conditions of the philosophic life. From this
point of view the man who is merely just or moral without being a philosopher appears
as a mutilated human being. It thus becomes a question whether the moral or just man
who is not a philosopher is simply superior to the nonphilosophic "erotic" man. It likewise
becomes a question whether justice and morality in general, in so far as they are required
for the sake of the philosophic life, are identical, as regards both their meaning and their
extension, with justice and morality as they are commonly understood, or whether mo-

rality does not have two entirely different roots, or whether what Aristotle calls moral virtue is not, in fact, merely political or vulgar virtue.[48]

We are struck by the conditional and interrogatory character of Strauss's formulation of the developed classical natural right teaching. But there are some reasons to think that Strauss's answer to each of these loaded "questions" is affirmative. I believe that such an account of philosophy is itself self-contradictory. It gives a content to natural right, the superiority of philosophy to non-philosophy, which radicalizes and one might suggest parodies the classical notion of the order of the soul. Intellectual virtue and moral virtue are not only distinct but the distinction between moral virtue and vulgar virtue, or some moralized version of collective self-interest or political ambition, is effaced. Philosophy is left with little to contemplate because the claims of the moral and political life are divorced from any access to nature or reason except indirectly or instrumentally. Strauss radicalizes the tension between the natural sociality and the natural rationality of men. I do not believe that Strauss's suggestion that a dialectical investigation of "the moral contents of life" reveals their merely instrumental character. Nor does his account square with Aristotle's presentation of the political philosopher as the umpire weighing and balancing rival but incommensurate partisan claims of justice which maintain a real if partial link to nature and the common good. Moreover, Strauss's second developed "Platonic" position is not compatible with any moral-political notions of the "common good." Nor can it generally accommodate those very *real* "copper coins" that were the starting point of Solzhenitsyn's resistance to and dissection of ideology. Strauss's *initial* and quite promising phenomenology of the soul on the other hand *can* accommodate Solzhenitsyn's experience and insights.

The dissident recovery of the experience of the soul through the confrontation with the totalitarian "lie" helps us better to appreciate the rationality and naturality inherent in the moral contents of life. It allows us to understand that the affirmation of the order of the soul does not entail the acceptance of rationalism narrowly understood. It is my suggestion that Solzhenitsyn's work in particular and in the dissident experience in general can provide powerful impetus and material for the Socratic imperative to "know thyself." It also allows us to appreciate the limits of Socratic rationalism, narrowly understood.

NOTES

1. For a competent intellectual history of totalitarianism, see Abbott Gleason, *Totalitarianism: The Inner History of the Cold War* (New York: Oxford University Press, 1995).

2. On the distinction between Machiavellian and ideological mendacity, see Alain Besançon's penetrating discussion in *The Rise of the Gulag: Intellectual Origins of Leninism* (New York: Continuum, 1981), 243–253.

3. Richard Rorty, *Contingency, Irony, and Solidarity* (Cambridge: Cambridge University Press, 1989), 169–188.

4. Aleksandr I. Solzhenitsyn, *The Gulag Archipelago 1918–1956*, Vol. 1, translated by Thomas P. Whitney (New York: Harper and Row, 1974), 161. Hereafter cited as *Gulag I*.

5. See Jan Patočka, *Heretical Essays in the Philosophy of History*, translated by Erazim Kohak (Chicago: Open Court, 1996), 135; and Václav Havel, "Politics and Conscience" in *Open Letters: Selected Writings 1965–1990* (New York: Knopf, 1991), 271.

6. Hannah Arendt, *The Origins of Totalitarianism* (San Diego: Harcourt Brace, 1979).

7. Arendt, *The Origins of Totalitarianism*, 459. See Eric Voegelin's review of *Origins* in *The Review of Politics* 15 (1953): 68–76; and Raymond Aron's essay "The Essence of Totalitarianism According to Hannah Arendt," in *In Defense of Political Reason: Essays by Raymond Aron*, edited by Daniel J. Mahoney (Lanham, MD: Rowman and Littlefield, 1994), 97–112. The original French version of this essay appeared in *Critique* (1954).

8. Solzhenitsyn emphatically declares that "a human being has a point of view." *Gulag I*, 131. For an excellent discussion of the meaning of "point of view" (*Tochka/zreniia* in Russian) see John Dunlop, "The Gulag Archipelago: Alternative to Ideology" in J. Dunlop, R. Haugh, and Michael Nicholson eds., *Solzhenitsyn in Exile: Critical Essays and Documentary Materials* (Stanford, CA: Hoover Institution Press, 1985), 164–175.

9. See Havel's "Politics and Conscience," especially 249–256.

10. Ibid., 257–258.

11. See Aleksandr I. Solzhenitsyn's Harvard Address of 1978, *A World Split Apart*, in *East and West* (New York: Harper Perennial, 1980), 39–71, esp. 69–71.

12. Solzhenitsyn, "The Nobel Lecture on Literature" in *East and West*, 25.

13. Havel, *Open Letters*, 208.

14. Ibid., 270.

15. Solzhenitsyn, *East and West*, 66.

16. See Part IV of Vol. II of *The Gulag Archipelago*, "The Soul and Barbed Wire," translated by Thomas P. Whitney (New York: Harper and Row, 1975), 597–672, esp. 597–617. Hereafter cited as *Gulag II*.

17. Raymond Aron, "Alexander Solzhenitsyn and European 'Leftism' " in *In Defense of Political Reason: Essays by Raymond Aron*, edited by Daniel J. Mahoney (Lanham, MD: Rowman and Littlefield, 1994), 115–124. The quotation is found on 123.

18. See Solzhenitsyn's account of "the lie as a form of existence" in *Gulag II*, 646–650.

19. See Solzhenitsyn's essay, "As Breathing and Consciousness Return," in *From Under the Rubble* (Washington, DC: Regnery, 1981), 25.

20. *Gulag II*, 615.

21. Ibid.

22. Ibid., 615–616.

23. This speech was delivered by Solzhenitsyn on September 25, 1993, in Lucs-sur-Boulogne, France, as part of a ceremony commemorating the massacre of rebellious peasants by the French revolutionary authorities in the Vendée region of France. Between 90,000 and 250,000 peasants were massacred between 1793 and 1795 in one of the most brutal episodes of the entire Revolution. Solzhenitsyn used the occasion of the commemoration of the Vendée massacre to examine the shared illusion of the French and Soviet revolution that "revolution could change human nature for the better." According to Solzhenitsyn, one conclusion is incontrovertible: "great revolution" of the Jacobin or Bolshevik variety is not to be wished upon any people. Solzhenitsyn writes as follows about the consequences of the revolutionary illusion:

That every revolution releases in people the unbridled instincts of primeval barbarity, the dark forces of envy, greed, and hate was all too obvious even to contemporaries. But it was in the twentieth century that the romantic aura of revolution still dominant in the eighteenth century became so drastically debased in human eyes. At a distance of a century and a half people became more and more convinced, on the basis of their own misery, that revolution overturns the set limits of society, ruins the naturalness of living, destroys the better elements of society while giving ample scope to the worse; that no revolution can ever enrich a country, but will only enrich the most unconscionable and cunning rascals in society; and that its principal gifts to the nation are death and widespread impoverishment to the masses—and in the worst case even the degeneration of its own people.

See "Solzhenitsyn in Europe: Extracts from Two Speeches" in *Bostonia* (Winter 1993–1994): 46–49 and 85.

24. *Gulag I*, 168.

25. *Gulag II*, 615.

26. *Gulag I*, 173.

27. Ibid., 173–174.

28. Ibid., 174.

29. Solzhenitsyn et al., *From Under the Rubble*, 25.

30. Ibid., 174.

31. *Gulag II*, 661.

32. *Gulag I*, 131.

33. Ibid., 414. On the incompatibility of communism and an "individual point of view," see Solzhenitsyn's discussion of Bukharin in *Gulag I*, 410–419.

34. See ibid., 175–178.

35. Ibid., 178.

36. Edward E. Ericson, Jr., *Solzhenitsyn and the Modern World* (Washington, DC: Regnery, 1993).

37. Aleksandr Solzhenitsyn, *Rebuilding Russia: Reflections and Tentative Proposals*, translated by Alexis Klimoff (New York: Farrar, Straus and Giroux, 1991). Part II of the essay "Looking Ahead" is peppered with references to a wide range of western sources from Plato and Aristotle to Montesquieu, Tocqueville, Mill, Spengler, Schumpeter, and Pope John Paul II. These references supplement and balance his equally numerous appeals to Russian sources and authorities. This rhetorical balance appears quite deliberate. Solzhenitsyn seems to be suggesting that there is a universal moral dimension to the task of responsible self-government even while highlighting the historical and cultural requirements of political liberty specific to the Russian context. He avoids both a deracinating enlightenment universalism and a cultural relativism that denies universally applicable moral principles and a human nature which transcends the boundaries of time and place.

38. See the concluding section of the Harvard Address in Solzhenitsyn, *East and West*, 69–71, especially the final paragraph of the address.

39. Aleksandr Solzhenitsyn, *The Gulag Archipelago*, Vol. III, translated by Harry Willets (New York: Harper and Row, 1976), 89–90.

40. Leo Strauss, *On Tyranny*, edited by Victor Gourevitch and Michael S. Roth (New York: Free Press, 1991), 178.

41. Ibid., 211.

42. Ibid., 209.

43. In his essay "Liberal Education and Responsibility" Strauss writes that the "grandiose failures" of Marx and Nietzsche, "the father of communism" and "the stepfather of fascism," respectively, "make it easier for us who have experienced those failures to understand again the old saying that wisdom cannot be separated from moderation and hence to understand that wisdom requires unhesitating loyalty to a decent constitution and even to the cause of constitutionalism." See "Liberal Education and Responsibility" in *An*

Introduction to Political Philosophy: Ten Essays by Leo Strauss, edited with an introduction by Hilail Gildin (Detroit: Wayne State University Press, 1989), 344–345. For a clear statement of Strauss's prudential defense of the superiority of liberal democracy to its modern alternatives, particularly communism, see the conclusion of "The Three Waves of Modernity," 98, in the same volume.

44. Leo Strauss, *Natural Right and History* (Chicago: University of Chicago Press, 1953), 127.

45. Ibid., 128.

46. Ibid., 129–130.

47. Ibid., 146–164.

48. Ibid., 151.

The Universal and the Particular:
Of Nations and Empires in
Raymond Aron's Thought

BRIAN C. ANDERSON

The advent of atomic weapons and the ruins of the twentieth century force us
to pose the question: Is it possible to leave international politics behind? While
international relations have always been possessed by the efficacity of immorality,
can we imagine a "historical transformation of states and their relations" so
profound as to constitute the preconditions for universal peace, ending the "im-
memorial order of collectivities"?[1] In the final pages of his longest book, the
French political theorist Raymond Aron asks what would be required for this to
take place and how plausible it would be for these requirements to be achieved.
As we reconstruct Aron's arguments on universal peace, we shall explore within
his thought the tension between the universality of human nature and the particularity of nationhood, raising the question of *what is common?*[2] In so doing we
will encounter the deeply political nature of Aron's reflection, its refusal to collapse the tensions which characterize the human world, and by extension, the
world of politics.

Aron set forth two categories through which power politics could be tran-
scended: *peace through law* and *peace through empire*. In each case sovereign states
submit their right to render justice to an external arbiter; without this submission
states "cannot live within a definitive peace, unless they have changed their very
nature or unless the world itself has *essentially* changed."[3] From the outset, Aron
points to the unlikelihood of either approach succeeding, and their possibly self-
undermining character. Industrial modernity had lessened the economic causes
of war by opening paths to growth for nations independent of blood and conquest.
But if we posit for the sake of argument the existence of an indisputable tribunal
or irresistible political will, will not the economic and social causes of conflicts

be magnified as a result? That is, if we abolish independent sovereignties in favor of a universal sovereign, do not the inequalities of economic development thereby become the responsibility of *one sovereign*? Yet such inequalities, if they exist within the political community, can lead to profound tension, even, on occasion, "explode into revolution." As Aron maintains, "Why should it be different within a universal state or world federation?"[4] The very project of universal peace is predicated on the transcendence, not just of independent political sovereignties, but of the political problem itself. Keeping this in mind will allow us to view any such enterprise with healthy suspicion.

Indeed this has been the problem with various historical attempts to establish universal peace through treaty or agreement. The Kellogg-Briand Pact, as well as the League of Nations Covenant established at the end of World War I and the more recent United Nations Charter have all failed because they have in effect ratified the dictates of force. To have found a home within the hearts of men and nations, global agreements of this kind would have to have had universal assent; but as Aron stresses, "neither victors nor vanquished could have specified which status would have been just in itself, without reference to the historical right of force."[5] There is, Aron is saying, a permanent dimension of force to political life, a *permanent political problem*. Collective security agreements have been consequently largely ineffective, with states preserving their sacred right to decide whether or not a particular agreement has been breached, if their security has been threatened, or their honor maligned.

This permanence of politics has been the source for what Aron calls the "essential imperfection of international law": states do not commit themselves unconditionally *in what concerns them most* to international agreements. And it is the states themselves, the independent sovereignties at the root of the anarchic life of international relations, that define what concerns them most. This refusal on the part of the world's political communities to abandon sovereignty, at least in the last instance, "has been and is an element in the unique character of relations among states."[6] "Geometric minds" might find it shocking, Aron adds, but war is thus not illegal in international law, which thereby, in the words of Julius Stone, "provides for its own destruction by the simple force of its own subjects."[7]

What was the likelihood of political communities abandoning their sovereignty? What kind of progress has been made by international law? Aron examined three variables as measurements of such progress: the emergence of transnational society, of the international system, and of the consciousness of the human community as a whole. Writing thirty years ago, Aron could see little progress in any of these three areas. It was undoubtedly true, as we have already addressed, that the world was being covered by grids of instantaneous transport and communication. People were traveling on a scale never before met with; and never before had "so many men, without leaving their own country, been capable of seeing, on large or small screens, the images of countries they will never visit."[8]

But these were not, in Aron's view, valid criteria of transnational society. For every sign of growing transnationalism, one could find a counter indication, a different line of evolution. At the time of *Peace and War*, the existence of the Soviet Union and a thoroughly communist China—in other words, the heterogeneity of the international system—made any talk of transnational society premature: "Exchanges across frontiers are, in the Soviet Universe, denied to private persons; they have become more international and not transnational."[9] In the aftermath of the fall of communism, with global capital markets spreading like wildfire, the Internet circling the planet instantaneously, and a growing cultural ubiquity, does Aron's pessimistic view of progress toward international law via transnational society still hold true? Writing somewhat later, in his neglected book *Progress and Disillusion*, Aron advanced an argument that holds as true today, as we open unto our post-Marxist history, as it did amidst the chaos of 1968:

[T]his unification, which we might call material, has less real impact than superficial observers are wont to believe. Even if all families had television sets—and this is far from the case on a worldwide basis—their interests would still be limited to a narrowly restricted social sphere. The poverty and misery of distant peoples, the daily catastrophes that occur all over the world, the strange customs the media purvey in such lively fashion—none of this, whether written or visual, affects the average viewer or reader as much as a quarrel with a neighbor or a colleague at the office, or the fluctuations of his own personal fortune.[10]

The material unification of the world, what Aron called the emergence of universal history, does not of necessity lead to a deeper unification, one which would leave politics behind. Moreover, if the heterogeneous nature of the international system during the long conflict with communism has given way to a more homogeneous system in 1997, new heterogeneities threaten to explode between the Islamic world and the West, and perhaps between various Asian societies and the West,[11] threatening to rip asunder the uncertain—and partial—peace of the post-communist world.

What then of a moral sense of universal humanity? Has this grown with time? Viewing the carnage of the century, Aron held it naive to assume a deepened moral sensitivity, despite the presence of an international human rights community. There *were* signs of universal human concern: "Men react to a *natural* catastrophe as to a misfortune which touches all humanity and the humanity within each man."[12] But these signs of universality, however important and hopeful, were weak beacons when confronted with the darkness of national passions, ethnic hatred, and ideological frenzy, which in our era of Bosnia and Rwanda seem as sadly inseparable from human nature as they have ever been. As Aron somberly put it, "One need merely attend a contest between national teams to realize that the identification of individuals with the group is powerful, the attachment to the human race or to the rules slight."[13]

In short, progress toward a system of international law has been insignificant, the prospects for perpetual peace through law slight. Aron held three conditions as essential for such peace to be achieved, at least in theory. First, if states were to agree to submit their external conduct to the rule of law, the rule of law must hold *within* political communities. Aron is making the Kantian argument, first set out in Kant's classic essay "Perpetual Peace," that in order for world peace to be possible, the internal constitutions of at least the major world powers must be *republican*, "based on the consent of the citizens and the exercise of power according to strict rules and legal procedures."[14]

If this first condition were to be established, the second would likely follow: the international system would be homogeneous, states would become increasingly aware of their relatedness, and a supranational community would gradually come into being. If a crisis arose, if a nation attempted to "opt out" of the supranational agreements, its fate would be isolation or worse. Even with these two conditions secured, however, Aron believed a third necessary: states must agree to renounce force, "and must agree without anxiety to submit their disputes to a tribunal, even those disputes whose object is the redistribution of law and wealth."[15] Is this *post-political world*, pacified by the rule of law, a world without nations—a global political community? Perhaps as important is the following question: Would this outcome be desirable?

In answering these questions of *peace through empire* or *world federation*, Aron felt the cardinal thing to be often overlooked: the persistence of politics and national identity. A world government achieved through empire unavoidably implied tyranny, particularly since, at the time Aron was writing, the Soviet Union was the more obvious candidate for carrying out the project of world unification. But the Soviet Union had a hard time keeping its own diverse nationalisms in check (how hard we have all come to see); extended across the globe, was this not a recipe for unending civil war? As Aron presciently observed, "Let the Russian and American armies withdraw . . . and each of the European states will tend to resume its own autonomy."[16]

Aron was acutely aware of the call to community and nationhood manifest in human nature, a fact that made him dubious toward all plans at creating a European "nation" or political community, let alone a world empire. Such views lost the "essential thing": that of "the community power, animated by a community desire, the state and nation, the human collectivity, conscious of its uniqueness and determined to assert and affirm it in the face of all other collectivities."[17] Political unification was not something cast up by the tide of subpolitical economic relations between political communities. Aron wrote presciently in response to the early enthusiasts of European union: "The hope that the European federation will gradually and irresistibly emerge from the Common Market is based on a great illusion of our times: the illusion that economic and technological interdependence among the various factions of humanity has definitively devalued the fact of 'political sovereignties,' the existence of distinct states which wish to be autonomous."[18]

Aron defined the nation as the conjunction of a community of culture—always pluralist in composition but never *absolutely so*—with a desire for political autonomy implying both chosen and unchosen elements. Nations were *real* and had ends in themselves, something denied by many liberal theorists, who, practicing a form of normative individualism, see only the individual and his choices as worthy of recognition. Aron even went so far as to speak of the "collective personality of a nation," something that grows and perishes across time. The nation, Aron continued:

has many conditions of a material, physical or biological order, but it asserts itself only by consciousness, being capable of thought and choice. Participating both in nature and in reason, these national personalities express the wealth of human possibilities. The diversity of cultures is not a curse to be exorcized but a heritage to be safeguarded.[19]

The nation was not a burden, then, something morally irrelevant, but the very precondition for human flourishing. To abstract away from the nation as many contemporary liberal theorists do, is not only to egregiously misunderstand the nature of political life, which in our time has been as dominated by nationhood as by any other force; it is to sanction the *impoverishment of human existence*. It is to deny that which is common in the quest for what is individual and abstractly universal, thereby robbing the universal of its resting place, its ground, its historical seedbed. As Aron tellingly phrases it: "how could the individual be obligated to all of humanity without being so with regard to the nation that makes him what he is?"[20]

But if the nation was on Aron's view both an ideal and a fact, nationalisms—the desire for power and glory on the part of nations—are not by that token automatically justified. Men and women had duties beyond borders as well as duties within. There were "universal and formal rules" bound up with human nature itself, respect for which had to be antinomically and imperfectly balanced with our duties to our own political communities. Pretending this antinomy did not exist, as idealists were wont to do, gets us nowhere: "This antinomy is real, it has lasted in one form or another since the dawn of history."[21] While not necessarily eternal, it has marked the human political condition long enough to make us wary of schemes to overcome it by rhetorical slight of hand.

The theoretical solution to the antinomy between community and universality, Aron suggested, was the institution of federation, the voluntary version of empire. In a federation, the community of culture is maintained, as in Switzerland, where the Helvetian Confederation holds sovereignty but groups and individuals within the confederation retain their freedom to belong to their communities of memory. Could not humanity as a whole be recast as a giant Switzerland? Aron uses the word "Utopia" to characterize this idea of world federation. While there were and are many historical obstacles to its realization, was the Utopia *ultimately* unrealizable? Did it run against the grain of human nature? Aron turned, perhaps surprisingly, to the German theorist Carl Schmitt to answer this second question.[22]

Schmitt's famous distinction between friend and enemy saw that alternative as intrinsic to political life, which would make any world federation a logical impossibility. As Schmitt wrote in his 1927 book, *The Concept of the Political*, "A world in which the possibility of war is utterly eliminated, a completely pacified globe, would be a world without the distinction of friend and enemy and hence a world without politics. . . . [T]he phenomenon of the political can be understood only in the context of the friend-and-enemy grouping, regardless of the aspects which this possibility implies for morality, aesthetics, and economics."[23] Aron agreed with Schmitt in stressing the difference between the broadening of political community and the unification of humanity. While Aron did not deduce the *impossibility* of world organization from Schmitt's distinction, he admitted, with Schmitt, that hostility was natural to man, and could be moderated and controlled only within the political community. But that control, Schmitt believed, was based on opposition: in order for a political community to exist, it had to be *other*, had to distinguish itself from what it was *not*. If Schmitt was right, and Aron was sympathetic to his argument, a world federation, deprived of an external other, would soon dissolve by internal friction, "by the action of internal conflicts."[24] In an interview from the seventies, Aron nodded in Schmitt's direction once again, without attribution: "[V]iolence has not vanished from the earth, and it is possible that violence within nations will increase, simply because larger conflicts seem to be ruled out. After all, one of the things that cement national unity is the threat from outside."[25]

Yet Aron hesitated to accede to this grim vision. To transcend the friend-enemy dichotomy, Aron mused in his most speculative mode, the universal history we increasingly live must give birth to three phenomena: the refusal to use nuclear weapons, the fair distribution of global resources, and the mutual tolerance of all of the world's peoples, nations, and creeds. Let us assume, implausibly but for the sake of argument, the first two have been achieved: will man still be wolf to man? To offer a positive answer to this question was to wager on the "conversion" of the human race; a negative answer "would leave no other hope of peace than the triumph of a race, a people, a Church, hence would enjoin us to sacrifice either peace or the wealth of diversity."[26] Peace versus the wealth of diversity: the end of history as boredom?[27]

Aron felt it best, in the face of these antinomies, to reaffirm an argument he first made in *The Opium of the Intellectuals*. To approach political life in the geometric spirit of abstraction, to expect more perfection from it than was logically possible, was not to embrace skepticism. The alternative to world federation or empire was not the endless tumult of the battlefield, the poison cup of the assassin, the death camps of Auschwitz. One must doubt the abstractions of the idealists and utopians, yes, but to doubt did not entail surrender to nihilism. Rather, Aronian doubt is based on "reasoning that confirms the imperfection of all social orders, accepts the impossibility of knowing the future, condemns the vain pretension of drawing up the schema of an ideal society."[28] It is, in short, a vision of antinomic prudence that Aron seeks to defend.

Antinomic prudence: a practical wisdom not rooted in an explicit return to the Aristotelian doctrine but instead in the knowledge, drawn from the social sciences and sustained reflection on the antinomies of human existence, about the limits of our power to transform the human world. While Aron hints through his phenomenological exploration of the political world at a philosophical conception of natural right, he does not flesh out that hint with a philosophical teaching, preferring to remain on the terrain of politics. That said, Aron's prudence is preferable to its alternatives of Machiavellian realism and utopian idealism. It is more in tune with the structure of the political and moral universe, where the uncertainty of human action is the first certainty, and political reason the best hope for preserving the genuine human goods made possible by political practice, than its feasible alternatives. It recommends "that we gradually improve what exists" rather than demolishing what exists in the vain hope that perfection can be built from rubble. Aron's antinomic prudence is an expression of his conservative liberalism, balanced between the demands of universality and the need for community, a *political* morality for an imperfect, and imperfectly knowable world. It is the voice of a modern Montesquieu that speaks through the pages of *Peace and War*.[29]

NOTES

1. Raymond Aron, *Peace and War: A Theory of International Relations*, trans. R. Howard (New York: Doubleday, 1957), 703.

2. I borrow this formulation from Pierre Manent, "Modern Individualism," *Crisis* (October 1995): 35–38.

3. Aron, *Peace and War*, 708.

4. Ibid., 708–709.

5. Ibid., 710.

6. Ibid., 724.

7. Quoted in ibid., 725.

8. Ibid., 731.

9. Ibid.

10. Raymond Aron, *Progress and Disillusion: The Dialectics of Modern Society* (New York: Praeger, 1968), 138.

11. This is the true kernel of an otherwise deeply problematic book by Samuel P. Huntington, *The Clash of Civilizations and the Remaking of World Order* (New York: Simon and Schuster, 1996). For an "Aronian" critique of Huntington's cultural determinism, see Pierre Hassner, "Morally Objectionable, Politically Dangerous," *The National Interest* (Winter 1996/1997): 63–69. See also John Gray, *Enlightenment's Wake: Politics and Culture at the Close of the Modern Age* (London: Routledge, 1995), 82–83.

12. Aron, *Peace and War*, 732.

13. Ibid.

14. Ibid., 735. For "Perpetual Peace," see Immanuel Kant, *Political Writings*, edited by H. Reiss (Cambridge: Cambridge University Press, 1991), 93–130. It is essential to note that Kant was far more hesitant about the feasibility of perpetual peace than many of his contemporary exemplars. Perpetual peace was an *idea of reason*, a principle which can

never be fully realized in history, but which serves as a regulative ideal toward which we can strive. Aron's understanding of perpetual peace is far closer to Kant than is, say, that of Charles Beitz or Martha Nussbaum. See also Pierre Hassner, *Violence and Peace: From the Atomic Bomb to Ethnic Cleansing*, translated by J. Brenton (Budapest: Central European University Press, 1997), 29–30.

15. Aron, *Peace and War*, 735.

16. Ibid., 737.

17. Ibid., 747.

18. Ibid., 748.

19. Ibid., 750.

20. Ibid., 751.

21. Ibid., 752.

22. Carl Schmitt's most important work is *The Concept of the Political*, translated by G. Schwab, with comments by Leo Strauss (Chicago: University of Chicago Press, 1996). For a superb commentary on this book, consult Heinrich Meier, *Carl Schmitt and Leo Strauss: The Hidden Dialogue* (Chicago: University of Chicago Press, 1996). Schmitt's central thesis, written at the time of Weimar Germany's greatest crisis, was that liberalism is fatally flawed by its unwillingness to recognize the violent heart of politics, that politics is a matter of life and death, inexorably opposing friend and enemy. The reception of this work has been tainted by Schmitt's subsequent involvement with the national socialist regime that rose from Weimar's corpse. Philippe Raynaud in an interesting essay has traced what might be called the "hidden dialogue" between Aron and Schmitt. See "Raymond Aron et le droit international," *Cahiers de philosophie politique et juridique*, No. 15 (1989): 115–128.

23. Schmitt, *The Concept of the Political*, 35.

24. Aron, *Peace and War*, 755.

25. Raymond Aron, *Thinking Politically: A Liberal in the Age of Ideology*, introduction by Daniel J. Mahoney and Brian C. Anderson (Rutgers, NJ: Transaction Publishers, 1997), 301.

26. Aron, *Peace and War*, 756–757.

27. See Francis Fukuyama, *The End of History and the Last Man* (New York: Free Press, 1992), Part V, "The Last Man," 287–339. Fukuyama, following Kojève, posits the possibility of history culminating in "secure and self-absorbed last men."

28. Aron, *Peace and War*, 757.

29. Aron opened his longest book with an epigraph taken from Montesquieu's *Spirit of the Laws*, "International law is based by nature upon this principle: that the various nations out to do, in peace, the most good to each other, and, in war, the least harm possible, without detriment to their genuine interests." On Aron and Montesquieu, see Simone Goyard-Fabre, "La liberalisme de Raymond Aron" in *Cahiers de philosophie politique et juridique*, No. 15 (1989): 59–97.

For Further Reading

Arendt, Hannah. *The Human Condition*. Chicago: University of Chicago Press, 1958.
Aron, Raymond. *Progress and Disillusion: The Dialectics of Modern Society*. New York: Praeger, 1968.
———. *Thinking Politically*. New Brunswick, NJ: Transaction, 1997.
Bell, Daniel. *The Cultural Contradictions of Capitalism*. New York: Basic Books, 1976.
Bell, Daniel. *Communitarianism and Its Critics*. Oxford: Oxford University Press, 1994.
Bellah, Robert, et al. *Habits of the Heart*. Berkeley: University of California Press, 1985. Updated edition, 1996.
Blankenhorn, David. *Fatherless America*. New York: Basic Books, 1995.
Bloom, Allan. *The Closing of the American Mind*. New York: Simon and Schuster, 1987.
Ceaser, James. *Reconstructing America: The Symbol of America in Modern Thought*. New Haven: Yale University Press, 1997.
Eberly, Don E., editor. *Building a Community of Citizens*. Lanham, MD: University Press of America, 1994.
Ehrenhalt, Alan. *The Lost City: Discovering the Forgotten Virtues of Community in the Chicago of the 1950s*. New York: Basic Books, 1995.
Elshtain, Jean Bethke. *Democracy on Trial*. New York: Basic Books, 1995.
Etzioni, Amatai. *The Spirit of Community*. New York: Crown, 1993.
Frohnen, Bruce. *The New Communitarians and the Crisis of Modern Liberalism*. Lawrence: University Press of Kansas, 1996.
———. "Robert Bellah and the Politics of 'Civil' Religion." *The Political Science Reviewer* 14 (1992): 148–218.
Fukuyama, Francis. *The End of History and the Last Man*. New York: Free Press, 1992.
Galston, William A. *Liberal Purposes*. Cambridge: Cambridge University Press, 1991.
Glendon, Mary Ann. *Rights Talk*. New York: Free Press, 1991.

Gray, John. *Enlightenment's Wake: Politics and Culture at the Close of the Modern Age.* London: Routledge, 1995.

Hertzke, Allen D. *Echoes of Discontent: Jesse Jackson, Pat Robertson, and the Resurgence of Populism.* Washington, DC: Congressional Quarterly Press, 1993.

Hirsch, E. D. *Cultural Literacy.* Boston: Houghton Mifflin, 1987.

Jardine, Murray. *Speech and Political Practice.* Albany: State University of New York Press, 1998.

Kautz, Steven. *Liberalism and Community.* Ithaca, NY: Cornell University Press, 1995.

Lasch, Christopher. *The Revolt of the Elites and the Betrayal of Democracy.* New York: W. W. Norton, 1995.

Lawler, Peter Augustine. *The Restless Mind: Alexis de Tocqueville on the Origin and Perpetuation of Human Liberty.* Lanham, MD: Rowman and Littlefield, 1993.

Lawler, Peter Augustine, and Robert Martin Schaefer, editors. *The American Experiment.* Lanham, MD: Rowman and Littlefield, 1994.

Mahoney, Daniel J. *The Liberal Political Science of Raymond Aron.* Lanham, MD: Rowman and Littlefield, 1992.

———. *De Gaulle: Statesmanship, Grandeur, and Modern Democracy* Westport, CT: Praeger, 1996.

Manent, Pierre. *Tocqueville and the Nature of Democracy.* Translated by John Waggoner. Lanham, MD: Rowman and Littlefield, 1996.

Mansfield, Harvey, Jr. *America's Constitutional Soul.* Baltimore: Johns Hopkins University Press, 1991.

McClay, Wilfred M. *The Masterless: Self and Society in Modern America.* Baltimore: Johns Hopkins University Press, 1994.

Murray, John Courtney. *We Hold These Truths.* New York: Sheed and Ward, 1960.

Neuhaus, Richard John. *The Naked Public Square.* Grand Rapids, MI: Eerdmans, 1984.

Nisbet, Robert. *The Quest for Community.* New York: Oxford University Press, 1953.

Novak, David, editor. *Leo Strauss and Judaism.* Lanham, MD: Rowman and Littlefield, 1996.

Phillips, Derek K. *Looking Backward: A Critical Appraisal of Communitarian Thought.* Princeton, NJ: Princeton University Press, 1993.

Popenoe, David, et al., editors. *Promises to Keep.* Lanham, MD: Rowman and Littlefield, 1996.

Putnam, Robert. "Bowling Alone: America's Declining Social Capital." *Journal of Democracy* 6 (January 1995): 65–78.

Rieff, Philip. *The Triumph of the Therapeutic.* New York: Harper and Row, 1987. Originally published in 1966.

Rorty, Richard. *Contingency, Irony, and Solidarity.* Cambridge: Cambridge University Press, 1989.

Sandel, Michael. *Democracy's Discontent.* Cambridge, MA: Harvard University Press, 1996.

Shain, Barry Alan. *The Myth of American Individualism.* Princeton, NJ: Princeton University Press, 1994.

Solzhenitsyn, Aleksandr. *Rebuilding Russia: Reflections and Tentative Proposals.* Translated by Alexis Klimoff. New York: Farrar, Straus, and Giroux, 1991.

Strauss, Leo. *Natural Right and History.* Chicago: University of Chicago Press, 1953.

———. *The Rebirth of Classical Political Rationalism.* Chicago: University of Chicago Press, 1989.

Taylor, Charles. *Sources of the Self*. Cambridge, MA: Harvard University Press, 1989.

Tocqueville, Alexis de. *Democracy in America*. Edited by J. P. Mayer. Translated by George Lawrence. Garden City, NY: Doubleday, 1969.

Walzer, Michael. *Spheres of Justice*. New York: Basic Books, 1983.

Index

About the Contributors

BRIAN C. ANDERSON is senior editor of *City Journal*. His book on Raymond Aron is forthcoming, and he is editing a series of Aron's writings with Daniel J. Mahoney.

BRUCE FROHNEN is a speech writer for United States Senator Spencer Abraham. His books are *Virtue and the Promise of Conservatism: The Legacy of Burke and Tocqueville* and *The New Communitarians and the Crisis of Modern Liberalism*.

ALLEN D. HERTZKE is Presidential Professor of Political Science and Assistant Director of the Carl Albert Research Center at the University of Oklahoma. He has written two acclaimed books on faith and politics, and is co-author of *Religion and Politics in America: Faith, Culture and Strategic Choices*.

MURRAY JARDINE is Assistant Professor of Political Science at Auburn University. He is author of *Speech and Political Practice*.

JOSEPH KNIPPENBERG is Associate Professor of Politics and Chair of the Division of History, Politics, and International Studies at Oglethorpe University. He is coeditor (with Peter Lawler) of *Poets, Princes, and Private Citizens* and has published on Rousseau, Kant, and contemporary liberal theory.

PETER AUGUSTINE LAWLER is Professor of Political Science at Berry College. Among his books are *The Restless Mind: Alexis de Tocqueville on the Origin and Perpetuation of Human Liberty* and the forthcoming *Postmodernism Rightly Understood*.

DANIEL J. MAHONEY is Associate Professor of Politics at Assumption College. He is author of *The Liberal Political Science of Raymond Aron* and *De Gaulle: Statesmanship, Grandeur, and Modern Democracy*.

WILFRED M. McCLAY is Associate Professor of History at Tulane University. He wrote *The Masterless: Self and Society in Modern America*, which won the 1995 Merle Curti Award of the Organization of American Historians.

DALE McCONKEY is Assistant Professor of Sociology at Berry College. He has published research in the sociology of religion, and is co-editor of *Social Structures, Social Capital, and Personal Freedom* with Peter Augustine Lawler (forthcoming from Praeger).

ROBB A. McDANIEL is a lecturer at Vanderbilt University and adjunct instructor at Belmont University. He is currently working on a project concerning religion and political theory in Heidegger, Strauss, and Levinas.

CHRIS McRORIE graduated Summa Cum Laude from the University of Oklahoma in 1997. He was an Undergraduate Fellow for the Carl Albert Research Center.

MARY P. NICHOLS is Professor of Political Science and Associate Chair for Graduate Studies at Fordham University. Her books include *Socrates and the Political Community* and *Citizens and Statesmen: A Study of Aristotle's Politics*.

BARRY SHARPE is Assistant Professor of Political Science at Northwestern College (Iowa). He has published a variety of articles on political theory.

MARC STIER teaches in the Intellectual Heritage program at Temple University. He is completing *Politics and Reason*, a three-volume work on contemporary political philosophy.

BRAD LOWELL STONE is Professor of Sociology and Director of American Studies at Oglethorpe University. He is the author of numerous articles and reviews, and his research on classical liberalism has been supported by an NEH Study Grant.

ALAN WOOLFOLK is Professor of Sociology at Oglethorpe University. His most recent publications include an edited volume of writings by Thomas Masaryk and articles on American culture and nationalism.

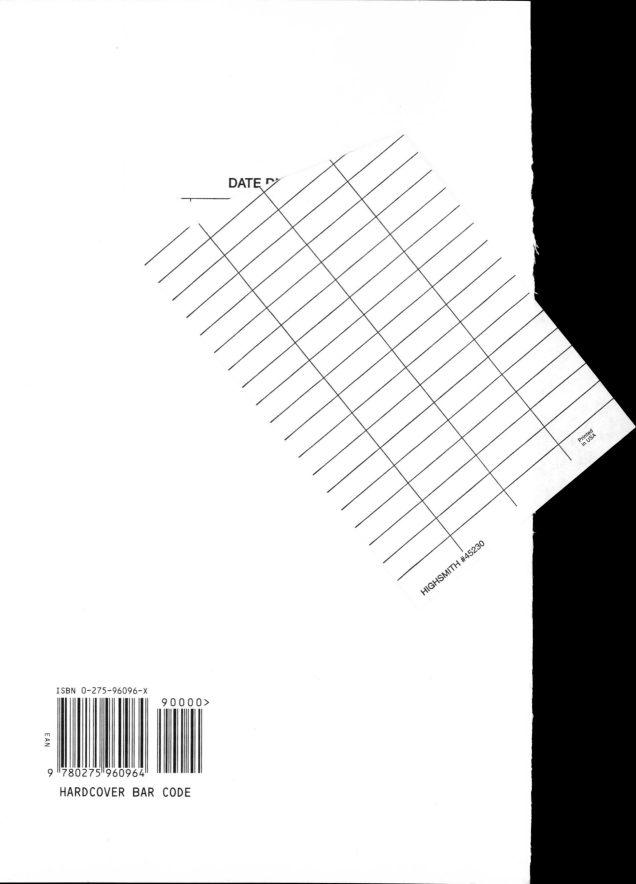

DATE D

HIGHSMITH #45230

Printed in USA

ISBN 0-275-96096-X

90000>

EAN

9 780275 960964

HARDCOVER BAR CODE